# European Logistics

# European Logistics

## Markets, Management and Strategy

*James Cooper, Michael Browne and
Melvyn Peters*

First published 1991
Reprinted 1992 (twice)

Blackwell Publishers
108 Cowley Road, Oxford, OX4 1JF, UK

3 Cambridge Center
Cambridge, Massachusetts 02142, USA

*British Library Cataloguing in Publication Data*

A CIP catalogue record for this book is available from the British Library.

*Library of Congress Cataloging in Publication Data*

Cooper, James.
    European logistics: distribution strategies for the 1990s / James Cooper, Michael Browne, and Melvyn Peters.
        p.   cm.
    Includes bibliographical references (p.   ) and index.
    1. Physical distribution of goods—European Economic Community countries—Management.   2. Shipment of goods—European Economic Community countries.   I. Browne. Michael.   II. Peters, Melvyn.
III. Title.
HF5780.E86C66   1991
382′.3′094—dc20
                                                                    91–27054
                                                                    CIP

ISBN 0–631–17347–1

Typeset in 11 on 13 pt Sabon
by Hope Services (Abingdon) Ltd.
Printed in Great Britain by T. J. Press Ltd, Padstow, Cornwall

This book is printed on acid-free paper.

# Contents

# Acknowledgements

A great number of friends and colleagues contributed to the completion of this book. We must, however, stress that the book reflects our views, and not necessarily those of the many people we consulted during our research. We would like to acknowledge the particular contributions of those listed below:

Rovelli Ambrogio, FAI, Milan
Peter Blok and Ronald Jorna, NEI, Rotterdam
Auke Boerema, Origin, Eindhoven
Stephen Byrne
Giorgio Caenazzo, Star Transport, Milan
Joe Canny and Ed Rastatter, Department of Transportation, Washington, DC
Paul Capella, DRI Europe
Mario Carrara, CSST, Milan
Robert Clark, Corporate Intelligence Group
Malory Davis, *Freight News Express*
Ulrich Engelbracht, Danzas, Paris
Vassilis Evmolpidis and George Emmanoulopoulos, Trademco, Athens
the staff at EVO, Zoetermeer
Richard Gadeselli, Fiat (UK) Limited
Ricardo Garoschi, Federcom, Milan
Hartmut Gasser and Rainer Mertel, Kombiverkehr, Frankfurt
George Giannopoulos and Telis Naniopoulos, University of Thessaloniki, Greece
Laurent Gregoire, Keyserberg, Paris

Paul Hanappe, INRETS
Lucille B. Hayes, PCL, London
Mike Hurn
Hironao Kawashima, Keio University, Japan
Christoph Kösters, University of Munster, Germany
Jelena Krivokapić, Belgrade
the staff at La Comité Belge de la Distribution
Trevor Larder, Lep Swift, Epsom
Barry Laver, McDonnell Douglas
Hervé Lionel-Marie, CAT, Paris
Jeronimo Maeso-Castrillon, Madrid
Gregory Marchant and Gerald Barton, Railfreight Distribution,
    London
Alan McKinnon, Heriot–Watt University, Edinburgh
Rene Mesure, France Distribution System, Paris
Allen Mottur, Temple, Barker and Sloane
Stavros Pangalos, Planet, Athens
John Parsons, Sony (UK) Limited
Martyn Pellew and Ivy Penman, Exel Logistics, Bedford
Pierre Pissoort, Mondia, Liège
the Trustees of the Rees Jeffreys Road Fund
Cees Ruijgrok, Catholic University of Brabant, Tilburg
Gert Schut, Nedlloyd, Rotterdam
Jean-Marie Sohier, Sealord Transport Consultants, Ohain, Belgium
Dean Stiles, *Motor Transport*
Jerzy Tarkowski, Bilspedition, Goteborg
Roel ter Brugge, INRO–TNO, Delft
the staff at The Institute of Grocery Distribution
Ilse Thomsen and Axel Hornung, Bundesverband des Deutschen
    Güterfernverkehrs, Frankfurt
Astrid Thygesen, Institut for Transportstudier, Padborg
Alan Treadgold, Templeton College, Oxford
Marinus van den Elshout and George Bordonis, NEA, Rijswijk
H. van Eerden, Intexo Veghel, Veghel
Sabine van Simaey, *Lloyd Anversois*, Antwerp
Jose Viegas, Technical University of Lisbon
Michel Violland, ECMT, Paris
N. J. Visser and T. Postma, Albert Heijn bv, Zaandam
Hans von Dewall, Rhenus, Dortmund
Matthew Walker, PE-International, Egham
Sten Wandel, University of Linköping

David Willis, ATA Foundation, Washington, DC
Robert and Catherine Worth, Park Avenue North, London

Finally, we wish to express our thanks to Richard Burton, our commissioning editor at Blackwell Publishers, for his helpful comments on the manuscript, and his patience in awaiting its arrival. Authors have used many excuses to justify delays. We prefer that attributed to Jane Austen by her brother Henry. He wrote that Jane never regarded a manuscript as finished 'till time and many perusals had satisfied her that the charm of recent composition was dissolved' (Austen, 1818) – our sentiments exactly.

*James Cooper, Michael Browne and Melvyn Peters*

## Authors' Note

Many readers will find it helpful to know how work on the book was divided among the authors. James Cooper and Michael Browne developed the analytical models and wrote the text, while Melvyn Peters completed much of the field work for the original research and contributed the majority of the case studies.

# List of Abbreviations

Benelux   Belgium, the Netherlands and Luxembourg.
CAD       Computer-aided design: systems used within the design area to generate and modify designs (such as generating a three-dimensional image of a product on computer screen instead of building a model by hand).
CAM       Computer-aided manufacturing: the application of computers to generate manufacturing data.
CAP       (1) Common Agricultural Policy: the policy of the EC by which farmers receive guaranteed prices for their production.
          (2) Controlled atmosphere packing: the use of gases in special combination to retard the deterioration of fresh produce in transport and storage.
CBI       Confederation of British Industry.
CFES      Computerized freight exchange systems: computer-based systems, used by shippers, freight forwarders and hauliers, to match available loads with spare transport capacity, especially in backloading.
CIM       Computer-integrated manufacturing: the use of computers to integrate the various stages in the manufacturing process and to coordinate these stages.
CMEA      Council for Mutual Economic Assistance: the formal name for Comecon.
Comecon   The trading bloc of command economies established in 1949, comprising the Soviet Union and many countries of eastern Europe, together with Cuba, Mongolia and Vietnam (*see also* CMEA).

| | |
|---|---|
| CVRS | Computerized vehicle routeing and scheduling: computer programs designed to allocate work to vehicles and devise routes for drivers to follow. |
| DRP | Distribution requirements planning: a method of reducing inventory requirements, especially for items with seasonal sales patterns, whereby forecast demand is used as the basis for inventory replenishment. |
| EC | European Community: the association of European countries, set up in 1957 mainly for trade reasons, but increasingly embracing wider economic and political ambitions. The key institutions of the EC are the European Commission (the executive), the European Parliament (democratically elected, but with restricted powers) and the Council of Ministers (the decision-making authority). |
| ECSC | European Coal and Steel Community. |
| ecu | European currency unit: the currency created within the EMS, against which the value of other currencies is expressed. The ecu is not in everyday use, although financial institutions do use it as the basis for transactions (*see also* EMS, ERM). |
| EDI | Electronic data interchange: a term usually given to an electronics-based system of communication whereby trading partners can both send and receive information related to their trading needs. Strictly, EDI refers to the computer-to-computer exchange of structured data. |
| EES | European Economic Space: a wider association of European countries, including EFTA and parts of eastern Europe, which have common trading interests. |
| EFTA | European Free Trade Association: an association of European countries, currently comprising Norway, Sweden, Finland, Iceland, Austria and Switzerland, which is based on mutual trading agreements. |
| EFTPOS | Electronic funds transfer at point of sale: a computerized system which enables funds to be transferred directly from a customer's bank account to that of the retailer at the checkout. |
| EMS | European Monetary System: the system for currency management used within the EC (*see also* ecu, ERM). |
| EMU | Economic and Monetary Union: the process of linking the economies of the 12 EC members and creating a single currency through a European central bank. |

EPOS      Electronic point of sale: a computerized system of recording sales at retail checkouts.

ERM      Exchange Rate Mechanism: the alignment at fixed exchange rates of currencies within the EC (*see also* ecu, EMS).

FTL      Full truckload: a term widely used in the USA to indicate that a single consignment fully occupies the capacity of a truck (*see also* LTL).

GATT      General Agreement on Tariffs and Trade: the forum for negotiating world trade agreements, with a special emphasis on removing barriers to free trade.

GIE      Groupe d'Intérêt Economique: a co-operative business grouping found in France. Small hauliers may belong to GIEs.

ICC      Interstate Commerce Commission: the regulatory body for inter-state trucking in the USA.

ICT      International combined transport: the use of more than one mode of transport for the international movement of goods. (The term implies that there is a high level of technical integration and management coordination between the modes of transport used.)

IT      Information technology: an ill-defined term with connotations of information being transmitted by electronic means, including robotics, automation, communications and so on.

JIT      Just-in-time: a production method in which components are produced and delivered according to immediate assembly needs. This eliminates inventories of components and reduces the need for storage space. Typically, this results in frequent deliveries of goods, in small quantities.

LTL      Less than truckload: a term widely used in the USA to indicate that many or several consignments together occupy the capacity of a truck. The nearest European equivalent is 'groupage' (*see also* FTL).

MRP      Material requirements planning: a system for forecasting or projecting component part and material requirements from a company's master production schedule and the bill of material for each end product or module. The time-phased requirements for components and materials are then calculated allowing for inventory in hand.

MRP II     Manufacturing resources planning: an approach to balancing demand through manufacturing and logistics channels using advanced integrated systems.

PTT     The abbreviation normally used to describe the national organization responsible for postal services and telecommunications.

RDC     Regional distribution centre: a large warehouse which is used to consolidate goods received by suppliers into consignments for supermarkets located in its catchment area.

SEM     Single European Market: the aim of the EC member states to create a common marketplace in which goods and services can be freely traded.

TKM     Tonne-kilometre. A measure of transport distance combining the weight of goods and the distance over which they are moved.

TQM     Total quality management: a method of ensuring that all activities associated with manufacturing processes contribute to high and predetermined levels of quality. TQM has important implications for logistics, not least in the service support activities of transport and warehousing.

TRO     Tarification Routière Obligatoire: the French system of setting tariffs for haulage operators, now abolished.

VAN     Value added networks: communications networks operated by companies such as IBM and GE which are used for the transmission of data and messages between subscribers.

VAT     Value Added Tax: a form of sales taxation used in the EC, under which transactions for goods and services are subject to a tax based on the value added since the previous transaction.

# 1

# Introduction

Readers rightly expect the title of a book to inform them of its contents. While the title of this book, *European Logistics: Markets, Management and Strategy* does describe what the book is mainly about, many readers will welcome some further clarification of its principal themes.

We use the word *European* primarily to mean the European Community (EC). This geographical focus is inevitable given the combined economic importance of the member states that make up the EC, and the far-reaching proposals for greater economic and political cohesion within the EC. Yet it is important to recognize that the EC is not an unchanging entity. Portugal and Spain joined as recently as 1986. The unification of the two Germanies[1] in 1990 has added to both the land area of the EC and its population. In the future, Austria may become a member.

Furthermore, it is important not to ignore European countries simply because they are not members of the EC. Countries belonging to the European Free Trade Association (EFTA) often have important links with the EC. Switzerland and Austria, for example, play a crucial role as transit countries for freight traffic between Germany and Italy, a major European trade route. Again, Switzerland is the country of origin for Danzas, the largest freight company (by revenues) in Europe, and one with extensive business interests throughout the continent of Europe.

Sweden also trades extensively with the EC, and many of its manufacturing multinationals (such as Electrolux and Volvo) have production plants in the EC. So, in many respects, Swedish companies can be counted as EC manufacturers, a distinction which is also shared by multinationals from other parts of the world, notably the USA and Japan. It follows that, when we consider the logistics of companies in Europe, it is the location of their activities which is often more important than their country of origin. Accordingly, the logistics activities of companies such as Kodak and Sony are just as relevant to the scope of our book as are the logistics activities of Agfa-Gevaert or Philips.

The term *logistics* is now widely used and understood throughout the business world, and refers essentially to the management of supply chains in commerce and industry. Although precise definitions of logistics will vary from author to author, the common thread will be a concern for the movement and storage of goods, together with associated information flows, from the beginning to the end of the supply chain. So, for a manufacturing company, logistics management will encompass the procurement of raw materials or components, production processes at both the semi-finished and finished stages, and the final distribution of products to clients. It is often convenient to divide logistics management into its three constituent elements; namely, procurement logistics, production logistics and distribution logistics. But the key point about logistics is that it is intended to be an integrative discipline; its separation into component parts will often be counterproductive. Many instances are cited in this book in which companies have greatly benefited from taking the integrative approach.

Few authors have so far used the word *markets* in relation to logistics. No doubt this is because logistics is usually written about more as a concept, rather than as a practice. However, we would argue that there is a vast market in Europe for *logistics services*, embracing transport, warehousing and information systems, which deserves to be considered in its own right. This market is subject to many changing influences, notably freight transport deregulation, the logistics needs of manufacturers and retailers, planning controls on infrastructure development, advances in computer software, and the application of logistics concepts within companies.

Furthermore, the pace of change for logistics services in Europe is arguably faster than anywhere else in the world, as companies respond to the dramatic challenge of completing the Single European Market (SEM), a process which may have been initiated in the late 1980s but which will continue to have consequences well into the next century. In view of these fundamental changes, this book considers at length the structure of the marketplace for logistics services and how it operates in Europe, an analysis which is long overdue.

Changes in the marketplace for logistics services must be a vital concern for *management*, both among the users of logistics services (such as manufacturers and retailers) and the providers (such as freight forwarders and hauliers). Only by developing an understanding of the market can managers from either side of the logistics divide make their businesses more effective. For users, the concern is to know what logistics services are being developed and how these might be used in future to build business. The providers want to know what opportunities can be exploited in the future; for example, by using information technology (IT) to control logistics service networks to better effect. And what will happen to the price of logistics services? Despite an increasing emphasis on quality in all areas of business, no manager can neglect price. Key management issues of this kind are addressed in many chapters of the book.

Management must also consider *strategy*, and the need for strategic initiatives within the marketplace for logistics services. We give special attention to possible strategic developments among providers of logistics services. Many providers see the need to expand, in order to have at least a pan-European capability. This needs to be underpinned by strategic initiatives in IT. The question is: 'How do we do it?' A strategy which is perhaps appropriate for, say, a freight forwarder may not work for a company which has its roots in liner shipping.

Having said what the book is about, it is equally important to say what it is not about. Above all, this book is not a technical guide to logistics, with comprehensive data about who does what. Nor is it narrowly focused on any one country. Our view is essentially a pan-European one. We may recognize the strengths of particular countries (such as manufacturing in Germany, or international haulage in Netherlands) but we have not set out to promote the interests of any one country in particular. Rather, we hope that by both informing and guiding the thoughts of logistics managers in Europe we can contribute not only to building upon strengths but also to correcting weaknesses within European logistics. Upon reaching the end of the book, readers will be able to judge for themselves whether or not we have succeeded in this aim.

# 2

# European Logistics in Context

## The Trading Organization of Europe

What the continent of Europe lacks in land mass it makes up in numbers of countries. In an area little bigger than Canada there are around 29 countries. (It is difficult to be precise about the number because some claims to independence, such as that of Lithuania, are not universally recognized.) This largely historical legacy has important implications for trade in Europe and, in consequence, for logistics.

In an era of fast-growing international trade, it is difficult for any one country, particularly if it is a small one, to be economically isolated from its neighbours and yet become prosperous. Albania is a classic case in point. Following the Second World War, Albania adopted a fiercely independent line, both politically and economically; it now has one of the most backward economies in Europe, in marked contrast to many of its neighbours. The logic of co-operation between countries led to the creation of three main trading blocs in the postwar years; the Council for Mutual Economic Assistance, more familiarly known as Comecon; the European Economic Community (EEC); and the European Free Trade Association (EFTA). It is important to understand something of the origins and purposes of each of these trading blocs, to provide a background for logistics developments in Europe.

*Comecon* developed in eastern Europe, dominated by the Soviet Union, as a trading bloc comprising planned (or command) economies. Within Comecon, the economic philosophy of all member countries (see figure 2.1) was based upon centralized

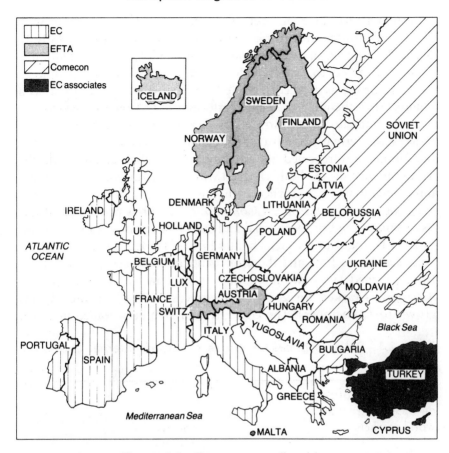

**Figure 2.1**   European trading blocs.

decision-making, especially in manufacturing and agriculture. In general, services were given a relatively low priority for economic development.

For a variety of reasons, including the use of non-convertible currencies and the production of low-quality goods, Comecon countries tended to trade more between themselves than the countries in western Europe. Moreover, particular emphasis was given to trading capital, rather than consumer goods; for one thing, the pricing mechanism was used to suppress demand for consumer goods. It is shown in table 2.1, for example, that in the USSR a car costs twice the world market price, with television sets three times as expensive.

Over time, the lack of consumer goods in shops, together with poor availability of staple foods, has caused major problems for governments in Comecon countries. Unfavourable comparisons with Western countries were increasingly made, especially in the 1980s. In particular, the European Community (the middle word, 'Economic', is now dropped to reflect wider ambitions) is seen by people in eastern Europe as a success, while Comecon is widely regarded as a failure. Also, the poor economic performance of Comecon economies was dramatically demonstrated at German unification. For many years, East Germany had been regarded as Comecon's star performer, but unification revealed the shallowness of that claim; with the Treuhandanstalt, the body charged with privatization, unable to find buyers for many state-owned companies.

In contrast, the *European Community* (EC) has prospered. It has its origins in the European Coal and Steel Community (ECSC), set up in 1951 by the countries which later formed the EEC, namely France, West Germany, Italy and the three Benelux countries. The Treaty of Rome, signed six years later, had as its aim the setting up of a 'Common Market' for goods and services. Since then, the EC has grown to 12 members. The UK, Eire and Denmark joined in 1973,

**Table 2.1**  Relative prices of goods on USSR internal and world markets

| Relative prices of goods on USSR internal and world markets[a] | Price[b] | |
|---|---|---|
| | Soviet internal market | World market |
| Oil | 1.6 | 5.0 |
| Copper | 66.0 | 127.0 |
| Scrap steel | 3.1 | 20.0 |
| Ammonia | 5.7 | 3.0 |
| Car (unit) | 500.0 | 250.00 |
| Meat (1 kg) | 0.3 | 2.0 |
| Wheat | 7.1 | 3.0 |
| Colour TV (unit) | 75.0 | 25.0 |
| Personal computer (unit) | 8,125.0 | 125.0 |
| Screw-cutting lathe (unit) | 311.0 | 232.0 |
| Video cassette recorder (unit) | 61.0 | 18.0 |

[a] Price of 1000 Kwh of electricity = 1.
[b] Per ton unless otherwise stated.
Sources: *Ekonomicheskaya Gazeta* and *The Economist*, 20 October 1990.

and in doing so had to leave EFTA. Greece joined in 1981, followed by Portugal and Spain in 1986. There are also three associate members which enjoy certain trading privileges with the EC without being full members (see figure 2.1). In an unexpected turn of events, the EC was enlarged in 1990, following the unification of the two Germanies.

The EC, then, has a far from static membership. It is even possible that some former members of Comecon might become future members. Czechoslovakia and Hungary seem two of the most likely candidates: while their incorporation might not be easy, it is by no means impossible. The EC is already a collection of quite dissimilar countries, and the addition of a further two is not widely regarded as difficult.

Size obviously divides the existing members. A united Germany has a population of nearly 80 million, while neighbouring Luxembourg has a population of only 400 000, little more than the city of Las Vegas, Nevada. Similarly, wealth is unequally distributed within the EC. People living in France or the Netherlands enjoy a much higher standard of living than their counterparts in Portugal or Greece.

Some of the most important differences are institutional. Legal systems may be based on different principles. Central banks may be independent from government or closely controlled by it, and welfare entitlements are better in some countries than others. The list is a very long one, and can reflect the different political complexions of countries. A major contrast developed between France and the UK during the 1980s. While France continued to attach importance to government intervention in its economy, the UK government under Margaret Thatcher aimed for a market-based economy, with a minimum of government involvement. It is important to note that the European Commission, which is playing an increasingly influential role within the EC, tends towards the French approach: this is hardly surprising since France was a founder member of the EC and the UK was not – arriving late at the party always has its penalties.

To many observers, the fact that the EC has been able to work at all, given its disparate membership, is something of a surprise. That it has worked so effectively is little short of a miracle. However, progress has been erratic. Perhaps the leanest period was in the late 1970s and early 1980s, when the policy thrust of the European Commission was to achieve 'harmonization of the terms of competition' between member states. This proved to be the wrong way to achieve a common market for goods and services within the EC. Jacques Delors, acceding to the presidency of the European Commission at the beginning of 1985, took a different approach. He charged one of his commissioners, Lord Cockfield, to prepare a white paper for the completion of the Internal Market. The result was a list of 300 directives (European laws) to achieve the Internal Market, and the date set for this achievement was the end of 1992. This date is now synonymous with the aim of promoting a much greater degree of integration, not just economically, but politically as well. *The Economist* best sums up the mood:

> Part of the power of 1992 is that it is so hard to reduce to essentials. At its simplest it is presented as a 'Europe without frontiers'; but to this graspable notion have been added extra after extra, all consistent with the aim of a single market but not necessarily vital to it: patent law, broadcasting standards, labelling rules, corporate structure, vocational training for young people, the pedigree of bovine animals, and so on and so on.
>
> (*The Economist*, 1988)

Some components of 1992 are highly relevant to logistics in Europe and especially its future development. The key issues are discussed below, but first we complete our short survey of trading blocs in Europe by examining the *European Free Trade Association* (EFTA).

EFTA (see figure 2.1) was formed in 1960, largely as a response to the foundation of the EC by countries which – for a variety of reasons – did not want to be part of such a close association of countries as membership of the EC implied. The UK, for example, still had important trading ties with countries in its former empire, now the Commonwealth. The loose association of EFTA presented no challenge to these ties. For Switzerland the reasons centred on political non-alignment. Fiercely neutral, the Swiss could accommodate being part of EFTA, but not the EC.

EFTA now comprises most of the Scandinavian countries (the Norwegian electorate voted in the early 1970s not to apply for membership of the EC), together with Switzerland and Austria. As its aims as a trading bloc were unpretentious from the outset, its achievements have been correspondingly modest. Essentially, EFTA made trading between member states easier by progressively reducing the impact of trade barriers such as tariffs and quotas. There is little in the way of the supranational machinery as represented in the EC by the European Commission or, indeed, the European Parliament.

The completion of the internal market of the EC by 1992 is of special importance to EFTA since the EC is EFTA's largest trading partner. Consequently, EFTA wishes to ensure that it is not disadvantaged by the 1992 programme. The proposed creation of the European Economic Space (EES) is designed to overcome some potential difficulties foreseen by EFTA, by providing reciprocal access to EC and EFTA markets. However, there are problems ahead. For example, Sweden and Norway say that they will not lower their standards on health and the environment to prevailing norms within the EC.

Given the regional dominance of the EC within Europe and the aim of some EFTA countries to achieve EC membership, it is possible that EFTA faces a limited future. Much depends on the willingness of the EC to admit new members. There is considerable debate on this issue. Some members (notably France) maintain that the first priority for the EC must be to deepen relationships between the member states, through the process of 1992 and beyond. Others (notably the UK) feel that free-market economies need to be encouraged throughout Europe by wider membership of the EC. Clearly, there must be a resolution of the 'deep and narrow' versus 'broad and shallow' conflict between existing members of the EC before the future of EFTA can be resolved. This will take some time.

# The European Community and 1992

The programme of initiatives designed to complete the Single European Market (SEM), as the internal market of the EC is often known, is far-reaching. As a consequence, much of the impact will be felt well after 31 December 1992, the date chosen for the implementation of Lord Cockfields's 300 directives. Then there is the prospect of economic and monetary union (EMU), which is not part of the 1992 programme, but could be implemented during the late 1990s. In providing for a European central bank and a single currency, EMU would do much to make the EC into a United States of Europe. It is important to consider the effects that these dramatic changes would have on business in Europe, and the consequences for logistics.

## Changes in progress

By dismantling barriers to trade within the EC, Paolo Cecchini calculated that output in the Community would rise by between 2.5 and 6.5 per cent (Cecchini, 1988). A major part of the '1992 effect' would therefore result from a once-and-for-all increase in GDP. This clearly has major implications for European business as it moves up a gear. Traded volumes would increase, particularly between EC member states, creating new demands for logistics services (such as transport and warehousing).

However, a subsequent study by Professor Richard Baldwin of Columbia University concluded that Cecchini had underestimated the gains that would result from the 1992 programme; the benefits might be five times as large as the Cecchini estimate (Baldwin, 1989). The difference in conclusion between the two studies rests on assumptions about long-term growth. While Cecchini makes no allowance for a rise in the long-term rate of growth, Baldwin believes that medium- or long-term bonuses in growth could result from 1992 (*The Economist*, 1989). The outcomes of these two different assumptions are illustrated in figure 2.2.

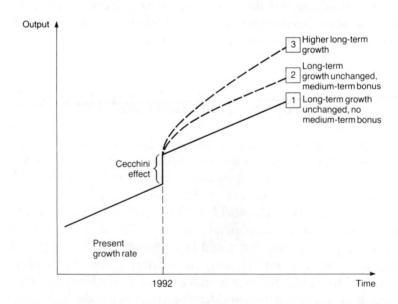

**Figure 2.2**   The EC after 1992: possible paths for economic growth.
*Source: The Economist*, 18 November 1989

Should Baldwin be proved right, then the consequences for both business and logistics would be dramatic. On the positive side, the growth in GDP would bring new opportunities both for the users of logistics services (such as manufacturers and retailers) and the providers (such as freight forwarders and hauliers). But there are also potential problems. There are already severe problems of traffic congestion on many parts of the European road network. Adding more freight to the roads would create further difficulties, particularly with respect to environmental deterioration and providing enough new road capacity to meet demand, not to mention worsening standards of performance in freight services (delivery delays, for example).

Completion of the SEM can also be counted upon to have micro-economic as well as macro-economic effects. Especially useful will be enhancements to the trading structure of European industries as companies increasingly regard the whole of the Community as their home market, rather than having their trading horizons restricted to a single country. Indeed, this is a central part of the logic of the SEM; to help create European companies with the critical mass to compete in the global marketplace. At present, Europe has too many companies – small by world standards – in traditional sectors of industry such as boilermaking; while in sunrise industries, such as information technology (IT), it has too few of any importance. This point is illustrated in table 2.2, based on research by W. S. Atkins, the management consultancy.

**Table 2.2** The structures of European industries (influenced by procurement)

| | Value of EC market (billion ecu per year) | Intra-EC trade | Number of EC producers | Number of American producers |
|---|---|---|---|---|
| Boilermaking | 2 | Little | 12 | 6 |
| Turbine generators | 2 | Little | 10 | 2 |
| Locomotives | 0.1 | Little | 16 | 2 |
| Mainframe computers | 10 | Extensive | 5 | 9 |
| Telephone exchanges | 7 | Moderate | 11 | 4 |
| Telephone handsets | 5 | Little | 12 | 17 |

*Source:* EC Commission, taken from *The Economist*, 9 July 1988

Importantly, the 'rules of engagement' in mergers and acquisitions have now changed in the EC. Whereas a merger or acquisition would once have been prevented if it resulted in a company which dominated a national market within the EC, the Directorate-General for Competition (DG IV) takes the view that it is the European marketplace, rather than the national one, which should be the overriding consideration. This opens the way for larger European companies, and the kind of home-based competition which can lead to world champions in business (Porter, 1990). Again, the implications for logistics are important. Three large companies are certain to have very different logistics requirements compared with, say, ten medium-sized ones.

In the process of creating larger European companies, changes to the rules of public procurement are also not to be forgotten. Since 1971 public contracts in construction worth more than one million ecus have had to be put out to Europe-wide tender. After 1977, the same applied to other categories of purchasing worth more than 200 000 ecu. But just 2 per cent of orders in each category go to other European countries (*The Economist*, 1988; see also table 2.2). The 1992 programme aims to widen sourcing in the public sector by taking a variety of initiatives, including better monitoring and allowing redress to suppliers who believe they have been unfairly treated by potential customers. However, the crucial development is to extend open procurement practices to businesses which have hitherto been protected. Notable among these are transport and telecommunications, two key elements of logistics.

The removal of non-tariff barriers is also a key element of the 1992 programme, and one which will help to stimulate trade between member states of the EC. The weapon that is being used to bring down non-tariff trade barriers is 'mutual recognition'. Essentially, this means that if a product or a service can be sold in any one member state of the EC, the sale of the same product or service cannot be prohibited in any other EC member state. According to *The Economist*, the origins of mutual recognition arise from an attempt to sell a liqueur in Germany. The account is an interesting one:

In 1978 along came a West German company called Rewe Zentral AG (which) wanted to import Creme de Cassis, a liqueur otherwise known as Cassis de Dijon, into West Germany. It found it could not, because the elixir did not contain enough alcohol to be deemed a liqueur by West German standards. Rewe started legal proceedings which led to the European Court of Justice in Luxembourg. The court looked at West Germany's claim that its liqueur norms did not discriminate between West Germans and foreigners, and ruled that it would not wash. West Germany had no right to block the import of a drink that was on sale in France, unless it could show that it was blocked for reasons of health, fiscal supervision, fair trading or consumer protection. West Germany could not.

(*The Economist*, 1988)

It is all very well to be able to sell a product in another member state of the EC – getting it there is another problem. To most people, delays at border crossings is what 1992 is all about. There is, of course, more to it than that, but the sheer visibility of border delays, with queues of cars and lorries waiting to cross, serves as a potent symbol.

An important point to recognize is that a border represents a convenient, but not essential, place to make checks. And the list of checks governments want to make is a long one, including:

- payments for Value Added Tax (VAT)
- payments to Customs and Excise
- animal and plant health
- illegal arms, drugs and immigrants
- trade statistics

The governments of EC member states have agreed to relocate many of the above activities away from borders, but this may take some time: there is no prospect of the EC being able to eliminate delays at all its internal borders from 1993 onwards. This problem is particularly acute for countries such as the UK which have sea rather than land frontiers. Ports (and also airports) are such convenient centres for checking passengers and freight that successive governments have preferred to exercise control mainly at these locations. As a result, there is little in the way of internal control (such as identity cards), which is commonplace in countries such as France, with extensive land borders that are difficult to police.

Progress towards a border-free Europe will probably be two-speed. The slowest countries to open their borders will probably include the UK, for the reasons outlined above, and France at its border with Italy, whose immigration laws are too lax for comfort. Those countries moving fastest towards eliminating mutual borders will be five of the founding countries of the Community, namely

France, Germany and the Benelux countries. Their shared desire to move quickly towards freer movement of goods and people is expressed in the Schengen Agreement of 1990, which is designed to sweep away many of the regular checks at borders.

A two-speed EC is also the prospect for some measures in the 1992 programme which directly affect the marketplace for logistics services. Foremost among these are the deregulation of haulage markets and the harmonization of rules affecting lorry operation. The deregulation of *international* haulage markets is planned to be complete by the end of 1992. Then all permit restrictions (both bilateral and multilateral) should be abandoned in favour of 'qualitative' entry into the international haulage market. In tandem with this additional operating freedom there will be relaxed controls on cabotage, which is wholly domestic work, carried out by an international haulier, in a country where he is non-resident (for example, an Italian haulier carrying goods between Hamburg and Frankfurt). Until July 1990, cabotage was banned by all Community countries. Since then an experiment in cabotage has been launched by the European Commission, against much opposition from national hauliers, with a view to fully liberalizing it during the 1990s.

In the above markets affected by deregulation, all EC countries have moved at the same pace. This is not true, however, for *national* deregulation. Here, the authority of the European Commission to force a country into national deregulation of its freight market is questionable. As result, countries such as Germany and Greece maintain strict controls on haulage capacity (and price in the case of Germany). By contrast, many other EC countries (such as the UK) are already deregulated or (like France) are close to full deregulation.

The deregulation of European freight markets is clearly less than seamless. A similar point applies to many rules affecting lorry operation. Take, for example, lorry weights and dimensions. According to the European Commission, these are harmonized throughout the Community because the relevant directives have been issued and accepted by member states. An observer may be forgiven for thinking that all member states allow lorries to operate to identical weights and dimensions. This is not so, because some countries have secured derogations from the Commission in respect of weights and dimensions, effectively allowing them to delay the national implementation of higher weights. So while, in theory, lorry weights and dimensions are already harmonized across the Community, the reality is revealed in table 2.3, which shows important

**Table 2.3**   Technical standards in the EC road freight transport sector

| Member state | Maximum width (m) | Maximum length (m) Artic. | Maximum length (m) Road train[a] | Drive axle tonnes | Maximum weight (tonnes) Artic. | Maximum weight (tonnes) Road train[a] |
|---|---|---|---|---|---|---|
| Belgium | 2.5 | 15.5 | 18 | 12 | 44 | 44 |
| Germany | 2.5 | 16.5 | 18 | 11 | 40 | 40 |
| Denmark | 2.55 | 16 | 18.5 | 10 | 48 | 48 |
| Spain | 2.5 | 16.5 | 18 | 13 | 40 | 40 |
| France | 2.55 | 16.5 | 18 | 13 | 40 | 40 |
| UK | 2.5 | 16.5 | 18 | 10.5 | 38 | 32.5 |
| Greece | 2.5 | 15 | 18 | 10 | 38 | 38 |
| Italy | 2.5 | 16.5 | 18 | 12 | 44 | 44 |
| Ireland | 2.5 | 16.5 | 18 | 10.5 | 40 | 40 |
| Luxembourg | 2.6 | 16.5 | 18 | 12 | 44 | 44 |
| Netherlands | 2.6 | 15.5 | 18 | 11 | 50 | 50 |
| Portugal | 2.5 | 15.5 | 18 | 12 | 40 | 40 |
| EC (inter-state) | 2.5 | 16.5 | 18[c] | 11.5 | 40[b] | 40[b] |

[a] Road train = drawbar–trailer combination.
[b] The maximum limit for intermodal work is 44 tonnes.
Note that the weight/dimensions in the table are standards applying in the EC and do not take account of special provisions (for example, the 2.6 m width for refrigerated vehicles).
[c] 18.35 m as of 1 Oct. 1991.
*Sources*: IRU *Handbook of International Road Transport*; Ford; EC Commission; DAF; Pegaso

differences between certain member states and standards set by the European Commission.

The progress of the EC towards common standards and all other 1992 objectives is often very confusing. Countries move at different speeds, and realities do not always accord with expectations. This should not really be too surprising, given the diversity of cultures represented within the Community and the need to make political compromises.

## Changes in prospect

Over the next few years, new initiatives are certain to come from the European Commission to promote the further integration of the EC.

Some possible initiatives are highly important, such as a common foreign policy and pooled defence arrangements, but have relatively little impact on logistics. Others, such as common standards for environmental control, would have an impact on both the users of logistics services (as in the case of emissions from factory chimneys) and the providers (as in the case of the siting of transport operating centres).

Given the uncertainty of future initiatives there is not much point at this stage in trying to evaluate the consequences for logistics, except in one instance. Possible economic and monetary union (EMU) is such a far-reaching and controversial goal that it cannot be lightly dismissed.

If it is achieved, EMU would result in two key events, namely the creation of a single currency for the EC and a central bank to manage it. The implications for national governments are profound, since this means a substantial transfer of economic sovereignty to Community institutions.

The foundations for EMU were laid in 1979 when the European Monetary System (EMS) was founded. Among other things, this involved the linking of currencies between member states through the Exchange Rate Mechanism (ERM). Each currency is only allowed to fluctuate within a narrow range. If a currency seems likely to breach the limits of the range then the national government must take corrective action.

In effect, the ERM acts as a straightjacket, and a government may be forced to change policy if its currency gets out of line with the others. France is a case in point. Following his election victory, François Mitterand launched an ambitious programme of economic initiatives, only to have to cut back on them when there was an adverse impact on the franc.

It is still uncertain whether EMS will lead to EMU in the 1990s. However, the prospects for EMU brightened considerably when the UK government finally took the pound into the ERM in 1990. For many people, the prospect of creating a single currency for everyday use within the EC is an exciting one. (The European Currency Unit, the ecu, does already exist, but is mainly restricted in its use to transactions between certain financial institutions.) For many businesses trading within the EC the single currency is a welcome prospect, since it is costly to remit money across borders within the EC; banking commissions for currency conversion can be high. Moreover, trading can be divorced from currency speculation; an exporter may gain from a windfall profit when his products are priced in a foreign currency which goes up in value relative to his own currency, but the reverse can also be true.

Fears of this kind can be held partly responsible for suppressing trading between EC countries; firms may simply feel more secure trading in their home markets. Similarly, currency fluctuations can have an impact on the service industries, such as international haulage. UK international hauliers, for example, suffered a major loss of business in the mid-1980s, partly because of the pound's rapid appreciation against other European currencies (Cooper, Browne and Gretton, 1987). Now that the pound is in the ERM, this is less of a problem.

What emerges clearly from the foregoing is that the creation of a single currency will do much to stimulate trade between EC member states and the services associated with that trade – especially logistics. Uncertainty over exchange rates and different national financial and fiscal policies have between them inhibited logistics services providers who are currently national from developing pan-European activities.

## R&D programmes and logistics

To conclude this discussion on the rapid transformations that are taking place within the EC, it is important to note the impact of programmes designed to promote improved efficiency in European logistics, particularly through developments in IT. From the mid-1980s onwards, the European Commission has sponsored a number of research programmes, mainly through DG XIII, the Directorate-General for Telecommunications, Information Industry and Innovation. The programmes are best known by their various acronyms, which include DRIVE, TEDIS, ESPRIT, EURET and COST, although others – such as PROMETHEUS – make affecting reference to symbols of European culture.

Most of these programmes are large-scale, with multimillion ecu budgets spread over a number of years. Two key objectives are common to all programmes: they aim to make European industry more competitive, notably in information technology (IT); and co-operation between European countries is promoted, especially in a north–south direction. Since IT is a very 'horizontal' activity (that is, it can link a variety of organizations, such as banks, retailers, finance houses) the spin-off from these R&D programmes is extensive.

Logistics, which also has many horizontal attributes, is a clear beneficiary. Take, for example, the first phase of the DRIVE programme. This featured two projects closely related to logistics. The FLEET project had as its focus in-cab technology for lorries, while the remit for the EUROFRET project was much wider, taking in freight exchange systems, customs clearance, vehicle routing and scheduling, among other things. Working on a 1.5 million ecu budget, over a period of two years, EUROFRET involved a consortium of consultants, operators and academics from five European countries, Belgium, Greece, the Netherlands, Sweden and the UK. Findings from the EUROFRET research were disseminated throughout the EC, both to inform about best practice, and to spur developments in the field of IT which are most likely to improve logistics efficiency.

Apart from the value of the R&D programmes themselves, what must also be considered is their contribution to European integration. The clear intention of the European Commission (and the European Parliament which must approve the programmes) is that the EC must be made a more cohesive entity by encouraging people from different countries to work with one another. The role model, once again, is the USA. Just as people from, say, Connecticut and California should readily be able to work together, the same should be true for people from Greece and Germany.

The logic of this aim applies, of course, not only to IT and logistics. It is particularly important in education, which is still largely pursued on a national basis. Higher education programmes such as ERASMUS aim to encourage the exchange of staff and students between universities, and so help foster a more European outlook among a potentially important group of opinion-formers. The fruits of all the Europe-wide initiatives are yet to appear, but there should be no mistaking the strength of purpose of those who want to see a unified Europe.

# Part I
# Demand-side Logistics

# 3

# European Manufacturing

## Introduction

The users of logistics services (such as manufacturers and retailers) play a critical role in shaping those services. As a consequence, change in the manufacturing sector must be an important focus of this book. Identifying the key changes, examining the underlying reasons for them, and analysing the implications for logistics services demand occupy this chapter and the next.

Increasing dominance in Europe of large corporations in many industries and Europe-wide mergers and acquisitions mean that logistics services providers such as road hauliers and freight forwarders must offer more diverse services over a larger geographical area – a tremendous challenge. But before we look at the changes in manufacturing in a European context and assess what they imply for logistics demand, it is vital to appreciate the role played by manufacturing industry in Europe, the various strengths and weaknesses of different sectors and indeed the key players – both companies and countries – in specific industries. Having established this we can then turn to the trends that are going to impact on the demand for logistics services, among which are: the effects of 1992 and market integration; corporate plans for growth, amounting sometimes to a desire for global status; and the need for large multinational companies to make their size count by concentrating their production facilities.

# Does Manufacturing Still Matter?

The relative importance of manufacturing and the service sectors has changed dramatically over the past 25 years. In most advanced economies the service sector now accounts for a greater proportion of employment and gross value-added[2] than does industry. Other measures such as employment also illustrate this change, and have been noted by many writers as providing a clue to the future. For example, between 1960 and 1985 employment in the manufacturing sector in the USA fell from 44 to 31 per cent of the total, and in Italy from 67 to 45 per cent (Handy, 1989) – a continuing trend with important implications for Western economies and societies.

Despite this decline in the relative importance of industry in many of the advanced nations, European manufacturers remain a major force both in Europe and in the wider world economy. For instance, within the EC, industry contributes 35 per cent of gross value-added, which is more than in the USA but less than in Japan (table 3.1). Reference to table 3.1 clearly shows the fall in the relative importance of industry's contribution to gross value-added, and this trend is most marked in the USA and EC.

**Table 3.1**  Percentage of gross value-added at market prices (current prices)

|        | Agriculture | | Industry[a] | | Services | | Total | |
|--------|------|------|------|------|------|------|------|------|
|        | 1976 | 1988 | 1976 | 1988 | 1976 | 1988 | 1976 | 1988 |
| EUR 12 | 4.7  | 3.0  | 41.0 | 35.4 | 54.3 | 61.6 | 100  | 100  |
| USA    | 2.8  | 1.9  | 33.8 | 28.5 | 63.4 | 69.6 | 100  | 100  |
| Japan  | 5.2  | 2.5  | 41.4 | 40.4 | 53.4 | 57.1 | 100  | 100  |

[a] Industry in the wider sense = manufacturing + energy + construction.
*Source*: *Basic Statistics*, Eurostat (1989b), Commission of the European Communities.

Four major countries – Germany, France, Italy and the UK – contribute between them more than 80 per cent of the value of the EC's industrial production. Germany leads by a considerable margin, with almost 30 per cent of the Community's gross industrial value-added – a figure that will rise if the productive potential of the former East Germany can be realized.

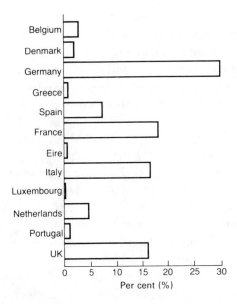

**Figure 3.1** Percentage of gross value-added by industry at market prices (current industrial prices), 1986. Industry in the wider sense is comprised of manufacturing plus the energy industry plus the construction industry.

*Source*: *Basic Statistics*, Eurostat (1989b), Commission of the European Communities

However, the importance of industry varies considerably from one country to another – industry contributed 40 per cent of gross value-added in the UK and Germany, 32 per cent in France and 35 per cent in Belgium and the Netherlands, while in Denmark it represented only 27 per cent (Eurostat).

## Which Industry Sectors are Important?

The value of production is a measure of the importance of various industry sectors. Published data on production values can be used to gain an insight into the absolute and relative importance of a number of industry sectors (table 3.2). The food sector is clearly the most important, accounting for 19 per cent of industrial production. Just four sectors (food, chemicals, motor vehicles and electrical and electronic goods) between them account for over 50 per cent of the total value of production. This has important implications for logistics services since the principal sectors will provide much of the demand for logistics services (such as transport and storage). The scale of the food manufacturing sector, combined with growing internationalization and concentration in grocery retailing (see chapters 5 and 6), explains why developments in grocery logistics have come to occupy such a prominent position in the thinking of many managers and academics.

The production index (table 3.2) shows that the most rapidly growing industry sectors within the EC are those producing electrical and electronic goods, in which the value of production rose by 18.6 per cent between 1980 and 1986. This sector is followed by chemicals, cars, food and paper. By contrast, it is the traditional sectors – timber, machinery, footwear and clothing textiles, iron and steel, and shipbuilding – which have declined (that is, all the 1986 indices are lower than those for 1980).

Four of the top ten European industrial companies are motor vehicle manufacturers and the European car industry is, in production terms, the largest in the world, ahead of both the USA and Japan. There are five major car-producing countries in the EC, and between

**Table 3.2**    Value of production by industry sector in the EC, 1986

| Sector | Value of production (million ecu) | Sector share of total (%) | 1986 Index (1980 = 100) |
|---|---|---|---|
| Iron and steel | 115 654 | 7 | 95.0 |
| Chemical industry | 229 938 | 13 | 116.8 |
| Office and data-processing equipment | 35 228 | 2 | n/a |
| Electrical and electronic goods | 178 123 | 10 | 118.6 |
| Motor vehicles | 178 370 | 10 | 109.3 |
| Shipbuilding | 12 770 | <1 | n/a |
| Food and drink | 334 822 | 19 | 107.3 |
| Textiles | 75 401 | 4 | 98.8 |
| Footwear and clothing | 51 852 | 3 | 90.8 |
| Steel products/tools | 124 929 | 7 | 91.3 |
| Machinery | 163 137 | 9 | 96.1 |
| Timber | 48 832 | 3 | 89.3 |
| Paper | 109 203 | 6 | 108.4 |
| Rubber and plastics | 68 910 | 4 | 112.2 |

*Source*: *Basic Statistics*, Eurostat (1989b), Commission of the European Communities.

them they account for 90 per cent of production (Germany 33 per cent, France 23.5 per cent, Italy 13 per cent, Spain 11 per cent and the UK 9 per cent). The car industry is a major exporter, but it faces very strong competition from Japan in all the world markets and within Europe itself. Since the late 1970s, Japanese exports have risen significantly while those of the EC have fallen (figure 3.2). Although European imports of Japanese cars have grown, there has been an uneven spread between different member states. For example, a long-standing arrangement between Rome and Tokyo allows Japanese car producers to export only 2550 cars a year to Italy, a nation that buys nearly two million cars annually (Friedman, 1988). By contrast, the UK imports almost one hundred times as many Japanese cars (213 067 in 1989), representing 9.3 per cent of

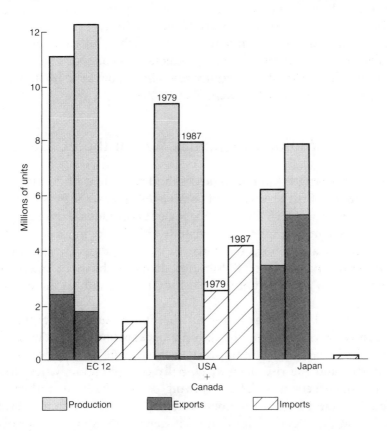

**Figure 3.2** Car production in millions of units, 1979 and 1987.
*Source: Basic Statistics*, Eurostat (1989b), Commission of the European Communities

the total new car market. Yet even this percentage figure is kept artificially low by a voluntary restraint agreement between the two governments on car imports from Japan.

Motor manufacturing can be seen as an intermediate sector between the traditional industries such as iron and steel and shipbuilding and the 'sunrise' industries such as biotechnology, information technology (IT) and telecommunications. The electronic components industry (making, for example, semiconductors and integrated circuits) employs over 260 000 people in the EC and is growing at a rapid rate. Four countries contribute 84 per cent of total production: Germany 35 per cent, France 21 per cent, UK 19 per cent and Italy 9 per cent.

But despite rapid growth the European electronics industry as a whole still trails behind the USA and Japan (CBI/PA Consulting Group, 1990). The European Commission is keen to stimulate European industrial competitiveness, and has noted with concern that European computer chip production accounts for just 10 per cent of the world market, compared with 52 per cent for Japan and 37 per cent for the USA (Kellaway, 1990).

# Major Companies Within the EC

National strengths and weaknesses, and the extent of dominance by particular industry sectors and companies, goes some way to explain the driving forces which influence logistics demands. For example, as we will see in chapter 6, the strength of UK retailing has acted as a very important innovative force in UK logistics. By contrast, in Germany, manufacturers' logistics demands have been far more important in driving change (reflecting the strength of the manufacturing sector).

The broad industrial profile of the EC outlined in the preceding sections provides an insight into the background of the demand for logistics services, vividly illustrating the decline of traditional heavy industry and the rise of new, globally competing activities such as consumer electronics. The following section looks in rather more detail at the big four member states of the EC (Germany, France, Italy and the UK) in order to form a view on the shape and priorities for logistics services demand in each country's manufacturing sector.

In many cases the largest companies in each country set a tone and standard which impacts on the nature of logistics demands. They do this first by direct involvement in logistics services demand (that is, as shippers, buyers of services) and second through their activities in professional institutes, trade associations and industry confederations (such as the CBI in the UK, and CONFINDUSTRIA in Italy). We have also concentrated on examining the larger companies since it is these companies, many operating in more than one European country, which will clearly have the most immediate opportunities to implement pan-European logistics strategies, a key development of the 1990s.

The importance of specific industry sectors is to a large extent mirrored by the size and relative importance of companies within those sectors; that is to say that large and important industry sectors contain large and important companies. Given the significance of the European automotive sector it is not surprising that three out of the top ten European companies are motor vehicle manufacturers (Daimler–Benz, Fiat and the Volkswagen–Audi Group). The top ten, measured by turnover, also includes two international oil giants (Shell and British Petroleum), two food processing companies (Unilever and Nestlé), a manufacturer of electrical equipment (Siemens), the German postal utility (Bundespost) and the Italian state holding company IRI (table 3.3).

Germany dominates two important industrial sectors in Europe – cars and chemicals. In each, German companies account for three out of the top six European companies. The top ten companies in each of the big four EC member states are shown in table 3.4. A striking feature is that the tenth largest German company (Tengelmann) is the 25th largest in Europe, while the tenth largest French, UK and Italian companies rank 49th, 58th and 96th respectively. Taken together, these points highlight the strength of the German economy and the extent to which it is by some distance the most dominant European economic force.

Having discussed the existing pattern of European manufacturing together with sectoral and country strengths and weaknesses, what is needed now is an assessment of the main forces which will change this pattern. Broadly, there are two categories of change which will impact on the logistics demands of manufacturing industry:

- external forces (such as the SEM)
- internal forces (such as mergers and acquisitions in the pursuit of scale)

It is perhaps rather artificial to try to separate the cause and effect. For instance, the cause of many mergers and acquisitions is a

**Table 3.3**   European top 30 by turnover, 1990

| | Company | Country | Turnover (US $m) | Year end |
|---|---|---|---|---|
| 1 | Royal Dutch/Shell | Anglo-Dutch | 89 264.2 | 31/12/89 |
| 2 | IRI | Italy | 54 490.3 | 31/12/89 |
| 3 | British Petroleum | UK | 50 720.4 | 31/12/89 |
| 4 | Daimler–Benz | Germany | 45 393.1 | 31/12/89 |
| 5 | Fiat | Italy | 42 117.6 | 31/12/89 |
| 6 | Volkswagen–Audi (VAG) | Germany | 38 833.1 | 31/12/89 |
| 7 | Unilever plc/NV | Anglo-Dutch | 36 825.8 | 31/12/89 |
| 8 | Siemens | Germany | 36 322.9 | 30/09/89 |
| 9 | Nestlé | Switzerland | 33 714.2 | 31/12/89 |
| 10 | Deutsche Bundespost | Germany | 33 520.7 | 31/12/89 |
| | | | | |
| 11 | BAT Industries | UK | 31 028.4 | 31/12/89 |
| 12 | Renault | France | 30 825.2 | 31/12/89 |
| 13 | Philips | Netherlands | 30 219.7 | 31/12/89 |
| 14 | ENI | Italy | 30 110.5 | 31/12/89 |
| 15 | Veba | Germany | 29 239.8 | 31/12/89 |
| 16 | BASF | Germany | 28 294.6 | 31/12/89 |
| 17 | Hoechst | Germany | 27 273.2 | 31/12/89 |
| 18 | Peugeot | France | 27 022.9 | 31/12/89 |
| 19 | Elf Aquitaine | France | 26 465.8 | 31/12/89 |
| 20 | Electricité de France | France | 25 814.1 | 31/12/89 |
| | | | | |
| 21 | Bayer | Germany | 25 728.8 | 31/12/89 |
| 22 | CGE | France | 25 422.6 | 31/12/89 |
| 23 | RWE | Germany | 23 157.2 | 30/06/89 |
| 24 | Imperial Chemical Industries | UK | 22 537.6 | 31/12/89 |
| 25 | Tengelmann | Germany | 22 104.7 | 30/06/89 |
| 26 | Metro International | Switzerland | 21 178.4 | 31/12/88 |
| 27 | British Telecom | UK | 21 072.9 | 31/03/90 |
| 28 | Marc-Rich | Switzerland | 21 055.5 | 31/12/89 |
| 29 | ABB Asea Brown Boveri | Sweden | 20 560.0 | 31/12/89 |
| 30 | Thyssen | Germany | 20 351.4 | 30/09/89 |

*Source: The FT European Top 500* (Week ending 11 January 1991)

company's desire to become bigger which, in turn, has been influenced by the perceived opportunities and challenges provided by the SEM. Accordingly, we have not sought to identify with any precision the sequence of particular events. What is of most importance is to identify the key influences on manufacturers and then to see how these impact on their logistics needs. The rest of this chapter addresses these issues in some detail under the following headings:

*External forces*
● effects of SEM
*Internal forces*
● concentration through mergers and acquisitions
● growth – from international to multinational to global
● making size count – the importance of concentrating production facilities

# Removing Barriers to Trade: a Stimulus for European Industry

In order to create the SEM, various barriers to trade between the member states must be removed:

● physical barriers (such as border crossing controls)
● technical barriers (such as product standards)
● fiscal barriers (such as different taxation regimes)

The processes involved in creating the SEM are illustrated in figure 3.3.

Elsewhere in the book we examine both the high-level implications of the Single European Market (SEM) and their effect on logistics strategies (chapters 2 and 8), as well as specific effects on certain sectors (such as greater freedoms to provide international transport services, in chapter 12). In the present chapter it is important to examine the implications for manufacturers of removing technical barriers.

It is evident that some technical barriers are considered by manufacturers to inhibit trade to a greater degree than others. We will concentrate on the two most significant developments:

● the opportunity for free movement of goods as a result of technical harmonization and standards and the approximation of laws
● the change to more open public procurement

**Table 3.4**  Top ten companies in Germany, France, the UK and Italy

| | Germany | | | France | | |
|---|---|---|---|---|---|---|
| Company | Sector | European rank by turnover | | Company | Sector | European rank by turnover |
| Daimler–Benz | 401 | 4 | | Renault | 401 | 12 |
| Volkswagen–Audi (VAG) | 401 | 6 | | Peugeot | 401 | 18 |
| Siemens | 541 | 8 | | Elf Aquitaine | 212 | 19 |
| Bundespost | 406 | 10 | | Electricité de France | 221 | 20 |
| Veba | 171 | 15 | | CGE | 533 | 22 |
| BASF | 622 | 16 | | Total | 212 | 31 |
| Hoechst | 622 | 17 | | Generale des Eaux | 221 | 34 |
| Bayer | 622 | 21 | | Usinor Sacilor | 633 | 35 |
| RWE | 221 | 23 | | Pechiney | 671 | 39 |
| Tengelmann | 491 | 25 | | Thomson | 551 | 49 |

UK

| Company | Sector | European rank by turnover |
|---|---|---|
| Shell[a] | 212 | 1 |
| BP | 212 | 3 |
| Unilever[a] | 451 | 7 |
| BAT Industries | 171 | 11 |
| ICI | 622 | 24 |
| British Telecom | 223 | 27 |
| Grand Metropolitan | 421 | 37 |
| British Aerospace | 523 | 40 |
| British Gas | 222 | 48 |
| BTR | 591 | 58 |

Italy

| Company | Sector | European rank by turnover |
|---|---|---|
| IRI | 171 | 2 |
| Fiat | 401 | 5 |
| ENI | 622 | 14 |
| STET | 171 | 44 |
| Enimont | 622 | 47 |
| Ferruzzi Finanziaria | 171 | 50 |
| Ferruzzi Agricola Fin. | 171 | 60 |
| SIP | 223 | 65 |
| Ilva | 633 | 90 |
| Pirelli Spa | 574 | 96 |

[a] Anglo-Dutch.

*Sector codes*

| 171 | Diversified holding companies | 523 | Aircraft manufacturers |
|---|---|---|---|
| 212 | Oil – internationals | 533 | Communications equipment |
| 221 | Electric utilities, water works and supplies | 541 | Electrical equipment |
| 222 | Natural gas utilities | 551 | Electronics |
| 223 | Telephone companies | 574 | Tyres and rubber goods |
| 401 | Vehicle manufacturers | 591 | Diversified industrial (manufacturing) |
| 406 | Diversified consumer goods/services | 622 | Chemicals (diversified) |
| 421 | Beverages – brewers | 633 | Iron and steel |
| 451 | Food processors | 671 | Fabricated metal products |
| 491 | Retail – department store | | |

*Source: The FT European Top 500 (Week ending 11 January 1991)*

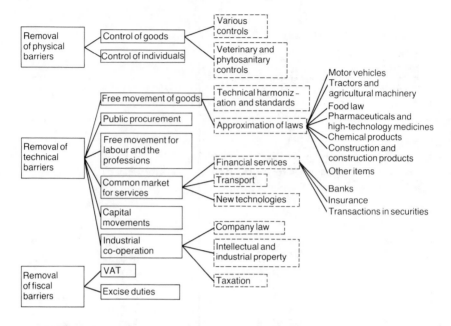

**Figure 3.3**   The process of creating the SEM.
Source: *Croner's Europe*, 1990, Croner's Publications Ltd,
Kingston upon Thames

Both of these initiatives are especially important to European logistics because they will further stimulate trade between EC member states, which is already growing faster than either national trade or trade with third countries. In turn, this new evolving trade pattern will impact on the logistics requirements of manufacturers.

The example of fruit yoghurts illustrates the type of product barrier that has often made it difficult to sell the same product in more than one EC country without changing the product in some significant way. In Germany the fruit used in the yoghurt may be coloured but the yoghurt itself cannot, whereas in Belgium the yoghurt may be coloured but the fruit cannot – an extreme example perhaps but, nevertheless, indicative of the sort of trade inhibitors which will certainly be removed by the mid-1990s.

At present, as this shows, the fact that a product is acceptable in one member state does not mean that it will be in another. Indeed, the acceptance procedures and the time needed to complete them vary considerably from one EC country to another. In order to resolve this difficulty it is proposed that there should be mutual recognition of technical and safety standards. This mutual recognition means that if a product is certified as acceptable in one member state it should be acceptable in others.

Clearly, mutual recognition will provide a mechanism for speeding up the acceptance of products by different member states, but it does raise issues of conflict with national policy. For example, a non-nutritive sweetener, aspartame, is used for the diet segment of the soft drinks industry in most, but not all, EC countries. In countries where aspartame has been banned (France and Spain) the diet sector has been far slower to take off. Mutual recognition of standards would make this type of 'discrimination' illegal. But whether this is universally a good thing depends on one's point of view – in 1990 a number of reports suggested that aspartame posed a health risk to certain people suffering from an inherited condition called phenyl-ketonuria (*The Economist*, 1990a). In an age when the power of the final consumer is becoming greater we can anticipate more rather than less concern about product safety and liability, no matter what EC mechanisms are devised to remove barriers to trade.

Intra-EC trade has been further inhibited as a result of the less than wholeheartedly European attitude shown by the public sector (such as nationalized industries and government departments and ministries) in many countries. The public-sector organizations of many EC member states are major purchasers of goods and services. Yet this sector has until recently had in place both explicit and unwritten rules to encourage them to buy only from companies from their own countries; regardless of whether that is really the best product or the lowest price.

As a result, within the EC, purchasing by the public sector is far more nationalistic than is the case in the private sector. This nationalism amounts to a form of protectionism for some national industries, and increases costs to the final consumer, while restricting opportunities for the most efficient European companies to grow. As part of the drive towards the SEM, legislation will force public-sector procurement to adopt a far more open policy (of course there are still some sectors, such as defence, in which for strategic reasons procurement is restricted to national firms). As Cecchini (1988) says 'certain high technology areas of telecommunications, power genera-tion, railways and defence are characterized by dominant public buyers, very few suppliers and little intra-EC trade'. The European Commission has proposed that companies should have legal redress in order to assert their rights under EC rules, and to ensure that public-sector buyers comply with them. In addition, open tendering and contract awards procedures which are currently restricted to certain markets will be widened to include the following sectors: energy, transport, telecommunications and water supply.

In brief, the removal of technical barriers will:

- increase intra-EC trade flows
- reduce product differentiation and complexity
- expand European branding and marketing
- reduce R&D costs
- reduce unit costs of production

The proponents of the SEM also point to two further developments which arise from removing technical barriers, and which they claim will make European industry more competitive:

- the increased scope for economies of scale
- opportunities for innovation by smaller companies

The reasoning for this has been extensively documented in the Cecchini report (Cecchini, 1988). The assertion is made that market integration will dramatically increase the scope for economies of scale. However, the report acknowledges that potential gains vary by industry, and amount to only 1 per cent in the petroleum products sector (most economies of scale having already been achieved) but some 6 per cent for heavy electrical equipment. Market integration will stimulate corporate restructuring within industry in each member state: the smaller and least efficient companies will disappear and new or more specialized companies will take their place. Savings within the manufacturing sector from restructuring are estimated at 48 billion ecu.

One of the most important implications of the SEM concerns the scope for innovation. Innovation is of crucial importance in an ever-accelerating global economy in which products have shorter and shorter life-cycles. But innovation appears to be stifled where industry has high entry barriers and low growth. The 1992 legislation and market integration should help to reduce barriers to entry. For example, large established firms (notably telecommunications and power generation) currently monopolize the European stage because of privileged links with national governments. The move towards common standards and regulations, mutual recognition of product standards and open public procurement will result in fewer barriers to entry, and opportunities for far more innovation by firms with new ideas and new competitive strengths.

While recognizing the important effects of the SEM, it would be as well not to lose sight of the way national governmental self-interest often seems to hamper the move towards an open and integrated market. This can be the case even when the government in question publicly espouses the cause of the SEM. Two examples of governments acting to protect narrow national self-interests – both taken from the car industry – illustrate how progress towards a truly integrated SEM with a 'level playing field' may be slower than expected, and the ultimate competitive benefits somewhat less than anticipated:

- The UK government was accused of favouring a British company (British Aerospace) when the decision was made to sell off the car manufacturer Rover Group.
- In Italy, Ford bid for Alfa Romeo, who favoured acceptance of the bid. However, it was reported that the powerful car manufacturer Fiat were able to influence the Italian government to bar the Ford bid – and ultimately Alfa was sold to Fiat.

Whatever the precise financial gains for European industry resulting from the SEM, an important point to note is that the creation of such a large market will further stimulate industrial concentration or the ownership by fewer companies of larger market shares – a feature of Western economies during the 1980s.

Frequently, the mechanism by which this corporate growth and the resulting industry concentration is achieved is through mergers and acquisitions. In order to gain some insight into who is buying whom, where they are doing it and what the effects will be for logistics, we now assess some recent data on this European trend.

# Growing Concentration Through Mergers and Acquisitions

Mergers and takeovers among manufacturers form another part of the jigsaw facing logistics services suppliers (such as road hauliers and shipping lines). What happens when two companies, which have until then been using different transport companies, merge? Usually there is a drive to rationalize activities and reduce the number of service suppliers. This can mean that a transport company loses an important part of their business for reasons that are essentially beyond their control. Or it may mean that transport and storage companies are faced with the opportunity of far more business if they become the favoured service provider following an acquisition by one of their current customers. This happened to Sutherlands (part of the Transport Development Group), which benefited from the British Airways merger with British Caledonian. Having been responsible only for British Caledonian's inter-airport trucking, Sutherlands subsequently took over responsibility for this activity for the new merged airline, replacing British Airways' in-house operation.

The scope for mergers and acquisitions and strategic alliances (where firms agree to pursue some common aim together, but remain operationally and legally separate) has been viewed by some European governments as having a special importance. In the UK since 1979, the government has adopted a 'hands off' approach, neither encouraging nor discouraging companies to merge. When this is combined with the ownership of UK companies which are equity-dominated, in contrast to many bank-dominated or private Continental European corporations, then it makes UK companies a relatively easy target for takeover. Alongside this must be placed the freedom from exchange control restrictions in the UK, which has made it easy for UK corporations to pursue an aggressive overseas corporate expansion strategy – most obviously in the USA.

France provides a striking contrast to the UK, with the French government adopting a much more interventionist approach; this is perhaps to be expected given the greater direct government involvement in industry in France. In mid-1990 the French Finance Ministry was reported to be encouraging French industry to use its strength (based on the record strength of the franc against the deutschmark) to buy up competitive parts of German industry (Translink, 1990). Both private-sector companies and French state enterprises were active acquirers in the period from January 1989 to March 1990, with the state companies alone completing a total of 41 deals in Europe worth 5 billion ecu (figure 3.4). When private investors are taken into account then it has been estimated that French investment outside France reached about 15 billion ecu in the year to July 1990.

Cross-border takeovers are not a new phenomenon, but the increased volume and value of cross-border deals within the EC, and by non-EC countries buying in the EC are striking, as KPMG Peat Marwick's Dr Sauer told a *Financial Times* conference (see Melly, 1990). The number of international deals in the EC grew from 847 – worth $31.6 billion – in 1988 to 1256 – worth $45.5 billion – in 1989 (table 3.5). Just over half of these deals (53 per cent) in terms of

**Table 3.5**　Cross-border merger and acquisition activity

| Buying region | $ bn | % | No. of deals | % |
|---|---|---|---|---|
| EC sales in 1988 | | | | |
| Other EC country | 11.2 | 35 | 547 | 65 |
| North America | 7.5 | 24 | 134 | 16 |
| Rest of world | 12.9[a] | 41 | 166 | 19 |
| | 31.6 | 100 | 847 | 100 |
| | | | | |
| EC sales in 1989 | | | | |
| Other EC country | 24.0 | 53 | 770 | 61 |
| North America | 13.1 | 29 | 217 | 17 |
| Rest of world | 8.4 | 18 | 269 | 22 |
| | 45.5 | 100 | 1256 | 100 |

[a] Includes Nestlé's acquisition of Rowntree for $4.9 bn.
*Source*: *Freighting World*, 18 May 1990.

value were between companies from EC member states. But investors from outside the EC have also been active: North American companies completed 217 deals with a total value of $13.1 billion, while Japanese companies invested $1.1 billion in the EC, of which $0.8 billion was in the UK (table 3.6). However, Japanese investment in the EC during 1989 was only about one-tenth of their investment in North America in the same year.

Companies from various EC member states were particularly keen to invest in Germany (104 deals were completed in 1989). But the value of these deals was very small (table 3.7), perhaps reflecting the considerable difficulty in purchasing German companies, with their bank-dominated ownership pattern. The figures suggest that British firms completed a great many relatively small deals, and Sauer notes that 'British companies do acquisitions much earlier in their corporate lifetime – and also small companies are making overseas acquisitions'. It is a moot point whether this represents a positive aspect of British business, implying far-sighted small companies, or whether it merely suggests that big UK companies are rather unadventurous in their attitude to the EC, preferring the English-speaking USA and Australia.

The discussion so far has focused on an important mechanism for growth, mergers and acquisitions. What we must also address are the

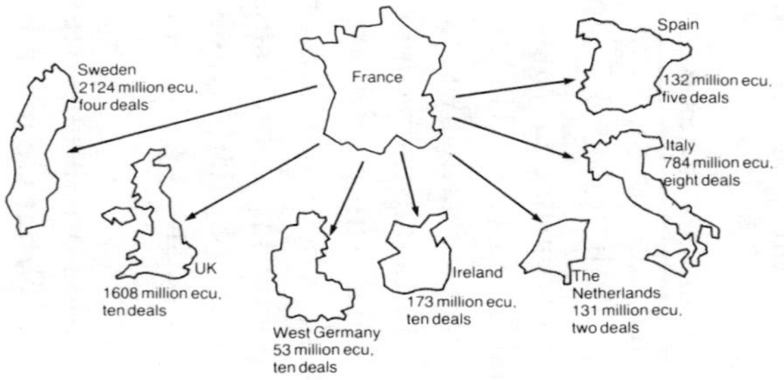

| Target industries | First quarter 1990 | | | | Full year 1989 | | | |
|---|---|---|---|---|---|---|---|---|
| | Number of deals | Ecu value (millions) | FF value (m) | Value as a percentage of all French acquisitions into sector | Number of deals | Ecu value (millions) | FF value (m) | Value as a percentage of all French acquisitions into sector |
| Automotive and aircraft | 3 | 2123.9 | 14.67 bn | 100% | 3 | 44.3 | 310.7 | 13% |
| Insurance | 3 | 261.9 | 1.81 bn | 53% | 7 | 680.0 | 4.77 bn | 25% |
| Services (miscellaneous) | 1 | 67.9 | 469.2 | 44% | — | — | — | — |
| Electronics, electrics and computers | 4 | 44.6 | 308.2 | 74% | 3 | 1470.1 | 10.31 bn | 98% |
| Chemicals | 2 | 22.5 | 155.5 | 100% | 9 | — | — | — |
| Mining and steel | 1 | — | — | — | 7 | — | — | — |
| Pharmaceuticals | 1 | — | — | — | 7 | 436.5 | 3.06 bn | 53% |
| Banking | | | | | 4 | 38.0 | 266.5 | 41% |
| Oil and gas | | | | | | | | |
| Totals | 15 | 2520.8 | 17.42 bn | 58% | 40 | 2668.9 | 18.72 bn | 28% |

Sweden 2124 million ecu. four deals

Spain 132 million ecu. five deals

Italy 784 million ecu. eight deals

The Netherlands 131 million ecu. two deals

France

Ireland 173 million ecu. ten deals

West Germany 53 million ecu. ten deals

UK 1608 million ecu. ten deals

**Figure 3.4** Outward investment by French state companies, January 1989 to March 1990. The following table shows the industries in which French state-owned and state-controlled companies made acquisitions during this period:

Note that prices were not disclosed for all deals. This compilation includes acquisitions by companies with state ownership in excess of 50 per cent.

*Source: Translink's European Deal Review*

potential benefits to manufacturers of this growth. Why should a company seek to move from a national base to become international, multinational or even global? The following section addresses this question and highlights some of the logistics implications of this trend to global scale.

# International, Multinational, Transnational or Global?

The terms *international, multinational, transnational* and *global* are often used interchangeably about businesses. A number of authors have commented on the difficulty of defining each one precisely (see, for example, Tugendhat, 1971; Dicken, 1986). Perhaps more important than any precise definition is the universal recognition that there has been a growing trend towards internationalization in the production and distribution of products.

**Table 3.6**  Japanese outward investment

|  | 1989 | | 1988 | |
|---|---|---|---|---|
|  | $ bn | No. of deals | $ bn | No. of deals |
| EC | 1.1 | 37 | 2.3 | 11 |
| North America | 10.9 | 89 | 8.4 | 62 |
| Other countries | 0.5 | 14 | 0.4 | 8 |
| Total | 12.5 | 140 | 11.1 | 81 |
| EC |  |  |  |  |
|   UK | 0.8 | 15 |  |  |
|   Germany | 0.1 | 3 |  |  |
|   Spain | 0.1 | 8 |  |  |
|   Belgium | 0.1 | 1 |  |  |
|   France | — | 5 |  |  |
|   Italy | — | 3 |  |  |
|   Other | — | 2 |  |  |
|   Total | 1.1 | 37 |  |  |

*Source*: *Freighting World*, 18 May 1990.

**Table 3.7** Intra-EC merger and acquisition activity, 1989

| | Purchases | | Sales | |
| --- | --- | --- | --- | --- |
| | $ bn | No. of deals | $ bn | No. of deals |
| France[a] | 7.8 | 183 | 3.9 | 163 |
| Germany[a] | 6.2 | 74 | 0.9 | 104 |
| UK | 4.6 | 295 | 11.1 | 116 |
| Belgium[a] | 1.6 | 24 | 1.3 | 64 |
| Italy | 1.1 | 50 | 1.6 | 81 |
| Netherlands | 1.0 | 61 | 1.9 | 89 |
| Ireland[a] | 0.8 | 39 | 0.2 | 13 |
| Spain | 0.2 | 17 | 1.4 | 101 |

[a] Includes some purchases made outside the EC.
Source: Freighting World, 18 May 1990.

Christopher (1990) suggests that 'A global business is one which does more than simply export' and that it will have the following features:

• typically, source its materials and supplies in more than one country
• often have widely spread production and assembly facilities
• market its products worldwide

Some of these features of a global business are clearly shared by multinational or transnational companies. But if pinning down the precise nature and definition of a global business is difficult, there nevertheless seems to be general agreement that global competition in fields as diverse as consumer electronics, computing, the fashion business and snack foods has been stimulated by:

• growing market integration
• a convergence of consumer tastes
• skilled marketing
• an almost frenzied search for new markets as product sales peak in their home markets

The opportunities generated by the increasing homogeneity and integration of the world's major economies, together with the accompanying development of global companies able to exploit them, has been noted (Levitt, 1983). However, as Zinn and Grosse (1990) have pointed out, in order to gain the benefits of globalization of markets, a manufacturer must be able to integrate and control international operations by centralizing and coordinating marketing, manufacturing and distribution. A global business approach enables firms to increase their competitiveness in world markets in a number of ways, each of which has important logistics implications:

- establishing specialized plants to supply regional as well as local markets
- implementing integrated transport and order processing systems
- responding to rapidly changing market conditions by switching products from one market to another
- using problem-solving originating in one market across all other markets
- sharing R&D costs, not only in product design and development but in the logistics area (say, inventory management or EDI implementation)

Sony provide an excellent example of a company seeking and achieving global scale and scope. By the mid-1990s the company seems set to become truly global, rather than simply a Japanese corporation with overseas subsidiaries. Globalization has indeed become a crusade for Akio Morita (Sony's chairman), who has defined his strategy as 'global localisation'. In the early 1980s some 70 per cent of the company's sales – but only 20 per cent of its products – were made outside Japan. This is changing, and in many instances Sony has 'gone local' in a big way; its European factories average 60 per cent local content (Cope, 1990).

Turning from consumer electronics to the related but distinct white goods sector (such as washing machines, cookers, refrigerators and dishwashers), there is also considerable evidence of growing global competition, driven by slowing sales in domestic markets and the ceaseless clamour for growth coming from the USA equity markets. In 1989 the US-based Whirlpool Corporation paid Fl525 million for a 53 per cent stake in the appliance business of Philips. Unlike many of its international competitors, Whirlpool is solely an appliance company and its target is global pre-eminence in that field. David Whitwam of Whirlpool has pointed out that – in the accepted sense – global markets embrace three main areas; the USA, Europe and Japan. Although Whirlpool is already strong in the USA, this desire to be global means that it will have to build considerable market share, first in Europe and ultimately in the Far East/Pacific Rim.

There is certainly considerable scope for white goods manufacturers to further build market share within Europe, since despite what has been referred to as a 'ten year orgy of mergers' (Parkes, 1990) there are still 300 appliance manufacturers in the EC. Mergers and acquisitions have left their mark on company ownership and control. For example, in the European market General Electric of the USA has taken a 50 per cent stake in GEC's appliance business, Maytag have bought Hoover, and Italy's Merloni Elletrodomestici has added Indesit to its Ariston business. Within Europe, Sweden's Electrolux is the market leader with over 20 per cent, Whirlpool/Philips has 13 per cent and Germany's Bosch/Siemens hold about 10 per cent.

Although there are many attractions to the idea of size and of marrying companies to obtain scale and create synergies, the strategy is not without its problems. Alliances, acquisitions, takeovers and mergers are all ways to get bigger and achieve Europe-wide, and ultimately global, scale. But there are difficulties, which should not be underestimated. The special cultural intricacies of Europe can create unexpected barriers, and these often seem to be derived from a clash of cultures rather than from specifically technical or managerial problems of exploiting potential synergies. These problems matter to the logistics sector, because logistics is increasingly becoming a truly Europe-wide cross-border activity, in which large manufacturers are placing a growing share of their business with a few key logistics services suppliers. The culture clash which occurred when the German car manufacturer Volkswagen took over the Spanish SEAT car company provides an example of some of the difficulties.

Volkswagen started buying into SEAT in 1986. By 1989 it had achieved a controlling interest and changed the company from a loss-maker into a profitable business. But the attitude of the Spanish workforce was also reported to have changed from having 'welcomed [Volkswagen] with open arms' to a relationship between Spanish workers and German management referred to as 'zero' (Hooper, 1989).

By late 1989, despite the introduction of quality circles, SEAT were producing just over half as many cars per worker as General Motors in Spain. Cultural factors underlay the reluctance of the Spanish workforce to adopt north European practices of continuous weekend production and relatively short summer plant shutdowns. SEAT's Zona Franca plant had traditionally closed down completely for the weekend and for the whole of August. However, there are reported to be signs of change (Hooper, 1989) and some 2000 workers at Zona Franca have adopted more flexible working practices. Nevertheless, productivity bonuses calculated by reference to time and motion study methods seem unlikely to be welcomed in the short term.

It is our view that the difficulties encountered in integrating different working practices and different cultural attitudes to work and leisure time are likely to decline as the SEM and growing integration becomes a reality. There seems almost certain to be a convergence of tastes, attitudes and business practices as a result of ever-increasing travel within the Community, and the important cultural influence of the media and information industries.

Although being big may bring problems for a manufacturer (either through the growth process or the ultimate operation) there is no doubt that it yields some potential benefits. One of these, the opportunity to concentrate production, is the focus of the final section of this chapter.

## Making Size Count: Concentrating Production

Increasing market integration does enable companies to pursue a number of strategies in order to make their size count. The scope to concentrate production at a small number of major locations is one that has a special importance within Europe, resulting from the move towards a single market and changes in eastern Europe. Going a step further than the decision to concentrate production at fewer sites is the move to single-product production lines, where specific factories are devoted to the manufacture of a single product type. Good examples of this development come from the fast-moving consumer goods sectors such as detergents and toothpaste, and from the consumer electronics and automotive industries.

There are a number of prerequisites in order for this concentration strategy to work:

- products must have a significant degree of commonality
- transport costs must be low relative to other resource costs (such as raw materials and storage)
- transport must be reliable
- the company must have centralized marketing control

Logistics strategy has a critical part to play in shaping each of these, and if all this can be achieved then there are a variety of benefits. Among the most important are:

- better quality control
- opportunities for more rapid product innovation

- economies of scale
- lower total costs
- longer production runs

The contrast between the manufacturing approach of the US company Procter & Gamble (P&G) and the Anglo-Dutch multinational Unilever in the detergents sector provides a good example of the benefits that can be gained from centralized production and distribution (Fraser, 1990). From the beginning of P&G's push into Europe in the late 1950s, they have launched standardized international brands that could be produced in one central location. For example, all P&G's heavy-duty liquid detergents for the European market (Ariel, Bold and Dash) are made in the UK and all its fabric softener in Germany. Provided that the economies of scale in production outweigh the potential transport cost penalty of moving relatively low-value items over longer distances, this will be a sensible strategy.

Unilever have traditionally manufactured different products in different local markets, and have not sought the benefits of very large-scale central production. This is partly the result of historical differences in the development of P&G and Unilever, with Unilever emerging much earlier in Europe and building a portfolio of national brands and companies though a series of acquisitions. In addition, the Unilever philosophy of decentralized marketing and independent profit centre responsibility has played a very strong role in their development, and produces a significant barrier to this type of focus strategy where production and marketing across national boundaries become subject to far greater central control. An organization structure based on autonomous local companies meant that Unilever concentrated on the differences that existed between markets rather than their similarities.

Unilever have decided to introduce some important changes to their decentralized policy, and are now seeking opportunities to produce and brand products in a much more coordinated European way in order to take advantage of the benefits of centralized production and concentrated inventory holding. Centralization does not have to lead to the complacency and the lowest common denominator approach. P&G has a 'totally harmonized' Ariel brand, which means it is made to the same specification for each European country. The company can, as a consequence, implement product innovation at a Europe-wide level more quickly, since it is able to concentrate its R&D efforts on a single well-branded product. This ability to innovate and maintain brand awareness, together with product quality control, all suggest that centralizing production and reducing the number of product lines produced at each site is, at present, the stronger strategy for a multinational company.

# 4

# Innovation in Manufacturing Logistics

## The Importance of Logistics

Themes of dramatic change, uncertainty and even chaos run through many recent books on industrial developments and management (see, for example, Peters, 1987; Handy, 1989; Dicken, 1986). Industry is said to be facing an ever more demanding future in which those working in manufacturing will have to cope with both increasing uncertainty and greater conflict; for example, conflicts between profit maximization and care for the environment.

Increasing competition, the rise of global markets and growing economic integration have between them contributed to a greater awareness of the importance of logistics in business strategy. For example, the completion of the Single European Market (SEM) will bring major opportunities for change in logistics strategies for companies which operate within Europe, whether they are European companies or subsidiaries of Japanese and American corporations with global ambitions. At present, the domain of logistics (sourcing, materials management and distribution) is often organized in a national way, with few companies adopting a Europe-wide – let alone global – approach.

Over the next few years, particularly as access to transport markets becomes easier (see chapters 8 and 10), more Europe-wide distribution networks will emerge. Some multinational companies already see Europe as a unified entity in production terms; with factory production and component suppliers coordinated at a European level. Integrated logistics networks are clearly a logical next step in smoothing the flow of products along the supply chain.

The previous chapter considered the principal trends in European manufacturing. It is evident that logistics both influences and is influenced by these trends. The logistics activities of sourcing, materials management and physical distribution both respond to change and can themselves be initiators of change in other parts of a firm's business (for example, new sourcing policy can impact on finance). Indeed, the logistics approach, which emphasizes the need to view the flow of material and information as a system, highlights the way change in any one area will affect all other parts of the system, in turn stimulating more change.

If we develop this concept further we can see that logistics cuts across traditional vertical boundaries (such as procurement, production and finance) in a manufacturer's activities. The crucial importance of logistics has led us to develop two hypotheses or propositions which provide a focus for this chapter. The first is that the trend towards international and ultimately global scale for many manufacturers has happened because companies have been able to count on logistics as a key support activity. Realizing the importance of logistics and the significance of its integrative function has enabled companies to pursue bold global strategies in the knowledge that sourcing, materials management and distribution could all be bound together by their logistics directors. An excellent logistics foundation has to be a prerequisite for success.

Second, the field of logistics has become a crucible for the techniques that many of the most innovative manufacturers regard as the leading edge of their competitive strategy – such as Just-in-Time (JIT), Quality Management, Materials Requirements Planning (MRP) and Computer-integrated Manufacturing (CIM). But logistics cannot be seen as a technological fix: there is no single logistics technique which can be put in place – no one right way to 'do logistics'. It is the need to think in depth about logistics and to pursue improvements in this area which enables companies to get it right and to continue to get it right. In this respect the best European companies are undoubtedly world class and able to compete in a global economy; others certainly lag behind.

Within this chapter we will deal first with the importance of the trend in many manufacturing sectors for the leading companies to seek global opportunities. We assess the way in which logistics has really been the enabler of change as companies strive to achieve wider geographical presence and, for a few, ultimately to become global players. Following that we turn to the view of logistics as the leading edge for corporate competitiveness. Finally, we consider the implications of these twin developments for the relationship between logistics services suppliers and logistics services users. Since these areas are interrelated readers may find it helpful to refer to figure 4.1, which also reflects the chapter structure.

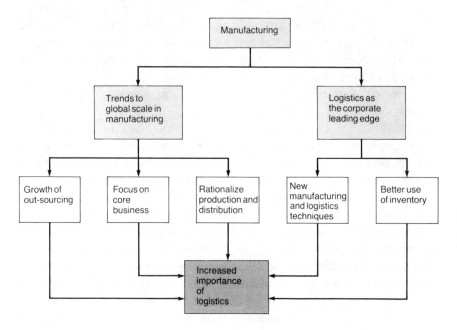

**Figure 4.1**  Driving forces in manufacturing logistics.

# Trends Towards Global Scale in Manufacturing

Drucker has pointed out that the two basic tendencies in this century are that the world is becoming more integrated economically and more fragmented politically (Flanagan, 1985). As he stresses, business should organize along product lines and not country lines, a statement that led the consulting firm A. T. Kearney to conclude that in the context of logistics 'Today the goal is not a fragmented multinational strategy but an integrated global strategy' (A. T. Kearney, 1987a). By implication it is not possible to have a global strategy without first having in place the underpinning logistics strategy.

When the desire for global scale is twinned with the opportunities provided by market integration in Europe (see chapter 3) then a number of implications become apparent. Of special interest to logistics are the linked corporate developments of:

- the decision to focus on core business
- the scope for manufacturers to alter their sourcing practices
- concentrating production and distribution

In passing it should be noted that while these developments are of particular importance to multinational and global companies, they will often be very relevant to companies with a much more limited field of operation.

## Concentrating on the core business

Ownership of industry became more concentrated during the 1980s (see chapter 3), leading to greater market share in fewer hands – with mergers, acquisitions and alliances all playing a part in changing the shape of manufacturing. The way in which corporations are 'desperately seeking synergies' has recently been analysed (Kanter, 1989). But, in contrast to this growth in conglomerates with diverse enterprises under one umbrella is the trend to focus on the firm's core business, divesting any but the most essential and central activities. This can be seen as a strategy to make the best use of corporate assets; in other words, simply concentrating on what the corporation does best.

At first sight, any move in this direction to a core business strategy seems to imply that the corporation has abandoned global ambitions and is prepared to defend a smaller patch of territory. However, the opposite may well be the case, and the focus on core business can be the prelude to launching a global attack in a far narrower range of products or services. After all, few companies will have the management skills and financial resources to match Sony's current attempts to achieve global scale together with product diversification.

Companies in industries as diverse as car manufacturing and grocery retailing have sought competitive advantage by concentrating on their core activities. Nevertheless, these corporations still want to retain control over essential products and services such as component supply and transport, although these will be supplied by third parties. In the 1990s the growth in sophistication and accessibility of information systems will enable more corporations to achieve their goal of control by information rather than control by doing.

Companies may have a number of reasons for wishing to opt out of running their warehousing and distribution. Of special importance can be a company's need for finance for expansion. When a company is expanding rapidly it may require all its capital to fund the growth. By contracting out various activities the company can open up internal sources of funds; for example, the capital will no longer be tied up in a vehicle fleet if the company contracts out the transport function. Other reasons may also have particular relevance in certain industry sectors. For example, consumer protection legislation has increased the pressure on manufacturers since makers need to keep information on model numbers and batches for ten years. This a big continuing clerical exercise, and some logistics services providers have seen it as an opportunity to offer top-line inventory management (Federal Express, quoted in *Motor Transport*, 1989).

## *Changes in product sourcing*

Many organizations, both within and outside the EC, have tended to see product sourcing in national terms rather than to look at Europe as a single market. The divergent national production standards and regulations have supported this piecemeal approach, many products being manufactured to specific standards for each separate country. Growing harmonization of technical standards and regulations will be a major encouragement to the adoption of a Europe-wide production and procurement policy.

A mark of the significance of these barriers across Europe is that it is difficult for some producers to manufacture a tractor that will sell in more than two or three of western Europe's 17 or so national markets without significant engineering alterations. Massey Ferguson have been quoted as saying that if just seven of these national markets in the EC and EFTA are considered (the UK, France, Germany, Austria, Sweden, Finland and Switzerland) at least 34 special modifications are required. For example, Switzerland insists on a larger separation between the headlights, while in Finland the cab roof must be fitted with an escape hatch (Garnett, 1988).

Out-sourcing is on the increase among European firms, while at the same time many are reducing the number of suppliers they trade with. Manufacturers must somehow match the search for low-cost suppliers internationally (global sourcing) with the desire to select local suppliers who can offer higher service levels, become involved in co-makership deals and support a just-in-time programme.

However, the trend in manufacturing to seek low-cost sources of supply and to serve dispersed high-growth markets adds complexity and cost to a firm's logistics supply chain, and a number of substantial criticisms have been levelled at remote suppliers in particular (Bulley, 1989):

- delivery times are longer and often less predictable than for local suppliers
- it is difficult to schedule frequent, small, JIT deliveries from distant sources
- quality problems impact dramatically because of the difficulty of handling return goods and the long time taken to activate replacement – the result is larger inventories to avoid production hold-ups
- regular up-to-the-minute communications are more difficult
- remoteness often implies supplying to many small customers – as a result, customer service will tend to be poor
- remote facilities are often large and burdened with expensive bureaucracy and low productivity

It is interesting that three out of the six criticisms outlined above essentially relate as much to problems of correct and timely information as to the supply of goods. Many observers have noted the trend towards growing internationalization or globalization of business. In parallel with this development has been the dramatic growth in information and communications technology. Logistics (one of a company's most information-intensive activities) benefits from this growth, and from the fall in the real cost of information. Logistics managers are increasingly able to substitute relatively inexpensive information for expensive inventory and transport.

The increased use of information technology (IT) – and in particular electronic data interchange (EDI) – will have an impact here. The widespread adoption of EDI will encourage Europe-wide sourcing. By removing much of the delay and expense from long-distance information flows EDI could help to make peripheral European regions, such as Scotland or southern Italy, effectively less remote from the central manufacturing regions. Any trends in this direction will have to be reinforced by improved transport between peripheral and central regions, but the point to stress is that improving transport without improving information quality will not overcome some of the inherent disadvantages and difficulties of out-sourcing.

Substitution of local products with products from distant markets means an enhanced role for gateway ports such as Rotterdam and services such as international road transport, but a diminished role for regional and even national warehousing and transport. Moreover, the distributor may decide that as, say, the shipping line NYK transported the goods from Japan they can also handle the responsibility of final delivery within Europe.

The foregoing discussion of the trend to focus on core business and the changes in sourcing practices shows clearly that there cannot be a single prescription for growth – each company and industry will approach the issue in a different way. What emerges is that there are two alternative strategies: one to grow geographically, and to develop and diversify the product area; and the other to get bigger by channelling corporate resources into the central or core business. Logistics will be a major consideration in the chosen strategy for innovative companies – as it should be for others.

## Concentrating production and distribution

There is much argument about the benefits of size to business. Peters (1987) has referred in critical terms to the US belief which predominated until the 1980s that if 'big is better then biggest must be best'. What emerges clearly from the debate is that being big is no longer enough for a manufacturer; they must find ways to get value from their size. In finding ways to do this, many companies have rationalized their production and distribution facilities. They have been able to do this and still maintain or improve levels of customer service, since logistics developments have kept pace with these changes.

The traditional way to take advantage of corporate size was through economies of scale; the scope for which was seen as the prerogative of large companies where such factors as automation, communications and better administration could be combined to produce lower unit costs. Being big meant that a company could produce at a lower cost than the smaller competition, and this could be used to satisfy strategies based on increased market share or profit maximization. But big is no longer enough: changes in manufacturing techniques, the need for greater and greater production flexibility, the spread of low-cost computing and communications power have all chipped away at the benefits of sheer size. Today large corporations must not only be big: they must be seen to gain from being big – otherwise shareholders start to ask awkward questions and corporate raiders appear over the horizon.

In the previous chapter we considered one way in which manufacturers try to make size count; that is, through concentrating production onto fewer but larger sites. But this trend puts pressure on the logistics function. For example, the fewer the production and storage sites used by the company, the fewer the alternatives if some factor beyond the company's control intervenes to prevent the normal flow of materials. The way in which Ford concentrated production in three factories for their Fiesta car is illustrated in figure 4.2. Vehicle assembly and final production takes place at Saarlouis, Dagenham and Valencia. Clearly, if there were, say, a port strike in the UK or a lorry blockade at the Spanish border, then production could be maintained in Saarlouis. However, if production were concentrated in just one plant for the whole of Europe the company would be somewhat more vulnerable to disruption from events beyond their control. It is evident that there is a trade-off between the economies of focusing production and the dangers of relying on one site for all vehicles of a particular model.

What is more, concentrating production at fewer sites will, generally, increase transport costs because products need to be carried further to markets. However, there is undoubtedly scope for saving through the better consolidation of out-bound loads and better vehicle utilization, if the company's logistics strategy is right.

However, making size count does not have to mean centralizing production at just a few sites. The quest for size – and the struggle to capitalize on that size – has underpinned the truck-maker IVECO's 15-year history and yet they have sought to avoid concentrating production in fewer locations (Lynn, 1990).

IVECO is currently number two in the European truck sector; its market share in 1989 was 22 per cent compared with the 25 per cent held by Mercedes–Benz. But IVECO is far more pan-European than its rivals, formed as it was from a merger of French, German and Italian companies (it is now also involved in a joint venture with Ford UK). Mercedes–Benz, for example, is a national company, while Renault, Volvo and Leyland–DAF must all be seen as only one- or two-country companies.

From the beginning of the merger in 1975 (between Fiat's truck division, Unic; a Fiat-owned French company; and Magirus, a German company) IVECO have faced the problem of how to make their size count. The obvious answer was to concentrate on a few big plants that could make trucks cheaply. Closing national plants would have meant selling Italian trucks in France and Germany – defeating

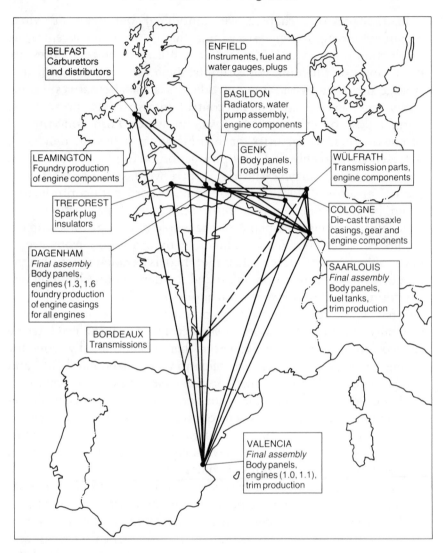

**Figure 4.2**   The Ford Fiesta production network in Europe.
*Source*: Dicken (1986) Copyright © by Peter Dicken. Reprinted by permission
of Harper Collins Publishers.

the object of the merger. But leaving the national producers intact
meant sacrificing the economies of scale that the merger was supposed
to produce (Lynn, 1990). The way round the problem has been to
assemble trucks in different places, but to make the components in
specific national production centres. This strategy places special

stresses on a company – stresses which only good logistics organization can resolve.

Not surprisingly, IVECO has been described as a sprawling company – production is spread over 18 plants and R&D is divided among nine centres. As a consequence, transport costs and border delays are a potential problem when a component may be manufactured in one country, built into an engine in another, and sold as part of a truck in a third country. Set against this apparently wasteful use of resources has to be the company's ability to stay in touch with local markets throughout Europe. At present, the truck markets have tended to behave in a rather parochial and national way, not surprising in view of the very fragmented haulage industry. However, increasing concentration in the haulage and transport sector has implications for the buying habits of transport companies and may, in future, reduce the benefits of IVECO's local approach.

Yet it is not only production sites which seem set for concentration; the same trend will also be observed in distribution centres. At present many manufacturing companies find themselves operating throughout Europe, but without the benefits of scale because of over-complex transport and product regulations; the consequence is that too much stock is held in too many warehouses (see the case study in chapter 7). This pattern will change: many national distribution centres will be replaced by international ones, with important implications for logistics. First, production at factories can be scheduled later, since supply lines to markets can be made more streamlined and efficient. Second, some final assembly tasks may even be transferred to the international distribution centres. For example, vending machines made in the USA for European markets can have instruction panels and coin operation mechanisms fitted – in line with national requirements – at the European distribution centre instead of at the factory. This can significantly reduce inventory levels. Rank Xerox has already focused its spares for Europe in a single central warehouse at Venray in the Netherlands. But perhaps a more dramatic example, because of the size of the company, comes from Philips. At present the company holds inventory in warehouses to satisfy national demands, but it has been suggested that after 1992 they will be able to reduce the number of inventory holding sites dramatically (figure 4.3).

Many other companies are also aiming to reduce their inventory costs while maintaining or improving customer-service levels. But reduced inventory levels place great demands on the transport and

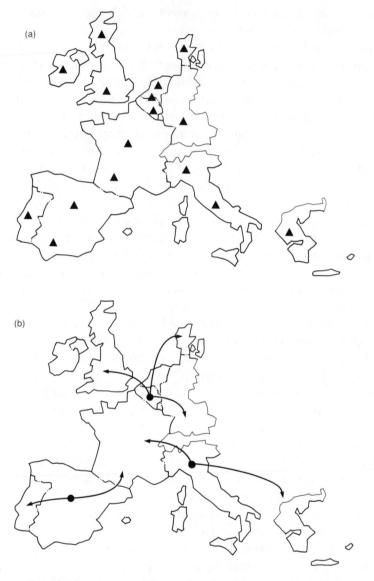

**Figure 4.3**   The scope to concentrate inventory after 1993: (a) Philips'
stock warehouses organized on a national basis (example); (b)
Philips' warehouses after 1993 – concentration and rationalization.
*Source*: A. T. Kearney Inc., *Road Transport After 1992*,
A. T. Kearney Ltd, London

information networks, in terms of both reliability and speed. The scale of the issue is in no doubt. In the UK capital tied up in inventory annually amounts to over £80 billion, representing about 20 per cent of the value of manufacturing output. It has been argued (Waters, 1990) that this has potentially important effects on international competitiveness (in Japan, for example, the corresponding figure represents only 10.5 per cent of the value of manufacturing output). One important way to reduce inventory costs is to concentrate inventory holding, which reduces costs for several reasons:

- Greater concentration of inventory implies a smaller overall inventory requirement. Using the square root law applied to inventory (Maister, 1976), it can be argued that under ideal conditions a single warehouse handling, say, 1 million units per annum should require only half as much stock as a system of four warehouses, each handling 250 000 units a year.
- If inventory is concentrated in fewer warehouses, the overall cost of operating the warehouses tends to fall because of economies of scale in warehousing (Williams, 1974).
- The administrative costs sustained by users of freight services (for example, order processing, invoicing and rate negotiations) are likely to decline as inventory is held in fewer places. Not only is the user likely to reduce the number of freight companies working on his behalf, but there will also be more opportunities to use IT in tasks which support distribution.

Inevitably, concentration of production and distribution centres has led to an increased need for transport – and the transport will in many cases need to be faster and more reliable in order to maintain customer service levels. Therefore, this emerging pattern of fewer production and distribution centres implies more complex logistics in the future, with a growing demand for high-quality transport linking more distant focal points in the supply chain.

## Logistics as the Corporate Leading Edge

Kanter (1989) has identified the importance of the corporate need to try to do more with less. As she has said, 'the imperative to do more with less is a common management theme across a range of industries. Budget cuts, organization chart trimming and programmes to eliminate staff are coupled with exuberant messages about becoming more entrepreneurial and growing new businesses.' The juxtaposition of conflicting aims makes the management task very difficult. For example, how do you achieve low-cost production together with small-batch flexibility?

Despite the inherent conflicts and contradictions, manufacturing industry has responded to this driving force in a variety of ways; in many of which logistics plays a central role, enabling manufacturers to get better value from their human, financial and technological resources. Global competition and shorter product life-cycles are twin stimulants to becoming a smarter manufacturer and using the support tools of modern manufacturing techniques to compete.

The concept of the product life-cycle encapsulates the idea that the demand for a product grows initially, but that ultimately – over time – it will decline (figure 4.4). In many industries product life-cycles have become shorter, so that there is a decreasing time interval between the introduction of a product onto the market and its eventual obsolescence and disappearance. The rate of innovation has increased dramatically in certain sectors, in turn accelerating product obsolescence. For example, in consumer electronics and computers, global companies may launch dozens of new products in a year. An ability to handle logistics activities efficiently is vital in enabling a company to reduce lead times and launch new products.

We consider manufacturing innovations under two broad headings. First, there are those relating to better use of inventory through improved resource requirements; here we can see the direct involvement of logistics skills. Second, we consider the use of computers in manufacturing and briefly outline the implications for logistics.

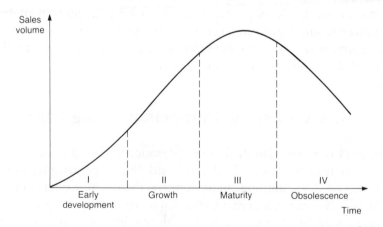

**Figure 4.4**  The theory of the product life-cycle.

# Better use of inventory: a key competitive advantage

We have already discussed one way to reduce inventory levels (centralizing stockholding) for companies which operate across a number of regions and countries. Another way to improve inventory use is through the adoption of requirements planning techniques. These techniques can be applied whether the company operates at one or many locations.

Since logistics cuts across company boundaries it has an important role in reducing lead times and coordinating sourcing, production and distribution. In order to achieve this complex task a number of techniques and concepts have been developed within the materials planning and control area; these have been referred to generically as requirements planning systems. Among the most well known are:

- JIT (Just-in-Time)
- TQM (Total Quality Management)
- MRP I (Material Requirements Planning)
- MRP II (Manufacturing Resource Planning)
- OPT (Optimal Production Technique)
- DRP (Distribution Requirements Planning)
- LRP (Logistics Requirements Planning)

Most of these techniques have been discussed in detail by Sohal and Howard (1987): here we use just two techniques to illustrate their importance in reshaping corporate logistics.

Christopher (1986) has defined MRP as 'a system for forecasting or projecting component part and material requirements from a company's master production schedule (MPS) and the bill of material (BOM) for each end product or module. The time-phased requirements for components and materials are then calculated, taking into account stock in hand as well as scheduled receipts.' The systems are usually made up of a series of modules which establish, maintain and derive priorities on the basis of regular reviews and updates. Christopher goes on to point out that 'these techniques have only really become practicable through the availability of computer programs capable of handling the complexity of information involved in managing multiple products, common components and materials and differing replenishment lead times'.

JIT represents an area of logistics in which many companies have taken an active interest. It complements simplified manufacturing by eliminating processes which do not add value. JIT will involve reducing machine set-up times, improving the flow of materials, reducing lead times, and improving customer service and product quality.

European references to JIT tend to emphasize rapid transport and control of suppliers. While the latter is also true of Japanese JIT, the transport requirements are usually simplified in Japan by the proximity of supplier and producer. Broadly speaking, in a European context JIT has the following implications:

- a closer relationship between supplier and manufacturer (which may approach co-makership, where the supplier and manufacturer approach design and manufacturing problems together rather than at arms length – as is typical of buyer–seller relationships in industry)
- a closer relationship between shipper and carrier (reduced or zero inventory, and therefore no margin for late or erratic delivery of raw materials or components)
- more frequent delivery, but of smaller amounts (which has stimulated manufacturers to turn from their own-account transport services to using high-quality less than truckload options provided by professional carriers)
- intensive information flows between supplier, manufacturer and carrier

The impact of JIT will not be evenly spread across different industry sectors and countries. For example, the degree of industry sophistication and the structure of buyer–seller relationships create important differences. However, some industries are clearly advanced; most obviously the European automotive sector.

A guide to the potential growth of JIT practices in Europe comes from a survey conducted in the USA during 1988 (LaLonde and Masters, 1990). Senior logistics managers (210 in all) were asked to forecast the likely changes for the years 1990 and 1995 in the percentage of product arriving under JIT conditions. They predicted that by 1995 some 45 per cent of in-bound product would arrive under JIT conditions (in 1988 the actual figure was 18 per cent).

Many European firms themselves have responded to growing competitive pressures by implementing JIT techniques. For example, Bostrom (a specialist manufacturer of anti-vibration seats for tractors and other work vehicles) has implemented a JIT manufacturing system (Bulley, 1989). The results have been dramatic, with inventory cuts of 30 per cent and improved customer response times. As part of the implementation effort the supplier base has been rationalized, and 11 companies which account for 40 per cent of Bostrom's in-bound supplier costs make JIT deliveries.

Rank Xerox provide a further example of the benefits of using a JIT approach. At their Mitcheldean factory in the UK four key JIT suppliers are committed to EDI, and are planning to reduce inventories from 25 days to 17 days (Ferguson, 1989).

Improved quality is a prerequisite for successful JIT implementation, and Sony in Bridgend (Wales) achieved a 70-fold fault reduction between 1985 and 1989 (Ferguson, 1989): the campaign has now been turned on their suppliers who have to show they are implementing their own zero-defects drive. Improved quality also enables companies to make other savings; for example, in staff who were previously required to inspect deliveries on arrival. By 1989 some 90 per cent of component deliveries were not inspected at Sony's Bridgend factory, and it was planned that in 1990 there should be no inspections at all.

Although there are clearly significant benefits from implementing techniques such as JIT, there is a downside. Many of the firms implementing, say, JIT or MRP have typically had high expectations, not all of which have been met. This is often as a result of the desire for a technological fix, whereas in reality the techniques are only as good as the underlying strategy and company philosophy – after all, there is ultimately little advantage to be gained by automating chaos.

Moreover, it has been pointed out (Wheatley, 1989) that the board of a company may regard it as their task to set customer-service levels and agree inventory policy. However, many of the materials requirements techniques rely heavily on computers and yet few, if any, board members will be involved in defining the decision rules within the computer which will turn their policies into practice. As a result, many companies have one stockholding policy while their computers have another.

## New technology in manufacturing

Although many of these requirements planning systems discussed above are implemented through the use of computers, they are in essence relatively simple techniques for minimizing inventory while ensuring that agreed customer-service levels are achieved. However, there are a number of techniques which are specifically derived from the use of computers in manufacturing. Among these are:

- CAD (Computer-aided Design): systems used within the design area to generate and modify designs. For example, CAD can be used to generate three-dimensional images of a product on a computer screen, instead of having to make a model by hand.
- CAM (Computer-aided Manufacturing): the application of computers to generate manufacturing data, including data for numerically controlled machines and robots.
- CIM (Computer-integrated Manufacturing): the use of computers to integrate the various stages in the manufacturing process and to coordinate these stages.

In the automotive industry, Western companies take six or seven years from drawing board to product launch while the Japanese can do it in three (Womack et al., 1990). Part of the solution to narrowing this gap will come from techniques such as CAD. By linking together the car manufacturer's designers and the component supplier's designers it should be possible to significantly reduce total product lead times. Although the precise nature of these techniques varies from industry to industry and company to company, the way in which Ford use them in Europe provides a good insight into their general attributes.

In design, Ford product development started with 28 CAD workstations in 1981, increasing to 300 by 1990 (CBI/PA Consulting Group, 1990). With each successive new model the CAD element has been increased, from 8 per cent CAD for the Sierra – launched in 1982 – to 25 per cent for the Scorpio. Ford expect that by 1992 up to 90 per cent of the design work for a new car will be done by computer.

In manufacturing, Ford started with one CAM workstation in 1981 and is expected to have 280 by 1992. Computer automation in sheet-metal die design, die model manufacturing and die manufacturing has cut four months from the design cycle.

Importantly, CAD/CAM means that companies such as Ford, with widely dispersed facilities, can develop joint design exercises worldwide (these can also include their suppliers), taking advantage of the scope to transmit design data from one computer to another.

CIM offers Ford the prospect of integrated manufacturing across Europe, planning production at individual sites, monitoring on-site production and quality and controlling JIT deliveries.

Manufacturers in some industries are trying to offer customers a 'bespoke' product, with a wide range of options selected by the customer. The use of CIM techniques can play a critical role here. In textiles, for example, it has been reported (Hodd, 1987) that advantage is currently taken of low-cost labour in developing countries. But using CIM techniques factories are able to make 180 bespoke shirts an hour, compared with the most productive worker's four. The effect of this will be to move the manufacture of textiles from distant suppliers to robotized factories nearer the source of demand. However, the individual nature of the customer order made possible by linking computerized information requirements with robotized manufacturing flexibility will boost the complexity of transport service requirements.

Yet, in a manufacturing context it must be stressed that it is little use automating 'business as usual' – automated chaos is still chaos. For example, the lead time advantage enjoyed by many Japanese producers is not solely a result of more computer use in manufacturing, but is a complex mix of advantages. In many cases it revolves around the concept of *kaizen*, or constant improvement through tinkering, and the strict policy of always implementing basic but boring solutions. By contrast, Western management typically rewards the more glamorous big-bang approach to problem-solving.

A further strategy to reduce lead times and manufacturing set-up times, and to reduce defects is to keep products as broadly international as possible until the last moment. This also increases the opportunity for national labelling and marketing functions to be spun off into the warehouse – which now tend to be larger and more centralized than before. Increased travel, global marketing and the information/media revolution combine to reduce regional and national differences. If harmonized technical standards are coupled with these developments then it is no surprise that products can be sold in the same form in more markets (for example, the rise of international brands such as Benetton). This development in turn reinforces the advantage of concentrating production and distribution in fewer sites and serving Europe-wide needs. It also gives the opportunity to third-party logistics specialists to provide certain added-value manufacturing services (such as labelling, installation and packing).

# All Change for Logistics Services in Manufacturing?

The growing importance of multinational and even global companies, combined with the increased emphasis on logistics management as a leading-edge technique for competitive advantage, all pose a tremendous challenge and a further opportunity for all those concerned with logistics services. Three key reactions to the challenge have important implications for the organization and purchasing of transport and storage services:

- rationalizing the vendor network
- contractual agreements between carriers and shippers
- 'quality' in freight service

*Rationalizing the vendor network* has spread to the transport sector. Manufacturers and retailers increasingly wish to concentrate a larger proportion of their transport expenditure with fewer, but inevitably larger, carriers (for example, Rank Xerox has stated that it wants one-stop shopping as far as transport by third parties is concerned). This development is reinforced by the growing ability of large companies to make international comparisons of their logistics services suppliers. The selected carrier (or prime contractor) will in many cases select a limited number of subcontractors for the actual trucking (control through information will be used to replace control by ownership). This represents a coincidence of interest, with larger carriers having to compete in an increasingly deregulated marketplace; they are looking for more defensible work other than general haulage.

It is interesting to compare these recent trends noted in Europe with work done in the USA. Details of a survey into anticipated changes in third-party relationships (LaLonde and Masters, 1990) are contained in table 4.1. The projected reduction in the number of carriers is striking.

Relationships between carriers and shippers are increasingly typified by *contractual agreements* rather than by a series of transactions. This leads to the carrier acting in much the same way as manufacturing co-makership arrangements (in fact, the Dutch have coined the rather inelegant word 'co-shippership' to describe this phenomenon). This more stable and long-term concept only becomes possible when firms deal with fewer carriers, so there is a strong link with the trend to reducing the number of transport suppliers. Moreover, the more sophisticated service requirements of users will mean that it will become harder to buy services at short notice from a variety of hauliers on the basis of price. The service requirements will be too complicated to allow that. Long-term contracts will be more usual, spelling out the terms of service and performance. This trend

**Table 4.1**  US logistics managers' expectations of change in third-party relationships

|  | 1988 (actual) | 1990 (forecast) | 1995 (forecast) |
|---|---|---|---|
| Average number of: |  |  |  |
| Carriers | 30 | 24 | 20 |
| Public warehouses | 6 | 5 | 5 |
| Contract warehouses | 3 | 3 | 3 |
| Percentage of freight volume: |  |  |  |
| Into public/contract warehousing | 8 | 9 | 10 |
| Out of public/contract warehousing | 18 | 19 | 20 |
| In-bound by contract carriage logistics services activity | 43 | 50 | 56 |

*Source*: LaLonde and Masters (1990), 'Logistics: Perspectives for the 1990s', *International Journal of Logistics Management*, Braybrooke Press Ltd., Henley on Thames

will be very much reinforced by the growing use of IT (such as EDI) which will have the effect of tying freight service users and providers more closely together.

Buyers are no longer concerned with transport price alone. There is already a considerable emphasis on *'quality' in freight service* purchasing by shippers. Although price will always be a very powerful determinant of purchasing decisions, quality is certain to become more important in all the European freight markets. This will often be a consequence of the introduction of new techniques to, say, manufacturing, such as JIT.

Raghunathan *et al.*'s (1988) study of motor carrier selection in the USA confirms the findings of previous research, in that transit time, reliability and door-to-door transportation costs are the most important carrier selection factors (table 4.2). Customer service has become the most important factor in transportation buying systems.

Volvo is one company in which transport value is the measure rather than transport price. For companies which operate in this way, there can be no question that the distribution and production functions are seen as complementary, and that co-operation is the order of the day. Evidence exists of the increasing importance attached to reliability and the decreasing significance of pure transport cost factors (figure 4.5).

Demand-side Logistics

**Table 4.2**  Mean importance and ranking of carrier selection determinants in the USA

| Rank | Description | Mean |
|------|-------------|------|
| 1 | Transit time reliability or consistency | 1.301 |
| 2 | Door-to-door transportation rates or costs | 1.405 |
| 3 | Total door-to-door transit time | 1.551 |
| 4 | Carrier willingness to negotiate rates | 1.611 |
| 5 | Financial stability of the carrier | 1.807 |
| 6 | Equipment availability | 1.878 |
| 7 | Frequency of service | 1.892 |
| 8 | Pick-up and delivery service | 1.899 |
| 9 | Freight loss and damage | 2.037 |
| 10 | Shipment expediting | 2.054 |

Mean scores based on 1 (very high importance) to 5 (very low importance) scale.
*Source*: Raghunathan *et al.* (1988).

It must be pointed out that our research suggests that companies which use value as the measure are the exception at present: for many companies – of all sizes – transport price is still seen as the only way in which a service can be evaluated. However, two quotes from suppliers of transport services show how they believe that service

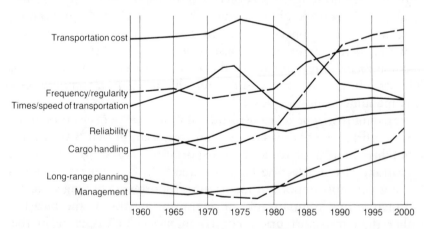

**Figure 4.5**  An analysis from Volvo Transport Corporation showing changes in the importance of factors affecting transport mode and carrier choice.
*Source*: M. Hodd, *Cargo Systems*, February 1987, CS Publications Ltd, Surrey

quality is the key to long-term customer service and loyalty (Fisher, 1990):

> BS 5750 (the UK British Standards Institute quality standard) reinforces the close working relationship with customers – all part of developing a total quality supply chain for industry.
>
> (R. Elviss, Managing Director of Reliance Tankers)

> A lot of our work is for ICI and they have stated that all hauliers who deal with them must have BS 5750 before the end of 1991. . . Of course the standard is attractive in several ways. We are a young company and BS 5750 is a way to show customers that we are a reputable and professional outfit. Plus the ground work required does make all your systems a lot better.
>
> (S. Dixon, Quality Manager, Dennis Dixon Limited)

Quality considerations will not, however, simply be restricted to the physical movement of goods. It is increasingly apparent that moving goods is the easy part of distribution; it is the communications in support of the movement that are most difficult to get right. Quality in communications (such as speed and accuracy) will be a vital part of future services in freight transport and logistics.

## Conclusions

The combined effect of the changes outlined above represent both opportunities and threats for providers of logistics services. For example, as buyers of logistics services shed a variety of activities, there is considerable opportunity for the larger providers of these services to add value to their basic activities of transport and storage by taking on new tasks, such as pre-delivery inspection, inventory management and installation.

However, any tendency by buyers to reduce the number of suppliers that they use could mean that small- and medium-sized enterprises (the typical size for many providers of logistics services) will be forced to perform only the simpler logistics tasks, such as inter-warehouse trunking. These 'dumb logistics' tasks would be controlled by the larger freight companies, who would act as logistics architects, also directly providing the 'intelligent logistics' (such as dedicated contract distribution) to the manufacturer.

Increasing global market integration will also pose a challenge for the strategic development of logistics services. Freight companies face a difficult choice: Do they try to provide all services to a widely spread range of buyers? Or do they opt for niche markets to which their special skills seem best suited? Both strategies clearly involve an element of risk. Niche markets may disappear in an increasingly integrated global economy, while an attempt to provide too great a range of services to too many buyers may be an inherently inappropriate strategy in an increasingly complex logistics world. This represents a real dilemma for logistics services suppliers. But it poses a problem for their customers as well, since they must plan in the face of uncertainty about the future shape of logistics markets.

## Case study    Sony: a manufacturer planning for change

The Sony Group is a worldwide manufacturer of electronic goods, with 21 manufacturing plants outside Japan, of which eight are in Europe. As a manufacturer competing in the global consumer electronics market, Sony has had to devise a logistics strategy for Europe in the 1990s. The objectives and the logistics implications underlying this strategy are the focus of this case study.

Since the mid-1980s Sony has adopted three objectives which fundamentally affect their logistic operations. They are:

• to reduce inventory to a minimum
• to adopt a global manufacturing and sourcing policy to take account of currency fluctuations, labour rates and tax incentives
• wherever possible, to manufacture within major economic markets such as Europe

The reasons behind the drive to reduce inventory highlights many of the issues facing manufacturers in the 1990s. Of special importance in this decision 'to do more with less' are:

• the shortening product life-cycle of electronic goods
• the decreasing value density of consumer electronic products
• increased consumption of electronic goods
• the 'replace rather than repair' philosophy of consumers

A marketable life of two to three years is now considered average, with some products only lasting for one selling season. There has also been a general decrease in the value of consumer products in this industry sector, brought about through technological advances and intense competition. As a result, distribution costs have increased dramatically as a percentage of sales revenue.

The 'replace rather than repair' philosophy of consumers, combined with reduced unit prices, has increased throughput not just of products but also of packaging. Consequently, distribution systems have to be both cost-effective and highly responsive to new market requirements and need to be constantly reviewed.

Given these changes, Sony has been implementing plans at the global, regional and national level. Here we focus on the plans for the UK and the wider, regional, plans for Europe.

## Sony UK's strategy study

Rapid growth brings problems as well as rewards. Sony's European sales rose from £6 million to £700 million between 1968 and 1988. In the UK, a regional logistics system with a nationwide network of depots had grown along with the business. A UK strategy study was undertaken in the early 1980s, resulting in significant rationalization and improvement. A key finding of the study was that although inventory levels were too high and had to be improved, customer service also had to be maintained. In order to achieve this, the decision was taken to move from a regional multi-warehouse operation to a central single stockholding operation. Sony UK set themselves a number of objectives.

The best site was identified as Thatcham, near Newbury, Berkshire, and this became the UK's National Operations Centre in 1986. From a geographical point of view the site was ideal for incoming goods; being relatively close to Bridgend, Wales (45 per cent volume of products sourced), Southampton (35 per cent) and the east coast ports (20 per cent). Furthermore, 70 per cent of Sony's delivery points were in London, the South East and the Midlands. The change to centralized inventory holding was accompanied by an increase in the use of logistics services suppliers, such as road freight companies, which in turn reduced fixed costs in favour of variable costs.

The decision to centralize inventory was successful, resulting in:

- a three-week reduction in lead times through the UK supply chain
- improved stock availability
- logistics costs reduced by £1 million per annum (not including interest charges on inventory)
- a standard service available throughout the UK (for example, videotape has a 24-hour order cycle delivery system)

## Sony Europa's pan-European strategy study

Turning now to the wider European sphere, we can see how Sony have evaluated the scope for concentrating inventory holding at a wider, regional, level. This planning is in response to changing manufacturing requirements (such as JIT), and to the changes which will result from the SEM (for example, the scope for much greater cross-border goods movement when time penalties from border delays are eliminated).

Sony Europa (in association with Locon Consultancy) undertook a logistics review of European operations. Since inventory accounted for 78 per cent of Sony's total physical distribution costs in Europe, a principal aim of the review was to look for ways of reducing this by concentrating inventory in fewer locations.

Having established theoretical demand, Sony estimated the likely product throughput in different areas of Europe and assessed the best locations for central warehouses. However, Sony's eight European manufacturing plants also had to be taken into consideration (see table 4.3).

**Table 4.3**  Sony's European manufacturing plants.

| Country | Place | Manufacturing |
|---------|-------|---------------|
| UK | Bridgend | Colour TV (1974) <br> TV tubes (1982) |
| France | Bayonne <br> Dax <br> Colmar Alsace | Audiocassette tapes (1980) <br> Videocassette tapes (1984) <br> CD players (1986) |
| Spain | Barcelona | Audio (1973) <br> Colour TV (1985) <br> Video (1985) |
| Italy | Rovereto Milan | Audiocassette tapes (1988) |
| Germany | Stuttgart | Audio (1975) <br> Colour TV (1980) <br> Video (1980) |
| Austria | Anif–Vienna | CD players (1987) |

Note: dates in brackets refer to factory start-up.
*Source*: Sony, 1990

In order to carry out the study, a number of assumptions were made. Of special interest from the logistics supply side was the assumption that there would be pan-European distribution companies which would be able to meet the demanding service levels required in the new logistics system.

Although having just one European stock location gave the cheapest overall solution, this was considered inappropriate due to:

- the very high forecast product throughput
- the risks associated with a single site (such as the consequences of a fire)
- the difficulties of maintaining customer-service levels across Europe

On the basis of the study, Sony have decided that their eventual European solution may be to have as few as four warehouses.

Sony recognize the problems of implementing cross-border solutions, but the study has helped the company to focus on the key issues and will provide the basis for further development during the 1990s. Sony believe that the physical requirements of an integrated approach to Europe can be achieved relatively easily, but that the issues of IT, management structure and corporate culture are in many ways much more difficult and complex.

Source: Presentation to the Institute of British Geographers by John Parsons (General Manager Logistics, Sony UK Limited)

# Case study   McDonnell Douglas: the switch to JIT

The US multinational company McDonnell Douglas Information Systems International manufacture and supply computers and a range of products to the information technology (IT) market. This case study concentrates on the switch by McDonnell Douglas in the UK from a conventional manufacturing system to a JIT system.

## Before JIT: efficient manufacturing but a hint of complacency?

In the mid-1980s McDonnell Douglas manufacturing in the UK considered itself efficient, and although this was a subjective view the company measured up well compared with most industrial standards. Products were built in a modular fashion for inventory based on forecast sales. Inventory was minimized by allowing final configuration of products to take place at the distribution stage. High product quality was crucial to this system, and although this was achieved the company had little idea how much this cost.

Various techniques such as MRP were applied to support the manufacturing process. By concentrating on accurate forecasting and the volume of finished goods in stock, overall inventories had been reduced year on year from the early 1980s. The company was considered to be performing well.

Interestingly, the UK part of McDonnell Douglas was first alerted to the opportunity of JIT by production difficulties in their sister company in California. Manufacturing problems in the USA had led to a decision to switch to JIT production. A small team from McDonnell Douglas in the UK visited the sister plant and decided that despite the teething troubles being experienced with JIT introduction in the USA, the technique needed to be investigated for application in the UK. Almost a year later, after intensive study within the UK company, they were ready to give JIT a trial.

## The switch to JIT

The UK team had the benefit of their US colleagues' experience, and decided to tackle first the process which had the smallest elapsed time – where it would be easiest to recover from any disasters. The area chosen was the final module assembly area which occurred in the middle of the manufacturing cycle. The UK team knew that the move to JIT would impact on work-in-progress (WIP) very significantly. The preparation to lay out a JIT-controlled process meant tuning lead times, changing batch sizes and laying out the kanban squares.

In 1987 'footprints' (kanbans) were laid out on the shop floor. The WIP, which had already been cut from £2.2 million to £1.7 million as a result of merely preparing for JIT, was further reduced over the next three months to £0.8 million.

Stores were placed at the point of use, and the traditional process of kitting started to wind down – as a result one-third of the workshop space was relieved. Although this had been predicted, the managers involved had not really believed that such a dramatic change could happen.

The tremendous pressure, and the need to get it right first time *every* time with the switch to JIT, revealed some problems in the area of quality. When McDonnell Douglas measured their 'right first time' hit rate it was only 45 per cent. Quality to customers had been maintained largely by costly re-working. In 1990 the 'right first time rate' is 90 per cent and is constantly under review.

Implementing JIT meant a considerable amount of extra training for the workforce. As groups of workers were trained, they in turn became trainers – with a significant change in people's roles and outlook.

Two other results of implementing JIT at McDonnell Douglas are of interest:

- Accounting processes had to change to a system known as 'back flushing', a method which accounts for materials at the point of production and not at an earlier stage when, say, a works order is issued in a non-JIT environment. Efficiencies here have reduced cost collection activities by 80 per cent.
- Since the need to 'get it right first time' has become paramount, designers have had to learn to consult with the production engineers and the quality controllers to a greater extent than ever before.

## JIT and suppliers

A fascinating point is that McDonnell Douglas did not focus on suppliers when they implemented JIT. As Barrie Laver, manufacturing director of McDonnell Douglas UK explains:

I believe many people make the mistake of thinking that if they organize their suppliers they will have established the JIT process. If one's own plant is not capable of working with JIT properly then we have the recipe for an enormous muddle.

But suppliers have not been forgotten. As Laver goes on to say:

1989 has seen us deeper into the process. With most of our house in order, yet far from perfect, our focus is now on raw materials and their supply.

What emerges clearly from the way McDonnell Douglas have implemented JIT is that it should not be seen as some sort of technical fix. Rather, to move to JIT production requires a fundamental re-think of the manufacturing process. The process that emerges clearly has implications for the methods used to transport and store raw materials, and semi-finished and finished products.

Source: Speech at the Exel Logistics Forum, 14 February 1990, by Mr Barrie Laver, Manufacturing Director of McDonnell Douglas UK

# 5
# European Retailing

## Introduction

The nature of retailing changes dramatically as an economy develops. Among other things, there is a huge expansion in the range of goods for sale, and branding becomes an important sales factor. Developments such as these combine to make logistics a crucial element of retailing in developed economies. No longer is it sufficient to source many goods locally; for example, in grocery retailing, out-of-season fruits must be imported from, say, Africa or South America, and clothing bearing fashionable designer labels must be bought from wherever it is made. As a consequence, supply chains in retailing have tended to become both longer and more complex, and logistics management has assumed a growing importance. This is true both within retail companies and indeed throughout supply chains.

The above observations are especially true of the USA and many countries in western Europe. However, it is much less true for countries such as Portugal and Greece where mass retailing has yet to become established. This makes it essential to qualify generalizations about retailing within the European Community (EC) and the logistics needs of retailers. So, while in grocery retailing there are large supermarket chains run by companies such as Ahold in the Netherlands and Tengelmann in Germany, no direct counterparts exist in parts of southern Europe.

The pace of development of retailing is clearly linked to income growth – as the population of a country becomes richer it purchases more goods and services. It is therefore important to realize that,

**Table 5.1**   Incomes in EC countries, 1989

|  | *Per capita* incomes (thousand US $) |
| --- | --- |
| Denmark | 20.4 |
| West Germany | 19.8 |
| Luxembourg | 17.5 |
| France | 16.9 |
| Belgium | 15.3 |
| Italy | 15.1 |
| Netherlands | 15.1 |
| UK | 14.5 |
| Spain | 9.6 |
| Ireland | 8.9 |
| Greece | 5.4 |
| Portugal | 4.4 |

*Sources*: UN; OECD

within the EC, there are major disparities in incomes, as table 5.1 shows.

Of course, table 5.1 tends to overstate the differences in purchasing power between countries; low-income countries often have low prices for, say, accommodation and services, which makes their population less poor than might first appear to be the case. In addition, over the long term, it appears that there will be some convergence between countries which are separated by large income gulfs at present. Political initiatives within the EC, such as completion of the Single European Market (SEM) and the planned creation of a single currency, are certain to make the economic characteristics of EC countries less dissimilar than they are at present. Similarly, business initiatives such as moving production from high-cost countries to low-cost countries could well mean, over the long term, that income differences will be reduced.

In its turn, retailing within the EC seems likely to become less differentiated than it is now. However, it is important not to attribute convergence in consumer taste solely to recent developments such as '1992' and the completion of the SEM. For example, two or three decades ago, the national markets for alcoholic drinks were substantially different. In France, wine was by far the most popular drink, while the English drank mainly beer. But as more people took

Mediterranean holidays, and promotion by retailers and wine-producers increased, there was a dramatic rise in wine-drinking in the UK during the 1970s and 1980s. Even the consumption of beer in the UK became more internationally oriented; German and Scandinavian light beers (lagers) have gained market share at the expense of traditional beers. Yet, despite increasing convergence in some consumer markets it is clear that, for many years to come, the EC will remain a much less homogeneous retail market than, say, the USA: language and cultural differences will always play an important part in retailing, and consumers will be French, German or Italian first, and European second.

# European Retail Markets

It is not the intention here to consider all aspects of retailing within the EC; rather it is to focus upon those which are most directly related to logistics. The characteristics to be discussed are as follows:

- *Scale of retailing by country.* The volume of retail sales, together with growth trends, indicates the potential demand for logistics services in the retail sector.
- *Concentration of ownership in retailing.* Large retailers will require a high degree of logistics organization and present good opportunities for technical innovation in logistics. The opposite is true when ownership in retailing is highly fragmented.
- *Forms of retail business.* Different kinds of logistics service will be attractive to different kinds of retailer. For example, small independent retailers will rarely require a warehouse to hold inventory for shops, whereas multiples will often have such a requirement.
- *Regulation of retailing.* Change in the retail sector is quite often crucially dependent on regulation which may, for example, restrict large store development. As a consequence, the need for particular types of logistics services will be affected.
- *Profitability of retailers.* Sufficient profitability is required to finance innovation and development, not just in retailing but also in logistics.

The *scale of retailing* by country within the EC is, of course, strongly related to the size of a country's population. Thus Germany and France, the two most populous countries, head the retail sales league, as indicated in table 5.2. Indeed, the Big Four of the EC (Germany and France, together with Italy and the UK) accounted for almost 80 per cent of retail sales within the Community in 1988. Yet,

**Table 5.2** Retail sales by EC country, 1988

| Country | Retail sales (billion ecu) |
| --- | --- |
| West Germany | 233.0 |
| France | 207.6 |
| Italy | 182.3 |
| UK | 156.9 |
| Spain | 81.9 |
| Netherlands | 39.3 |
| Belgium | 34.8 |
| Portugal | 18.8 |
| Denmark | 17.7 |
| Greece | 17.6 |
| Ireland | 7.1 |
| Luxembourg | 1.4 |
| EC total | 998.4 |

Note that estimates are for 1988 sales and have been adjusted to exclude motors and fuel. Ecu exchange rates at 1988 annual average.
*Source*: Corporate Intelligence Group, *Retailing in Europe*, 1990

while Luxembourg had the smallest of retail sales in total, it is a wealthy country, and per capita sales there were second only to West Germany (see table 5.3).

*Concentration of ownership* in retailing is evidenced by the growing importance of large companies in many EC countries. As table 5.4 shows, eight out of the top 20 retailers in the EC, ranked by revenues, are based in Germany.

Interestingly, there are no Italian retailers represented in table 5.4. Although Italy is one of the Big Four countries of the EC in terms of population and the size of its economy, it has a retail sector which remains highly fragmented. The most telling contrast is with the UK which has an economy and population of about the same size. Yet, in 1983/4 the UK had only about *one-third* of the retail outlets of Italy: 342 022 compared with 1 033 725 (*Euromonitor*, 1987). Moreover, while about two-thirds of UK stores are independently owned, almost all Italian stores are independents of one kind or another (see below). In terms of numbers of persons per store, Italy had 55 compared to 165 in the UK (*Euromonitor*, 1987), figures which

Demand-side Logistics

**Table 5.3**   Retail sales per person in EC countries, 1988

| Country | Sales per person (ecu) |
|---|---|
| West Germany | 3810 |
| Luxembourg | 3750 |
| France | 3724 |
| Belgium | 3519 |
| Denmark | 3442 |
| Italy | 3176 |
| UK | 2750 |
| Netherlands | 2670 |
| Spain | 2107 |
| Ireland | 2017 |
| Portugal | 1838 |
| Greece | 1759 |

Notes as for table 5.2.
*Source*: Corporate Intelligence Group, *Retailing in Europe*, 1990

further underline the fragmented nature of Italian retailing. Indeed, Italy has by far the lowest number of persons per store of any country in the EC.

Concentration of ownership is closely linked to the third of our EC retailing characteristics, namely *forms of retail business*. For simplicity it is best to begin by examining four major kinds of retail organization, broadly following the classification used by Treadgold (1989).

*Multiples* are retail companies which operate a number of (often large) retail outlets. Interpretations vary on how many retail outlets are required before a retailer can be classified as a multiple; anything between two and 25 has been suggested. UK official statistics, for example, use nine outlets as the benchmark for status as a multiple, whereas five will be considered sufficient elsewhere (EC Commission, 1989).

Multiples usually specialize in a particular range of commodities, such as groceries. Indeed, grocery multiples are well represented in the top 20 retailers in the EC (table 5.4) and dominate grocery sales in some countries. In the UK, for example, five grocery multiples account for about 60 per cent of grocery sales, which probably represents the highest degree of concentration among EC countries.

Yet, in neighbouring Eire, the growth of multiple retailers has been much slower than in the UK, partly because the population is based in rural areas, a demand configuration which is relatively unattractive to multiple retailers.

In many retail sectors it is evident that multiple retailing has represented one of the more successful formulas. From food to furniture, multiples have taken an increasing share of retail sales within the EC; and at the expense of wholesalers, who become

**Table 5.4**  The EC's 20 largest retailers ranked by annual revenues[a]

| Rank | Company | Country of origin | Financial year ending in | Group revenues[b] (million ecu) |
|---|---|---|---|---|
| 1 | Tengelmann | West Germany | 1989 | 17 986 |
| 2 | Rewe–Leibbrand | West Germany | 1989 | 14 203 |
| 3 | Leclerc | France | 1989 | 12 386 |
| 4 | Intermarché | France | 1989 | 12 101 |
| 5 | Aldi | West Germany | 1989 | 12 040 |
| 6 | Edeka | West Germany | 1989 | 10 628[c] |
| 7 | Promodes | France | 1989 | 10 550 |
| 8 | Carrefour | France | 1989 | 10 516 |
| 9 | Sainsbury | UK | 1989 | 10 294 |
| 10 | Casino | France | 1989 | 8 442 |
| 11 | Marks & Spencer | UK | 1990 | 8 329 |
| 12 | Tesco | UK | 1990 | 8 023 |
| 13 | Vendex | Netherlands | 1990 | 7 666 |
| 14 | Ahold | Netherlands | 1990 | 7 566 |
| 15 | Karstadt | West Germany | 1989 | 7 150 |
| 16 | Asko | West Germany | 1989 | 7 034 |
| 17 | Gateway | UK | 1989 | 6 758 |
| 18 | GIB Group | Belgium | 1989 | 6 408 |
| 19 | Otto Versand | West Germany | 1989 | 6 397 |
| 20 | Kaufhof[d] | West Germany | 1989 | 6 288 |

[a] Including buying groups but excluding co-operatives.
[b] Group revenues include sales of affiliated companies where appropriate and in some instances sales taxes (where separated data are not available).
[c] Retail sales only (that is, excluding wholesaling turnover).
[d] Owned by Metro. Metro is not included in this table since the bulk of its revenue comes from cash-and-carry operations.
*Source*: Corporate Intelligence Group, *Retailing in Europe*, 1990

excluded from the supply chain, and the other three main kinds of retailer, namely co-operative societies and small independents which are either affiliated or unaffiliated to some kind of buying group.

For any one country there are usually a number of separate *co-operative societies*, each of which controls a number of retail outlets selling food and other basic commodities. Importantly, the co-operative societies will usually be linked to a central buying organization, such as Interco-op, which was founded in Copenhagen, but has since spread its activities to other European countries.

The co-operative movement is an important force in retailing in some countries. This observation holds true particularly for the smaller EC states (notably Greece and Denmark) and the EFTA countries (see table 5.5). For example, Migros in Switzerland has around 40 per cent of total domestic food sales.

Co-operative societies operate through a wide range of retail outlets, from high street shops to hypermarkets. There are also wide variations between countries in the way that co-operatives are run. For example, in Portugal co-operatives are mainly small shops, whereas in Greece the only co-operative outlets are supermarkets in rural areas operated by local agricultural co-operatives on behalf of their members (EC Commission, 1989).

**Table 5.5**   Co-operative societies in Europe, 1986

| Country | Number of outlets | Selling area ('000 m²) | Number of employees | % share of all retail outlets |
|---|---|---|---|---|
| Austria | 1032 | 598 | 20 120 | 9.6 |
| Denmark | 1599 | 736 | 17 981 | 6.34 |
| Finland | 3179 | 1008 | 34 087 | 20.5 |
| France | 3100 | 540 | 20 000 | 2.0 |
| West Germany | 2992 | 2134 | 63 000 | 3.0 |
| Italy | 1352 | 442 | 19 050 | 0.8 |
| Norway | 1544 | 550 | 12 930 | 10.5 |
| Sweden | 1843 | n/a | 35 134 | 16.1 |
| Switzerland | 1334 | 624 | 27 082 | 12.0 |
| UK | 5200 | n/a | 80 600 | 4.7 |

*Source*: Inter Co-op.

*Affiliated independent retailers* belong to one of two types of purchasing group, namely voluntary chains or buying groups. A voluntary chain (or symbol group, as it may often be called) is an organization owned by a wholesaler which distributes basic products – usually groceries – to small retailers. The advantage to small retailers is that they benefit from the buying power of the wholesaler: purchasing direct from the main producer is generally more expensive. In addition, there are marketing advantages from being associated with the voluntary chains, which usually seek to promote a corporate image on behalf of independent retailers affiliated to them. Spar and VG are widely recognized voluntary chains trading throughout the EC.

In contrast to the voluntary chain, a buying group is a joint purchasing organization set up by independent retailers to secure discount prices from producers by buying in bulk. Buying groups are, in general, less often found in non-food retailing. This is because product differentiation can be a very important consideration (for example, in clothing) which reduces the scope for joint purchasing by independent retailers.

The purpose of establishing a buying group or voluntary chain is, of course, to compete more effectively with larger competitors, mainly the multiples, and especially on price. However, there is frequently some flexibility in affiliation; some buying groups and voluntary chains do not compel affiliated retailers to make all their purchases through them. Other sources, such as cash-and-carry, may be used as required.

As may again be expected, the pattern of affiliated retailer trading is variable across the EC. Affiliated retailers are particularly strong in Germany, and the Rewe and Edeka buying groups are ranked two and five in the top 20 EC retailers by revenues (see table 5.4). In Greece, there is government support for grocers and other small retailers to form affiliated groupings to improve their competitiveness. By contrast, in France, the government has been examining the activities of some buying groups to ensure that the interests of the consumer are not being compromised by unfair trading practices (EC Commission, 1989).

Unlike their affiliated counterparts *unaffiliated independent retailers* are strictly independent and are not associated with any kind of purchasing group. They are often run as family businesses, sometimes being passed on from generation to generation. There may be some degree of specialization, especially in urban areas where fishmongers, bakers and butchers are typically run on an independent basis. However, many independent retailers will sell a wide variety of products, notably in rural areas, but also in urban areas where the 'corner shop' is convenient for local residents who wish to buy a few essential items, often ones forgotten in a shopping trip to a more distant superstore.

As table 5.6 shows, independents still have a major share of the market in some European countries, but this share is under sustained attack, notably from multiples. As far as grocery retailing is concerned, Euromonitor has constructed a format life-cycle (figure 5.1), which shows that outlets typically operated by small retailers (small 'supermarkets', corner shops, butchers, and so on) are in decline. By contrast, the kinds of outlet typically run by the multiples (freezer centres, large supermarkets and hypermarkets) are mainly at stages of rapid or steady growth.

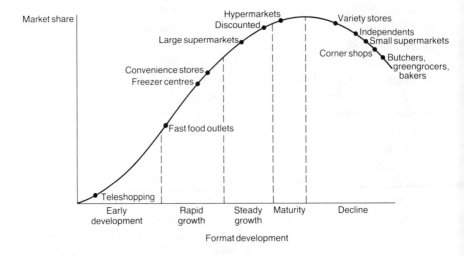

**Figure 5.1**   Grocery retail format life-cycle.
*Source*: Grocery Distribution in Western Europe, 1987 Report,
*Euromonitor*

Should the life-cycle for grocery retailing be repeated in European retailing as a whole, then it is clear that some erosion of the overall importance of the independent retailer remains in prospect. It is shown in table 5.6 that, for some countries, there could be a steep fall in the number of independent retailers; Spain seems to be especially vulnerable in this respect. Yet in the UK and, to a lesser extent in the

**Table 5.6** Retail trade by form of organization – % total retail trade

|  | Co-op | DVS | Mult | Affi | Inde | Total | Notes |
|---|---|---|---|---|---|---|---|
| EC members |  |  |  |  |  |  |  |
| Belgium | 0 | 6 | 13 | 12 | 69 | 100 |  |
| Denmark | 18 | 6 | 18 | 33 | 25 | 100 |  |
| France | 2 | 7 | 30 | 19 | 42 | 100 |  |
| West Germany | 4 | 11 | 24 | 40 | 21 | 100 |  |
| Greece |  |  |  |  |  |  |  |
| Ireland | 1 | 6 | 38 | 7 | 48 | 100 |  |
| Italy | 2 | 5 | 10 | 83 | 0 | 100 | a |
| Luxembourg | 0 | 6 | 10 | 20 | 64 | 100 |  |
| Netherlands | 0 | 5 | 28 | 33 | 34 | 100 |  |
| Portugal | 4 | 3 | 32 | 8 | 53 | 100 |  |
| Spain | 1 | 4 | 14 | 4 | 77 | 100 |  |
| United Kingdom | 5 | 16 | 51 | 5 | 23 | 100 |  |

[a] Affiliated includes Independents
DVS    Department and variety stores, mail order
Mult    Multiples, including hypermarkets
Affi    Voluntary associations and buying groups
Inde    Non-affiliated independents
*Source*: *European Marketing Data and Statistics*, 26th Edition, 1991. *Euromonitor*

Netherlands, it is possible that in many areas of retailing the nadir for independent retailers has already been reached. This, in turn, presents a challenge to the multiple retailers who will increasingly find that their domestic markets are saturated. Retailers in this position have tended to opt for one of four choices for further business development:

1 *Retail diversification in the home market*, which involves selling new product ranges as well as the established ones. In the UK, for example, Sainsbury's the food multiple, has set up a chain of do-it-yourself stores called Homebase. Similarly, a number of French hypermarket groups have gone into fast-food retailing.
2 *Non-retail activities*, where new business is sought in unfamiliar sectors. A good example is the Burton Group which has diversified from retailing into property and financial services.
3 *Improving supply chain efficiency*, in order to gain a competitive edge over retail rivals. Many UK companies have chosen this route, as illustrated in chapter 6.

4 *Internationalization of retail operations*, where the same, or some similar, retail format is introduced into other countries. The Belgian retailer GB-Inno-BM has greatly expanded its international operations, with substantial trading interests in France, Spain and the USA. One reason for this was the restrictive Loi de Cadenas in Belgium, which has inhibited large store development and hence the development of its multiple retailers.

The future structure of retailing within the EC is, therefore, crucially linked to *regulation* which affects development in the retail sector. Regulation which acts to inhibit the activities of the multiples is mainly of three kinds. First, there is regulation which is contained within the planning controls exercised by local government. It is common to most countries of the EC that planning permission is required to erect new buildings or change the use of existing ones. Planning controls have had a major impact on the number of hypermarkets and superstores in some countries because suitable greenfield sites are so rarely made available for development. For example, in the UK it has proved very difficult to obtain sites in the 'Green Belt' around London because this land has effectively been set aside for amenity purposes. However, the Green Belt continues to be eyed jealously by developers, who see considerable potential for hypermarket development in such close proximity to large population centres. French multiple retailers face similar restrictions but, on the whole, multiple retailers in both France and the UK have had considerable success in developing sites for supermarkets (and hypermarkets in the case of France), although not always quite where they wanted. By contrast, in Belgium, where the high population density makes land scarce, the problems of expansion for the multiples have been altogether more severe.

A second form of control on retail development is to restrict the entry of new commercial enterprises into the retail market. This was the purpose of Law 426 which was introduced in Italy during the 1970s. In effect, Law 426 has fossilized the structure of the Italian retail market; it remains fragmented and characterized by independent retailers (EC Commission, 1989). Change may result as a consequence of retail deregulation: the rapid expansion of multiple retailers in Denmark only took place following the repeal of a law which restricted the number of retail outlets that could be owned by any one retailer in a particular area. Similarly, the retail multiples may develop in Italy, should Law 426 be repealed, but their prospects remain uncertain. There is some feeling that Italian consumers will continue to show a strong preference for using independent retailers, despite the best efforts of the multiples to win business.

A third type of regulation which can affect retail development is legislation affecting opening hours. For example, the success of multiple retailers in the UK's do-it-yourself sector is, in part, due to the lack of enforcement of Sunday trading restrictions. Recent crackdowns have seriously affected the earnings of these multiples, for whom Saturday and Sunday represent the best trading days of the week. But again, there is wide variation across the EC. In France, for example, there are no restrictions on the hours of opening. As long as employment regulations are satisfied, then a retailer may stay open at all times. Yet, in neighbouring Germany, there are very strict limits: many shops are closed from Saturday lunchtime through until Monday morning, simply on account of the regulations. A recent slight relaxation now allows retailers to remain open late on one night of the week: however, they may still be required to close earlier or open later in the morning on other days.

It would, however, be misleading to suggest that retailing hours in the different European countries will remain as they are – powerful forces for change are at work. Consumers, and their representative associations, are pressing for a relaxation of restrictions on opening times. As more women go out to work, it is a major inconvenience if shops are only open from, say, 09.00 to 17.30 because of legal restrictions. Furthermore, with more people travelling to other parts of Europe, either on business or on holiday, more comparisons are made between home and abroad. This leads to much more questioning of the need to restrict the choice of the customer by legal means.

Another powerful force for change in retailing results from the activities of the retailers themselves. For many years, while European manufacturers established an international presence, most retailers stayed at home. Often there was the belief that retailing simply did not 'travel' very well – and there was a degree of truth in this belief. Attempts to export a successful formula devised in one country to other countries did sometimes fail. But those early failures were instructive. Retailers learned by their mistakes and now there is an unmistakable trend towards internationalization in retailing. It is a trend that is likely to have a profound effect in retail business in Europe, as will be discussed in the following section.

However, to conclude the present discussion on retail markets in

Europe, it is important to have an appreciation of the *profitability* of retailers. It is all very well for retailers to engage in a wide range of activities, but unless they are profitable, retailers will have restricted opportunities for future development. As in any other area of business, retailers depend on being profitable to finance innovation and development. Yet, as shown in table 5.7, there were wide variations in profitability during the mid-1980s for selected European retailers.

Rather surprisingly, perhaps, table 5.7 contains no German retailers. There appear to be three reasons. First, in common with many other enterprises in Germany, private shareholding is high in retail companies. This means that retailers have a restricted obligation to publish data on business performance, including profitability. Second, when there is reporting of business perform-ance, accounting conventions in Germany tend to make profitability appear low, compared with other countries. Third, businesses in Germany tend to take a long-term view of profitability. Rather than seeking high profits in the short term (which may be the priority of institutional shareholders), German business culture prefers to see a solid profit base developed over the long term, with allowances made for short-term losses. German retailers conform to this approach: Aldi, for example, one of the more internationally oriented retailers in Germany, often invests overseas without any expectation of profit in the first few years of trading; it ran at a loss for 12 years in Denmark before turning in a profit in 1988 (Institute of Grocery Distribution, 1990). This committed approach gives Aldi a sustained and developing market presence, but does little to enhance its profitability record.

Table 5.7 can therefore give a misleading picture of the relative success of retailers in Europe, if profitability is used as the sole criterion for judgement. If anything, high levels of profitability can expose UK retailers to takeover by overseas corporate raiders who perhaps do not fully understand the differing nuances of business culture within Europe. The evidence of strong profitability makes a number of UK retailers especially tempting targets (*Retail and Distribution Management*, 1988).

Clearly, then, a track record of impressive profits is going to be a mixed blessing in retailing. Profitable retailers are able to finance expansion programmes for retail development which can increase market share in the home country or expansion in other countries, but they also risk takeover.

**Table 5.7** Net profit as a percentage of sales among selected European retailers[a]

| Company | Country | 1984–5 | 1985–6 | 1986–7 |
|---|---|---|---|---|
| Storehouse | UK | 6.2 | 5.3 | 7.9 |
| Next | UK | 9.5 | 9.1 | 7.5 |
| Burtons | UK | n/a | n/a | 7.3 |
| Dixons | UK | 4.1 | 4.1 | 7.0 |
| Boots | UK | 6.6 | 6.4 | 7.0 |
| Marks & Spencer | UK | 5.7 | 6.0 | 6.5 |
| Sears | UK | 5.4 | 5.2 | 5.7 |
| Harris Queensway | UK | 4.3 | 4.3 | 5.6 |
| Ward White | UK | 4.5 | 4.1 | 5.3 |
| Asda MFI | UK | 3.9 | 4.6 | 4.9 |
| Darty | France | 3.0 | 3.6 | 4.5 |
| J. Sainsbury | UK | 3.6 | 3.7 | 4.1 |
| Woolworth | UK | 5.2 | 2.1 | 3.8 |
| Tesco | UK | 2.0 | 2.3 | 3.3 |
| W. H. Smith | UK | 2.4 | 2.3 | 2.8 |
| K. Bijenkorf Beheer | Netherlands | 1.1 | 1.8 | 2.6 |
| Argyll | UK | 1.7 | 0.6 | 2.5 |
| Dee | UK | 1.8 | 2.3 | 2.1 |
| Nouvelles Galeries | France | 0.7 | 0.9 | 1.6 |
| Carrefour | France | 1.2 | 1.2 | 1.3 |
| Ahold | Netherlands | 1.0 | 1.1 | 1.2 |
| Casino | France | 0.8 | 0.9 | 1.1 |
| GB–Inno–BM | Belgium | 1.4 | 0.8 | 1.1 |
| Printemps | France | 0.6 | 0.7 | 0.9 |
| Euromarché | France | n/a | 0.6 | 0.9 |
| Delhaize | Belgium | 0.5 | 0.7 | 0.8 |
| Promodes | France | 0.7 | 0.5 | 0.7 |
| Galeries Lafayette | France | 0.6 | 0.8 | 0.1 |

[a] In the late 1980s and early 1990s, some of the top-ranking companies in this table suffered huge drops in profitability. This is particularly true of the two at the top in 1986–7, Storehouse and Next.
*Source*: Musannif and George (1987)

As yet, the balance between threat and opportunity remains difficult to determine; much depends on non-financial factors, such as the managerial skills of retailers. The certainties are that competition in European retailing will become fiercer, rather than more relaxed, and that the source of competition will increasingly be international, rather than domestic. There is also the prospect of spectacular success by some retailers, and expensive failure by others who are unable to adapt to different retailing cultures or gain acceptance of new retailing formats from fickle consumers.

# The Internationalization of Retailing[3]

No retailer can contemplate the internationalization of its operations without giving serious thought to logistics. In particular, lengthening supply lines is a crucial consideration. However, a first consideration in the internationalization of retailers must be their *motivation* for developing outside their own countries. Treadgold (1989) finds it useful to distinguish between 'push' and 'pull' factors, although a certain degree of overlapping is inevitable. The main push factors are:

- intense competitive pressures within the domestic marketplace
- the prospect of saturation in the domestic marketplace, leaving little room for business development by the retailer
- sluggish performance in the domestic economy, resulting in flat home sales
- restrictive legislation on new store developments

To a large extent, many retailers opt for internationalization by being reactive to the above push factors. By contrast, other retailers take an active approach through being attracted by opportunities elsewhere. Here, there are a number of pull factors at work, including:

- the identification of fragmented, underdeveloped or niche marketing opportunities in other countries
- the opportunity to establish a bridgehead for further expansion
- the presence of attractive acquisition targets

In addition, there are some important *facilitating* factors which come into play, including improved data communications, the international mobility of managers and the accumulation of company experience in international trading (Gibson and Treadgold, 1990).

It may, of course, be argued that many of these factors have long been in existence; in themselves, they cannot be responsible for the wave of retail internationalization that is now taking place. The crucial difference compared to the past seems to be that retailers are becoming increasingly active in identifying and exploiting opportunities in other countries *before* opportunities for expansion at home are exhausted. Furthermore, according to Treadgold, 'this wave of internationalization is unique in its scale, geographical orientation and motivations from earlier efforts to develop an international presence' (Treadgold, 1988).

In table 5.8, 43 retailers are identified which have established an international presence. While the compilers of the listing do not claim that it is exhaustive, they nevertheless point out that it does include all the principal players in international retailing, together with a number of companies which demonstrate particular approaches towards developing international retail business. One notable feature of table 5.8 is that it contains relatively few US retailers. As Treadgold (1988) notes, 'in 1988, only four of the ten largest retailers in the USA had retail interests outside North America. Furthermore, some, including Sears Roebuck, JC Penney and F. W. Woolworth, have substantially divested themselves of their overseas interests, to concentrate instead on developing differentiated trading formats in their domestic marketplace'. Treadgold goes on to suggest two reasons for this small international presence by US retailers. First, the size of the North American retail market is much larger than for, say, any one European country: this in itself has presented US retailers with many more home opportunities for retail development than their European counterparts. Second, the European interests of US companies have often performed rather poorly, which goes some way to explaining the process of retrenchment. Having said that, it is also known that a number of US retailers are looking afresh at the SEM with a view to business development, this being especially true of the specialist retailers such as The Gap, Levi and Toys Я Us.

There is no single path to developing an international presence in retailing. On a geographical basis, retailers can take one of four approaches to internationalization (Treadgold, 1988). These are:

- *Concentrated internationalization.* This comprises 'border hopping' into adjacent countries with similar (and therefore familiar) conditions to those prevailing in the domestic market. The German retailer Aldi's move into Denmark is one example of concentrated internationalization. The expansion of French hypermarket groups into Spain is another.
- *Dispersed internationalization.* Here retailers have developed a presence in a number of markets which are geographically remote and culturally

**Table 5.8** Selected retailers with an international presence

| Name | Country of origin | Main trading activity |
|---|---|---|
| Ahold NV | Netherlands | Food retailing |
| Alain Manoukian | France | Fashionwear |
| Albrecht Group (Aldi) | West Germany | Food retailing |
| Asko | West Germany | Food and clothing |
| Auchan | France | Food retailing |
| BAT Industries | UK | Department stores, catalogue showrooms, drug stores |
| Benetton | Italy | Knitwear |
| Body Shop | UK | Cosmetics, skin care |
| Boots | UK | Dispensing chemists, variety stores |
| Brenninkmeyers (C&A) | Netherlands | Clothing |
| Carrefour | France | Food retailing |
| Coles Myer | Australia | Food, department stores, discount stores |
| Courts | UK | Household furnishings |
| Dee Corporation | UK | Food, sports goods |
| Delhaize | Belgium | Food retailing |
| Dixons | UK | Domestic retailing |
| Docks de France | France | Food retailing |
| Fastframe | UK | Speciality |
| GUS | UK | Mail order, household furnishings, DIY |
| GB–Inno–BM | Belgium | Department stores, food, DIY, sports goods, fast food |

| Grand Metropolitan | UK | Food and drink |
| Ikea | Sweden | Flat-pack furniture |
| John Menzies | UK | Newsagents |
| Laura Ashley | UK | Clothing, soft furnishings |
| Marks & Spencer | UK | Clothing, food, household |
| McDonalds | USA | Fast food |
| Nordiska Kompaniet | Sweden | Department stores |
| Otto Versand | West Germany | Mail order |
| Printemps | France | Department stores |
| Promodes | France | Food retailing |
| Ratners | UK | Jewellers |
| J. Sainsbury | UK | Food retailing |
| Sears Roebuck | USA | Department stores, mail order |
| Southland Corporation | USA | Convenience stores |
| Stefanel | Italy | Fashionwear |
| Storehouse | UK | Household, clothing, babies' and children's products |
| Tengelmann | West Germany | Food retailing |
| W. H. Smith | UK | News, recorded music |
| Ward White | UK | DIY, vehicle parts and accessories |
| Safeway Stores Corporation | USA | Food retailing |
| Tandy Corporation | USA | Domestic electrical |
| Toys Я Us | USA | Toys |
| Vendex | Netherlands | Department stores, fast food, DIY, bookshops |

*Source*: Davies and Treadgold (1988)

diverse from their home market. A striking example of dispersed internationalism is that of Carrefour in Taiwan.

- *Multinationals.* Retailers in this category have developed a more extensive presence than retailers in the two preceding categories. Examples of multinational retailers are Ikea, Toys Я Us and Laura Ashley.
- *Global.* Multinational retailers sometimes develop into global retailers, which have a presence throughout the world and operate in a highly diverse range of trading environments. Current examples of global retailers are McDonalds, Benetton and Southland Corporation (as '7 to 11' stores).

Different geographical approaches are also complemented by a range of methods for gaining entry to new markets. Among retailers trading internationally, there is apparently no consensus on the most appropriate method for a particular market. Different kinds of company have their own preferences, and what might work for one company may not work so well for another. On the whole, retailers with limited overseas experience appear to choose high control entry strategies, often involving acquisition. Mass merchandisers, in particular, seem to prefer acquisition. By contrast, specialty retailers appear to have a preference for organic growth, particularly through franchising, which represents a low-cost, but low-control, method of entry into overseas markets.

Figure 5.2 has been constructed by classifying international retailers according to their geographical presence and their entry strategy for new markets. From this classification, Treadgold identifies four clusters of companies, which may change their membership of any one cluster as their business interests change over time (Treadgold, 1988):

- *Cluster 1: 'The Cautious Internationalists'.* This is the largest grouping of international retailers, which have chosen a high-cost strategy to develop a limited international presence. Companies from the UK are notably well represented in Cluster 1.
- *Cluster 2: 'The Emboldened Internationalists'.* Retailers in this cluster usually have longer experience of international retailing than those in Cluster 1. The uniting factor of retailers in the two clusters is an unwillingness to loosen control over their overseas interests. Carrefour is, perhaps the archetypal Emboldened Internationalist.
- *Cluster 3: 'The Aggressive Internationalists'.* Although few retailers are currently placed within Cluster 3, it appears that an increasing number of retailers aim for membership. Typically, the Aggressive

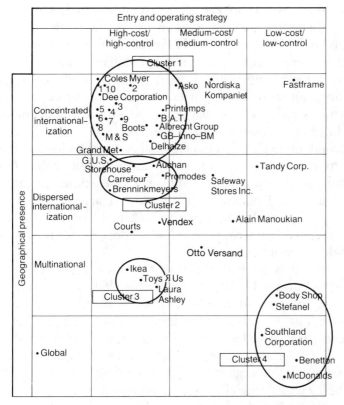

**Figure 5.2** A typology of transnational retailers. 1, Ahold N.V.; 2, Sears Roebuck; 3, J. Sainsbury; 4, John Menzies; 5, Tengelmann; 6, Docks de France; 7, Dixons; 8, W. H. Smith; 9, Ward White; 10, Ratners.

*Source*: Treadgold (1988)

Internationalists find a market niche which they exploit with an effective combination of product placement and brand promotion.

- *Cluster 4: 'The World Powers'*. Retailers in this cluster occupy a special place in international retailing. Above all, they are selling products and/or trading formats which have universal appeal, whatever the country. In many cases, new markets are created where none previously existed. Typically, franchising is used to develop quickly on a global scale. However, characteristically, the World Powers exercise a high level of control over the supply chains. Benetton, for example, is the largest manufacturer of woollen garments in the world, as well as trading from more than 4000 shops.

Here, then, we have one of the many anomalies of European retailing. Benetton, an Italian company, is one of the few retailers that can be classified as a 'World Power' with around 4000 (mostly franchised) stores in 80 countries. Yet Italian retailing, in general, remains largely undeveloped, partly as a result of regulatory restrictions on store development. It would therefore be wrong to make too strong a link between the strength and innovatory capabilities of a company and its origins.

A second anomaly concerns regionality and retailing. Often there is an expectation that retailing in the northern half of the EC will be more advanced than in the south. Yet restrictions on large store development in Belgium have severely retarded the growth of multiple trading within Belgium; leading retailers such as GB-Inno-BM (now called GIB Group) have had to look outside the country for worthwhile opportunities.

The anomalies serve to illustrate the unevenness of patterns of retailing in Europe. Different states in the USA, say, may have their own distinctive styles of retailing, possibly arising as a result of local regulation, but the variability in Europe is much the greater. As we have seen, there are often major differences, particularly with respect to the scale of retailing, concentration of ownership, forms of retail business, regulatory impact and the profitability of retailers. In their turn, these factors crucially affect retail logistics in a variety of ways which will become apparent in the following chapter.

However, to end this discussion of retailing in Europe, it is necessary once again to emphasize the importance of the process of retail internationalization and the resulting need for excellence in logistics. Retailing in Europe is no longer self-contained, either for a member country within the EC or within the boundaries of the EC itself. Retailers from Europe are, in ever increasing numbers, exploring opportunities in other parts of the world. In turn, retailers from the USA and Japan are establishing presences in Europe. Developments in eastern Europe are also an important source of change. The state-run shops of eastern Europe are unlikely to adapt readily to a change to a market economy, and retailers from the West are looking to take their place. In particular, western German retailers are well placed to gain new business, especially in eastern Germany. Tengelmann has already formed a number of joint ventures, and Kaufhof has acquired sites for development. It is also believed that the secretive Aldi chain is looking East for opportunities. If it follows previous patterns of business development, Aldi will probably buy sites and operate them itself, rather than enter into, say, joint venture agreements.

The pace of internationalization in retailing, particularly with respect to the EC, is therefore likely to quicken. A crucial consideration in the process of internationalization will be logistics. Business ventures will succeed or fail on the strength of a retailer's grasp of logistics in an expanded marketplace. To reinforce this point, we conclude with an illustration from Benetton, one of the World Powers of retailing, on the importance of logistics in its approach to international retailing:

> Benetton's order system is 'just-in-time' as production runs are not started until orders have been received. A key aspect of its system is the dyeing of knitted goods after production rather than dyeing yarn prior to knitting. This allows Benetton outlets to delay commitment to particular colours until later in the production cycle. Since each selling season typically begins with about ten alternative colours with only about three usually resulting in high demand, the delay in colour affords Benetton an opportunity to respond directly to market demand. The retail system itself provides valuable information to Benetton for production planning via daily orders. These feed production with current demand, on which replenishment schedules for designs and colours may be based. The timeliness of this order data is crucial since popular colours will often sell out in the first ten days of the new season. This rapid response system gives Benetton retailers a competitive edge over their less responsive competitors. The order information is digested and fed back to those customers whose orders appear to be out of line with others in their area. Further, Benetton uses CAD for design and cutting in order to respond to dynamic demand as rapidly as possible. Finally, the company's marketing strategy promotes simple colour fashion with heavy advertising support, which in turn maximizes the benefits from delayed dyeing production process.
>
> (Montgomery and Hausman, 1985)

# Case Study   Aldi

Aldi is a remarkable example of a company which has succeeded through persistence, both in sticking with a tried-and-tested formula and in waiting for investment to pay off. The origins of Aldi are fairly recent, which makes its expansion all the more impressive. Two brothers, Karl and Theo Albrecht, launched the company from their mother's grocery shop in Essen, just after the Second World War. By 1955 their retail operations were expanding rapidly, with shops throughout the Ruhr.

The two key features of the retail operation are that it is based on discounting and that growth is achieved organically, rather than by buying other retailers. When Aldi had outgrown the German retail market, it set up in other countries using the same formula of discounting and organic growth; except in the case of Austria, where it bought the Hofer Group. By late 1989, Aldi had 3097 shops in eight countries (see table 5.9).

In each of these countries, Aldi operates a no-frills policy in its retailing. Products are displayed in their packing cases and are stacked on simple steel shelving. Shops stock a limited range of products, typically only 600 basic food items, predominantly own-label. As a result, Aldi is able to charge very competitive prices which are especially attractive to budget-conscious shoppers. Even so, more than 75 per cent of western German householders regularly buy from Aldi.

Many retail analysts consider Aldi to be one of the most conservative of retailers; it has been slow to expand its limited range of fastest selling products, lines of fresh and frozen foods are few, and non-food products such as clothing have been limited to one-off bulk purchases sold through discount bin displays in shops.

By not changing its retail format according to fashion, Aldi has achieved some solid success, although it is often a long time coming; it took its Danish shops 12 years to return a profit. Part of the reason

**Table 5.9** Numbers of shops operated by Aldi, by country (to December 1989)

| Country | Number of shops |
|---|---|
| Germany | 2158 |
| The Netherlands | 271 |
| USA | 225 |
| Belgium | 220 |
| Austria | 103 |
| Denmark | 102 |
| France | 15 |
| UK | 3 |

*Source*: Institute of Grocery Distribution, taken from 'European Fact File' and Key Account Profiles

for Aldi's international success is that it often enters retail markets by occupying niches vacated by other retailers. The UK is a case in point. Tesco, which was once the major player in discount grocery retailing, has steadily gone up market from its 'pile it high, sell it cheap' origins. Aldi's entry into the UK market in the late 1980s is well timed to occupy the niche once dominated by Tesco, and will test the assertion that shoppers now expect more than just low prices.

Experience from other countries would suggest that it would be wrong to underestimate the importance of price in shoppers' buying decisions. For example, Aldi initially found it difficult to become established in the Benelux countries, but now it has emerged as the largest discounter in the Netherlands, accounting for 50 per cent of all discount sales. Aldi's firm belief that persistence brings reward seems likely to guarantee a special role for it as an international discount retailer.

## Case Study   Groupe Casino

Groupe Casino has diversified interests in food processing, hyper-markets and supermarkets, convenience stores, autocentres, restaurants and property (see figure 5.3). Most of its activities are concentrated in France, but there is also a cash-and-carry operation in the USA. The Casino retailing division accounts for 77 per cent of Groupe Casino's total sales, and the contribution of the different types of retail outlet is shown in table 5.10.

Casino provides a good example of a company whose ambitions are vested in co-operation rather than a go-it-alone approach. Its decision to co-operate is partly a function of size; Casino is a medium-sized retailer and joint ventures with other, similar retailers can make good sense when they are competing against much larger rivals. In a number of respects, the planned completion of the SEM has sharpened the threat from larger competitors. First, some of the larger European retailers are using the SEM as an opportunity to internationalize their operations and gain a greater share of the pan-European market; Casino does not want this to be at its expense. Second, a number of suppliers of goods to retailers are becoming bigger, by merger, acquisition and organic growth, again in response to expanded opportunities in the SEM. This tips the balance of power in purchasing more in favour of the suppliers rather than the retailers, and this is especially so for small and medium-sized ones.

As a result of these developments Casino, along with two similar retailers, Argyll from the UK and Ahold of the Netherlands, co-founded the European Retail Association (ERA). The aim of the ERA is

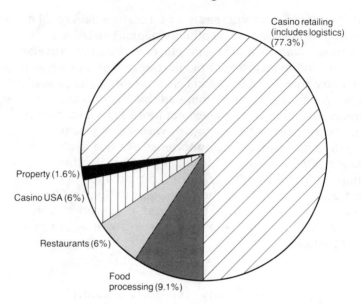

**Figure 5.3** Groupe Casino sales by operating division, 1989 (total sales were US$ 9316.6 million)

*Source*: Groupe Casino Annual Report, 1989

not just to pool purchasing, but also to co-operate in the fields of marketing, logistics and IT. Ties between the partners were consolidated by an exchange of shares in September 1989.

Only three months before, Casino had taken a separate co-operative step, this time with La Rinascente, a subsidiary of the Fiat Group, for the development of the Italian supermarket chain Rinascente/SMA. With a 35 per cent shareholding, Casino is committed to developing

**Table 5.10** Total Groupe Casino retail sales by store type, 1989

| Store type | Number of stores | Total sales (million US$) | Sales as a percentage of total |
|---|---|---|---|
| Hypermarkets | 40 | 2820 | 50.2 |
| Supermarkets | 122 | 1235 | 27.2 |
| Convenience | 2216 | 881 | 19.4 |
| Affiliates | 278 | 68 | 1.5 |
| Other | — | 82 | 1.8 |

*Source*: Groupe Casino Annual Report, 1989

the supermarket/superstore concept in Italy, whose retail market is still largely characterized by small independent shops.

It is still too early to say whether or not Casino's strategy of co-operation will work. In the circumstances, the logic is appealing enough, and co-operative strategies have been successfully adopted by many other medium-sized companies threatened by larger competitors. Yet, as in all co-operative ventures, success is critically dependent upon practical considerations, such as the choice of partners. Logic is just part of the story.

# 6
# Innovation in Retail Logistics

## Key Areas of Logistics Innovation

Most sectors of retailing can provide at least one example of excellence in logistics. In clothing, Benetton has evidently used innovative approaches to logistics to develop and sustain its position as a 'world power' in retailing, as the quotation at the end of the previous chapter shows. Similarly, in furniture retailing, Ikea would have been unable to expand from its Swedish home market without a sound grasp of the importance of logistics in developing new business.

At the conceptual level, logistics has a similar importance for all kinds of retailer. For example, considerable importance must be attached to the quality of logistics services. Products need reliable delivery to stores and the availability of the bestselling lines must always be assured; considerations of this kind are central to the success of every retailer. Invariably, some sectors of retailing are ahead of others in their innovative approach to logistics. One sector which has consistently led with new ideas is grocery retailing, particularly in countries where the multiples dominate.

Among the Big Four countries of the European Community (EC), France and the UK emerge as leading innovators in grocery retailing. Italy remains characterized by independent retailing (see chapter 5) and German retailers tend towards conservatism. By contrast, French retailers pioneered the hypermarket concept and have recently introduced this form of retailing into other countries, notably Spain, with success. There is also a fascination in France with information technology (IT), potentially important applications of which are to be found in grocery retailing, including EFTPOS, which allows the use of smart cards in some French supermarkets (EC Commission, 1989).

Grocery retailing in the UK has developed along different lines from those in France. Hypermarkets are less common, not least as a result of planning restrictions on large retail development. Instead, grocery retailing is based more on supermarkets and superstores, many sited in urban high streets. The key to innovation in UK grocery retailing has been fierce competition between multiples, now numbering five since the takeover of Safeway by Argyll. Indeed, it is interesting to draw parallels with Japanese manufacturing, in which major companies, especially in cars and electronics, are locked in fierce competition with rivals in the domestic marketplace. Porter (1990) has noted that competition of this kind has been an important factor in promoting innovation. This is certainly true of UK retailers in the field of logistics, where it is widely used as a competitive weapon.

There have been three major areas of logistics innovation in UK grocery retailing, each of them interlinked, namely:

- using IT to maintain better control over the supply chain
- releasing more sales space in retail outlets by eliminating storage space
- contracting out to specialist companies those logistics activities such as transport and storage which are not 'core' business

It must, however, be recognized that these particular innovations will not necessarily transfer in an unmodified form to retail outlets other than supermarkets. In hypermarkets, for example, storage space must often be adjacent to the sales space because, in provincial France, say, there is no scope for serving several hypermarkets from a *separate* distribution centre used for storage. Nonetheless, the three areas of logistics innovation identified above do serve as a useful framework for further discussion, with appropriate qualification according to country, retail sector and type of retail outlet. Furthermore, the case study of Ahold, at the end of this chapter, shows in detail how a particular retailer is adapting its retailing and logistics activities according to local changes in trading conditions. Ahold mirrors many of the logistics innovations taken up by its counterparts in France and the UK, but has refocused to take account of the special needs of the Dutch marketplace.

## Information Technology

The importance of IT in retail logistics cannot be underestimated. Spectacular advances in both computer hardware and software have made IT a key component of logistics planning in the retail sector.

A major contribution of IT in logistics is that it increases *transparency within the supply chain*. At one time, the established way of discovering how much product was held in a retail outlet was by a physical counting. For any particular product line, staff would need to count the number of items that were left on shelves, and how many further items of the product were held in the storeroom, before they could judge whether a replenishment order was necessary. Within this routine the main uncertainty was the quantity on the shelves, since paperwork records could usually be used to determine how much was still in the storeroom. But the rate at which customers took stock from the shelves of supermarkets was uncertain due to poor monitoring.

The introduction of electronic point of sale (EPOS) systems completely changes both how retailers check quantities at the store and re-order new supplies. As customers pass through checkouts at supermarkets, light pens or bar-code readers are now widely used to identify the products purchased. Whereas once the checkout operator had to enter the price of an individual item into a cash register, the EPOS system is used to check the price of the item and automatically add it to the total of other goods purchased by the customer. At the end of the transaction, the customer receipt is printed out to include descriptions of the goods bought, together with prices of individual items.

This is all very helpful for the customer, not least because the time through the checkout is reduced by the automatic identification of purchased items using the EPOS system. But for the retailer, there is an immediate registration within the EPOS system of goods sold. When this data is matched to data for goods delivered to the store, it is possible to have a immediate and up-to-date understanding of items held at the store for any given product line. Electronic refinements can be made to EPOS upstream of the checkout. For example, Argos, the UK catalogue showroom retailer, no longer uses paperwork as the basis for recording deliveries to its stores. Instead, vehicle drivers hand in floppy disks at the store when making a delivery so that incoming goods can be entered into the store computer terminal without data having to be keyed in (*Materials Handling*, 1989). This procedure both saves time and reduces the frequency of error.

Furthermore, EPOS can eliminate waste in association with other logistics innovations. Boots, the UK chemist, has a very extensive range of products, up to 40 000 lines in the largest stores (Murrell, 1988). Under these circumstances, there is a high risk of oversupply of products to an outlet, relative to demand at the outlet or, alternatively, of running entirely out of stock. However, EPOS, in association with just-in-time (JIT) delivery, has transformed the position for Boots, making both of these occurrences much more unlikely. Redesign of the supply chain has meant that deliveries are now tightly controlled to points along it; products are received only a very short time before they are required to be moved on from that point. This has the effect of both speeding up the movement of goods along the supply chain (and so reducing overall inventory requirement) and giving Boots the flexibility to supply quickly any retail outlet which has an unexpectedly high demand for a particular product. Transparency therefore goes hand-in-hand with improved control of the supply chain to give an improved logistics service to retail outlets.

Neither of the above examples of companies using EPOS to achieve greater transparency in the supply chain are from the grocery sector. But it is perhaps in grocery retailing, which accounts for so much retail expenditure, that the impact of EPOS will be greatest. Crucially, there is a growing demand for fresh food to contain less preservatives and this means that product life is shortened. As a result, there is pressure on retail logistics to maximize the life of fresh food on the shelves of supermarkets and in the customer's home (Boatman, 1989). EPOS, in association with controlled atmosphere packing (CAP) and controlled environments for the growing of fresh food will help in the realization of this goal.

For example, one UK supermarket chain is investigating the possibility of reducing waste in the production and sale of salad vegetables, demand for which is sensitive to changes in weather; if it is hot, then demand tends to increase, and vice versa. Using the much-improved weather forecasts which are now available, demand for salad vegetables over the coming week can be assessed more precisely than before. This means that demand forecasting, linked with EPOS to monitor actual sales, can be used to notify growers (especially local ones) of short-term requirements. If, say, there is a forecast fall in demand for lettuce, the grower will then be able to delay harvesting of his lettuce crop by adjusting heat and light combinations in the greenhouse to postpone maturity. In this way, food production and demand can be better harmonized so that there is less product waste within the supply chain. The freshness of food products such as meat and fish, as well as vegetables, can be prolonged during transit by the use of vehicles with controlled environments, again contributing to longer shelf life. Here IT is combined with food handling technology to bring fresher food to the consumer.

IT, often in the form of EPOS, can also be used to provide better measures of *trading performance* in retailing. By capturing data at the checkout, EPOS enables the retailer to calculate a whole range of performance indicators relating to retail business (MacPherson, 1987), including:

- sales by department and/or item
- fast movers and non-movers
- hourly sales
- sales by transaction type (such as cash, cheque or credit card)
- sales by location of retail outlet
- sales by customer
- sales by staff
- overs and shorts reports
- analysis of exception reporting
- inventory analyses

Retailers benefit from information of this kind in two ways; there are both hard and soft benefits (Sparks, 1987). The hard benefits are essentially quantifiable, such as the need for fewer staff to carry out certain tasks around the store (the checking of inventory quantities, for example). Soft benefits, however, are those benefits which are practically impossible to quantify. For example, the retailer may be able to improve the marketing effort by having better sales information. But it is extremely difficult to quantify the impact of any marketing campaign based on this better information.

A further application of IT in the form of EPOS is to provide better *merchandising support*. While certain sectors of retailing have enjoyed this advantage for some time, it is now penetrating the more traditional areas of retailing, such as bookselling. Books have long had good potential for EPOS, since each published book is given an ISBN, a number which uniquely identifies it anywhere in the world. Increasingly, ISBN numbers are being bar-coded, making books ripe for EPOS. As a result, there is now a departure from the established practice of a publisher's representative making a periodic call to the bookseller, taking an order and getting the ordered books to the shop within 3–4 weeks. Penguin Books, in going over to EPOS, now manages to deliver ordered books to shops within 24 to 48 hours (Hitchin, 1987). In particular, this reduced lead time for delivery has proved to be especially important in the case of bestsellers and school texts for literature. Non-availability of these product lines almost invariably means sales being lost to another retailer. When the average Penguin bookshop can sell up to 300 copies of a bestseller within a week of publication, the importance of quick replenishment of titles becomes very clear.

Increasingly, electronic data interchange (EDI) is being used as a way of enhancing merchandising support in retailing. A major objective of many EDI systems is to replace traditional methods of placing orders with suppliers: telephone calls and paperwork are invariably time-consuming, expensive and prone to error. By sending electronic messages to suppliers though EDI, retailers anticipate the elimination of these disadvantages.

However, while the concept of EDI may be stated simply enough, the practice is an altogether more difficult proposition. Trading partners often not only have different trading procedures, but also incompatibilities between computer systems. In the UK, these difficulties were resolved through TRADACOMS standards promoted by the Articled Numbers Association (Fenton, 1985). A key function of TRADACOMS was to set out a standard structure and sequence of data for the documents essential for trading: orders, delivery notes, invoices and remittance advice, along with formats for product, price and customer master files.

TRADANET evolved from TRADACOMS to provide a communications network for trading partners which allowed them to exchange information. An essential function of TRADANET is to provide the necessary protocol conversions to allow otherwise incompatible hardware to exchange data (Peters, 1990). Each trading partner has its own 'electronic mailbox' which enables it to see what information has been received or withdrawn for processing. TRADANET is now becoming well established as a communications link between trading partners, and this has clear implications for logistics and the providers of logistics services suppliers, such as freight companies, since many are now having to develop their links to the network.

IT can also be applied to improve the *efficiency of supply chain management* in retail logistics. One case in point is the scheduling and routing of delivery vehicles. In many countries throughout Europe, the standard practice is for a delivery planner to allocate consignments to particular vehicles on a manual basis; he takes details of consignments that must be delivered on any given day, and then allocates those consignments to vehicles in the fleet according to the carrying capacity of individual vehicles and the characteristics of products making up consignments (for example, weight, size and volume). The delivery planner (or the driver) then decides a routing for the vehicle on the road network: this will depend on customer locations and any constraints upon delivery (for example, the time of day when deliveries would not be accepted).

This process of scheduling and routing for vehicles is not only laborious, but is relatively inefficient. As a result, there have been various attempts over the years to computerize the process and so drastically reduce the human element. Early attempts were not notably successful (anecdotal evidence points to instances of vehicles being routed by the computer over a river – at a point where there was no crossing). However, refinements in software and dramatic improvements in the abilities of hardware have transformed the situation. It is now possible for computerized vehicle routing and scheduling (CVRS) to be used on a daily basis, although many users still prefer to work with it at the strategic level (for example, to plan fixed delivery schedules for a particular time of year, or to establish future fleet requirements).

For daily operations, companies use CVRS to allocate vehicles to sets of delivery locations and build routes linking these locations. In most cases CVRS is linked to sales order processing systems to speed computation and minimize the occurrence of error. It is also noteworthy that most companies now using CVRS on a daily basis first used it in a strategic planning capacity; overall cost savings of 5–10 per cent over manual planning have been reported in some cases (Peters, 1990).

One of the earliest UK users of CVRS on a daily basis was the grocery retail multiple, Argyll. Christensen and Eastburn (1985) reported on the use of daily CVRS at Argyll's Felling distribution centre in the north-east of England. Felling served 95 retail outlets, mainly within a radius of 30 miles. Using the PARAGON system of CVRS on a daily basis, Argyll achieved the following:

- a significant reduction in transport costs
- greater vehicle utilization, both in the use of vehicle capacity and the use of available time for delivery
- an improved and more responsive service to the retail outlets
- a significant reduction in capital investment for vehicle and trailer replacement
- the ability to ask 'what if . . .?' questions without carrying out an expensive operational trial (for example, a night-time delivery was implemented following computer simulation)

Paradoxically, as a retailer grows and its outlets become larger and more widespread, the need for CVRS may in fact diminish because deliveries will increasingly be consolidated into full vehicle loads for delivery to single locations. Sophisticated routing and scheduling techniques are not required for this kind of straightforward work.

It has to be said that UK interest in CVRS, not just from retailers, seems to be more positive than in other European countries. Research carried out under the EC's DRIVE programme by the Eurofret consortium indicates that, in many countries, there is a failure to appreciate the potential benefits of CVRS in delivery operations (Eurofret, 1990). Given the established benefits reported by Argyll, it seems that widespread acceptance of CVRS will occur, but the diffusion rate in Europe as a whole will be slow, as negative perceptions of many potential users have to be reversed.

# Maximizing Sales Space

The second major area of retail innovation for discussion is the release of more sales space in retail outlets by eliminating storage space. At first sight, this may appear to be a relatively mundane innovation next to the 'high-tech' diversity of computer-based logistics, but the opportunity cost of storage space will often be substantial in high street locations. Converting this storage space into sales space has important implications for both retailers and the suppliers of logistics services.

Most retailers will be united in the belief that retail outlets are for sales, rather than storage. But many retailers feel they are forced to retain storage areas at retail outlets for fear of running out of essential product lines. If the shelves are empty, they can be filled by a short visit to the storeroom at the back of the shop: for many retailers this is preferable to the uncertainties of waiting for deliveries from a supplier.

However, keeping products in store at the shop has a number of important disadvantages. Most important of all is that it reduces the sales area and hence the revenue-earning potential of a given retail outlet. In a competitive retail environment, this can be a very serious consideration. A second factor is that keeping products in the shop's storeroom is expensive. Once the retailer has taken delivery then he has to finance the cost of keeping the products even before they are ready to go on sale. This is clearly bad for both cashflow and profitability. But what is the solution, given the fear of not having products available for sale?

*Unaffiliated* independent retailers have little option other than to keep products in reserve at their shops, unless their suppliers (often including wholesalers and cash-and-carrys) provide a first-class delivery service at an acceptable cost, a condition which may be doubtful. The unaffiliated independent retailer could keep products in store elsewhere – say, in a lock-up – where the rental cost of floorspace will be less than for the shop. But shelf-filling is inconvenient if products are stored at some remote location; this represents a cost to be weighed against possible savings.

The prospect of eliminating storerooms at shops is better for an *affiliated* independent retailer if, say, the voluntary group to which he belongs is prepared to innovate in logistics. Essentially what is required is a frequent delivery service from the voluntary group acting as wholesaler. Daily deliveries may have to replace deliveries every, say, two or three days. Furthermore, support will have to be forthcoming from other independent retailers affiliated to the same voluntary group to ensure sufficient volumes for economic delivery on a more frequent basis.

Overall, the *multiple retailers* have the best prospect of eliminating storage space at shops and, indeed, many of them have already done just that. In some cases, however, the opportunity to do so may have come about as a consequence of first following other priorities. The UK is a case in point. In table 6.1 is shown the sequence of events that led to the elimination of storage space at many supermarkets. As indicated, regional distribution centres (RDCs) were established in the first instance as a way to discipline deliveries to shops by suppliers. In effect, each RDC acted as a consolidation point for supplier delivery to a number of shops. Later developments were the contracting out of distribution services (see below) and then the centralization of all storage at the RDC. So, in effect, the elimination of storage areas at supermarkets came about because the retailing multiples had *already* established RDCs as part of the supply chain to supermarkets.

In the UK there has been a substantial move by the retailing multiples towards the use of RDCs; the process is usually referred to

**Table 6.1** Sequence of major logistics innovations by multiple retailers in the UK

| Period | Problem | Innovation | Consequences |
|---|---|---|---|
| 1960s and 1970s | Disorderly delivery by suppliers to supermarkets; queues of vehicles led to both inefficiency and disruption | Introduction of regional distribution centres (RDCs) to channel goods from suppliers to supermarkets operated by retailer | (1) Strict timing of supplier deliveries to RDC imposed by retailer (2) Retailer builds and operates RDC (3) Retailer operates own delivery fleet between RDC and supermarkets within its catchment area |
| Early 1980s | Retailers becoming too committed to operating logistics services in support of retail activity | Operation of retailer-owned RDCs and vehicle fleets to specialist freight companies | (1) Retailer can concentrate on 'core business' of retailing (2) Retailer achieves better financial return from capital invested in supermarkets than in RDCs and vehicles |

**Table 6.1** (*cont.*)

| Period | Problem | Innovation | Consequences |
|---|---|---|---|
| Mid-1980s | Available floorspace at retail outlets being under-used; too much floorspace used for storage | Conversion of storage floorspace at supermarkets to sales floorspace | (1) Better sales revenue potential at retail outlets<br>(2) RDCs absorb products formerly kept in store at supermarkets<br>(3) Just-in-time (JIT) delivery used from RDC to replenish supermarket shelves |

as 'centralization', reflecting the pivotal role of RDCs in management of the retail supply chain. Moreover, there are wider consequences of centralization than those listed in table 6.1, which concentrates on the major logistics innovations. Numbered among these wider consequences are:

- *Quantity purchase discounts achieved as a result of bulk purchasing.* Instead of store managers from each supermarket placing orders with suppliers, joint orders are placed through the RDC or a central purchasing office. This, in effect, means making larger orders and gaining improved discounts from suppliers.
- *Better control of levels of inventory.* There are advantages in centralization since inventory held at an RDC can be released to supermarkets according to the changing levels of demand at each supermarket. As a result, there should be less risk of keeping too much inventory within the supply chain as a whole or, conversely, of running out of particular products at some supermarkets when faced with unexpectedly high demand. Furthermore, the centralization of inventory can, in itself, reduce the inventory requirement for the multiple retailer according to the square root law (Maister, 1976). By eliminating storerooms at supermarkets and keeping all inventory at RDCs, there should be a reduced overall inventory requirement within the retail supply chain.

• *Reduced shrinkage and breakage.* Converting space from supermarket storerooms into sales space means that goods delivered to the supermarket are put straight on to the shelves. This reduction in handling means that there is less likelihood of breakage and less opportunity for shrinkage (the retail trade's euphemism for theft).

• *Opportunities for mechanization.* Large RDCs, by breaching through-put thresholds and exploiting economies of scale, make it economic to introduce more mechanization to materials handling. This reduces the retailer's dependence upon labour and makes maximum use of storage volumes within RDCs (*Materials Handling*, 1989), especially with respect to height.

Clearly many UK retailers, including Sainsbury, Mothercare, Boots, Asda and Argos, have found the benefits of centralization impossible to resist. Consciously or unconsciously, they have been following the advice of Bowersox (1988) to use 'logistical competency to gain competitive advantage'. And, given the pivotal role of inventory in promoting the centralization concept, retailers have also recognized the importance of yet another observation of Bowersox, that 'inventory is the focal asset of business'.

The skill of UK retailers in logistics innovation is well documented in the literature. Sainsbury, pioneer of the RDC concept, now has 23 distribution centres strategically located throughout the UK and responsible for handling 780 million cases (85 per cent of the volume) each week to 280 supermarkets (Quarmby, 1988). Then there is Argos, whose efficient distribution enables it to achieve a 95 per cent level of product availability on a 3500+ product range throughout the year at all of its 250 catalogue showroom outlets (*Storage, Handling and Distribution*, 1990).

But the point of this chapter is not so much to illustrate the individual achievements of retailers, but to outline the way in which success in retailing can be achieved through logistics. Consequently, it is important to emphasize the extent to which logistics innovation may be restricted, or take a different form, according to circumstances. Variations in retailing format between European countries mean that centralization is a logistics option open only to retailers in some parts of Europe. In the grocery sector, retailers in the Netherlands (such as Ahold) have tended to follow the supermarket/superstore model of retailing rather than the hypermarket one. Use of RDCs has developed in tandem with supermarkets and superstores, but without the degree of contracting out of logistics functions associated with the UK retailers. The supermarket model works well in a largely urbanized country such as the Netherlands; it undoubtedly would work as well in Belgium, another largely urbanized country, if large store development had not been restricted. It follows that the RDC concept is mainly appropriate to wholesalers in Belgium, simply because there are too few supermarkets/superstores to support many retailer-operated RDCs.

Hypermarket development in Spain has largely followed the French pattern. Two factors are at work here. First, high street development by the multiples has been restricted by the continued existence of 'traspaso' leases, initially granted in the Franco era. These, in effect, maintain low rents for family-run independent retailers. Further, since traspaso leases only lapse with the sale of the business outside the family, there is continuity of ownership among the independents, and a consequent lack of suitable high street sites for multiple chains to develop. Hence the best opportunity has been to develop out-of-town shopping centres, such as hypermarkets and malls, although restrictions on new schemes have recently been tightened. Second, retailing in Spain has been led by French interests. Around 19 per cent of Carrefour's turnover comes from its 24-hypermarket Pryca operation in Spain. Similarly, Alcampo is owned by Auchan and Continente/Saudisa is owned by Promodes.

Both French and Spanish retailing, being mainly based on the hypermarket retailing format, gives the RDC concept limited appliction. Hypermarkets often have a largely 'stand-alone' status within a region, so it does not always make sense to serve them from a separate distribution centre. Inventory control therefore has to be sought in different ways: exercising tight discipline over suppliers with respect to order quantities and frequency of delivery are options which are particularly relevant.

The drive towards maximizing sales space therefore has a different priority rating depending upon the style of retailing adopted in any given country. In broad terms, in countries where multiple retailers trade mainly from supermarkets located in high streets (such as the Netherlands, Germany and the UK), there will be a strong motivation, either actual or potential, to translate storage space into selling space at stores. By contrast, in countries with hypermarkets (such as France and Spain) the motivation is less.

For a third group of countries in the EC, retailing is either too small in scale (as in Luxembourg) or too fragmented in ownership (as in Italy or Belgium) to benefit substantially from the RDC concept in retailing, especially as a means to maximizing sales space.

The future application of RDCs in retailing therefore depends crucially upon trends in retailing itself. Increasing competitive pressure may mean that retailers will have to increase their sales areas in shops in order to realize the full revenue potential of their locations; changing legal frameworks for retailing may favour, say, hypermarket development over trading from supermarkets; the internationalization of retailing may mean a blurring of national patterns of retailing and a bias towards the organization of retail trading on a regional basis, with national frontiers becoming less consequential than they are now. However, all of these potential developments are extremely difficult to predict, with respect to both the frequency of their occurrence and timing. In all probability, the established patterns of retailing in the major economies of Europe will suffer no abrupt change over the next decade or two, not least because the scale of investment in the current retail infrastructure, notably the shops, is enormous.

Few retailers would voluntarily accept or initiate a major change in retail trading formats unless significant advantages for them were to result. So hypermarket-led retailing will tend to predominate in Spain and France, with supermarkets setting the pattern for northern Europe. In turn, these different retailing formats will tend to dictate the pattern of logistics support. Yet it is important to emphasize that some innovations in logistics (such as RDCs) can be seen as the outcome of a struggle for control of the supply chain among retailers, wholesalers and suppliers. The creation of RDCs means that retailers take control of more of the supply chain, provided that manufacturers are willing or can be persuaded to relinquish some of their responsibilities. Furthermore, the existence of RDCs helps to provide a better definition of logistics responsibilities; some logistics activities, such as the running of the RDCs, can even be contracted out. As retailing becomes more international, then skills in the manipulation of the supply chain may mean that retailers from some countries will have a competitive edge over others.

## Contracting Out Within the Logistics Function

The third major innovation in retail logistics is the phenomenon of contracting out parts of the logistics function to specialist service providers. Contracting out often means employing specialists to undertake transport work; frequently it means making specialists responsible for warehouse operations. Sometimes the specialist will even be made responsible for inventory management, perhaps taking legal title to the goods. In many instances a specialist will perform more than one of the logistics functions, say transport and warehousing combined, on behalf of a retail client (Cooper and Johnstone, 1990).

In table 6.1 we identified one reason why UK retailers are keen to contract out logistics work; they achieve better financial returns from capital invested in supermarkets than in warehouses and vehicles. Yet it is vital to recognize that IT is a crucial factor in contracting out. Only by using IT to make supply chain management more transparent are many retailers prepared to relinquish direct management of logistics functions. The retailers' own fleets, for example, can be replaced by contractors' fleets because IT makes it possible to exercise 'control by information' rather than have 'control by doing' (Quarmby, 1985). In effect, IT can be used by retailers to make contractors 'mimic' the high standards of operation established by the retailers' own fleets. Data output from logistics operations gives retailers the opportunity to take early corrective action if anything goes wrong. Any sign of bad habits being developed by the contractor can also be acted upon quickly, simply because IT can be used to give the retailer the relevant information almost immediately (Quarmby, 1988).

The specialist contractors have also seen demand for their services rise on account of the increasing complexity of logistics in retailing. For example, in food retailing temperature control has assumed a critical importance, and specialist skills are being developed by contractors to meet new demands. Now 'composite' facilities in both warehousing and transport are being developed so that a variety of food produce can be carried or stored simultaneously, but with each type of food maintained at an appropriate temperature. In the UK, Asda's temperature control requirements are shown in table 6.2.

The rise of the specialist distribution contractor has been especially prominent in the UK, where they have gained a substantial share of grocery retailing, as illustrated in figure 6.1.

Figure 6.1 simultaneously emphasizes the dominance of UK multiples in grocery retailing, with a 69 per cent share compared with 50 per cent in Germany, the next highest. But whereas specialist contractors have about 44 per cent of the share of retail logistics for grocery multiples in the UK, this share falls to only about 17 per cent in the case of France and Germany. In Italy, specialist contractors

**Table 6.2** Temperature control requirements for retail logistics in Asda

| Asda temperature standard | Temperature range | Food products carried within temperature range |
|---|---|---|
| Ambient | Not controlled | Tinned food and so on |
| Schedule 1 | 0° ± 2°C | Fresh meat |
| Schedule 2 | 5° ± 2°C | Fresh product and stocked provisions |
| Schedule 3 | 10° ± 2°C | Fresh produce and citrus |
| Schedule 4 | −25°C | Frozen |

*Source*: Stanton, 1989, taken from *Motor Transport*, 29 November 1989

appear to have no presence at all within grocery retail logistics.

The reasons for this varying pattern are complex. In some countries, such as Germany, capacity restrictions in the haulage sector, combined with tariff control, may have restricted the development of specialist contractors. Furthermore, the cautious approach of many German retailers has been expressed in a preference for running logistics on an in-house basis, rather than contracting out.

In France, the hypermarket pattern of retailing has restricted the need for contractors in logistics. With few RDCs there is only a small need for transport by retailers; most goods will be delivered by suppliers in bulk, direct to each hypermarket. While grocery retailers in the Netherlands do operate both supermarkets and RDCs, the use of specialist contractors appears to be relatively limited compared with the UK. Part of the reason may be that Dutch grocery retailers are much less profitable than their UK counterparts, while Dutch hauliers tend to be more profitable. As a result, there is the feeling that it is not necessarily worth concentrating on the core business of grocery retailing in the Netherlands, since there is no great disparity between rates of return on investment in retailing and transport/distribution.

Within Spain, many retailers are not confident about the capacity of locally based hauliers to provide sophisticated logistics services on contract. A number have turned to foreign contractors to undertake logistics work. Pryca, for example, uses Christian Salvesen for chilled food distribution, while Galeria Preciados, a Madrid-based department store, uses Exel Logistics to control its supply chain.

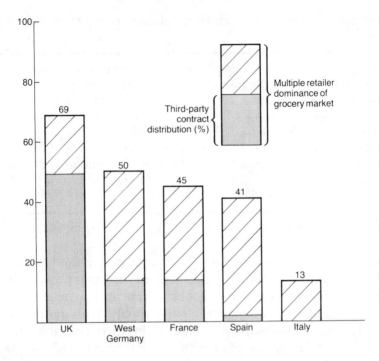

**Figure 6.1**  Grocery market share held by multiple retailers, and share of grocery retail distribution held by third-party operators.
*Source*: NFC Contract Distribution Report, 1989

The factor which may be the most important in determining the future contribution of the contractors may well be IT, because of its revolutionary impact on retail logistics. As Quarmby (1985) has already noted, there are no significant economies of scale in transport (beyond the size of vehicles being filled); costs tend to be linear with volume. But there are economies of scale in computer systems, and especially in the management effort spent in planning and implementation. This does present the opportunity for specialist logistics contractors to move upstream and downstream within the supply chain, particularly in terms of computer-based systems.

Indeed, it might be rather more than coincidental that UK retailers not only have a high level of use of specialist contractors (see figure 6.1), but also are important users of EPOS (table 6.3).

IT therefore seems to be developing as a common thread to unite retailers and specialist logistics providers, a theme which is expanded upon more fully in chapter 11. Here it is sufficient to conclude with the observation that the interaction of IT between retailers and their

**Table 6.3**  Country shares of European EPOS installed base (installed terminals, not orders)

| Country | Percentage |
|---|---|
| UK | 46 |
| West Germany | 24 |
| France | 13 |
| Italy | 13 |
| Others | 4 |
| | 100 |

*Source*: Walman, 1989

suppliers has important implications for specialist contractors in logistics. A similar situation exists in manufacturing. The potential rewards for specialists in logistics are enormous and the race is on to determine which companies will succeed and which will fall by the wayside.

# Case Study   Ahold

Ahold is primarily a retailing conglomerate which trades in the Netherlands, its country of origin, and the USA (see table 6.4). Albert Heijn is Ahold's flagship in the Netherlands, where it operates 549 shops, 106 of these being on a franchise basis. Shops range in size from 300 square metres to over 3000 square metres, and are usually

**Table 6.4**  Ahold retail sales for 1989 (million Dutch guilders)

| Store | Sales | Number of locations |
|---|---|---|
| *Netherlands* | | |
| Albert Heijn | 6902 | 443 |
| AH Franchise | 654 | 106 |
| ETOS | 207 | 143 |
| Gall & Gall | 351 | |
| Other | 172 | |
| | | |
| *USA* | | |
| Bi Lo | 3033 | 178 |
| First National Supermarkets | 3897 | 112 |
| Giant Food Stores | 1676 | 52 |

*Source*: Company Annual Reports.

located in high streets and shopping malls. Virtually all Dutch towns have an Albert Heijn shop.

Ahold plans to strengthen the regional presence of its three US retail chains, which are located in the eastern states. In part, this is seen as an alternative to developing Ahold chains in EC countries other than the Netherlands: Ahold perceives the European retail market to be near saturation and therefore a difficult proposition for a medium-sized player such as itself.

In order to gain better positioning for future trading in Europe, Ahold has joined forces with Groupe Casino from France and the Argyll Group from the UK, two other medium-sized players in the field, to form the European Retail Association (ERA; see also the Groupe Casino case study in chapter 5). Furthermore, Ahold has been the driving force behind Ahold Marketing Services (AMS), which comprises the three ERA members together with Dansk Supermarket (Denmark), ICA (Sweden), La Rinascente (Italy), Migros (Switzerland), Kesko Oy (Finland) and Mercadona (Spain). The overall aim of AMS is to increase co-operation between producers and retailers to help reduce the costs of both production and distribution (that is, logistics).

The approach to logistics taken by Albert Heijn, in its own right, is reasonably typical of Dutch multiple retailers. All warehousing is operated in-house, with the exception of frozen food, which is handled by subcontractors. In total, Albert Heijn have 11 warehouses – four regional, one central, five for produce and one for cut flowers. Approximately 80 per cent of supermarket deliveries originate from the regional distribution centres; only a limited number of products are delivered direct.

Albert Heijn's senior managers have strong reservations about contracting out their warehousing activities for dry goods. The company believes that it has built up considerable competitive advantage in this area, and it is reluctant to allow a third-party contractor to take over warehousing for fear that the contractor will learn valuable skills which could then be used to benefit a rival retailer. However, Albert Heijn does concede that there are also benefits from contracting out warehousing and does not discount the possibility of so doing, at least on an experimental basis.

Transport, by contrast, is largely contracted out, although a small own-account fleet is kept for the purposes of comparing costs and service levels. Typically, transport from a regional distribution centre (RDC) will be divided between a number of contractors; Albert Heijn believes that there are too few contractors in the Netherlands able to provide a complete transport service from any one of its RDCs. Nonetheless, the small- to medium-sized carriers working for the company essentially provide a dedicated service, using their trucks exclusively to serve the needs of Albert Heijn.

Managers at Albert Heijn are well aware of developments in retail logistics in markets outside the Netherlands. Yet, while recognizing UK retailers as being among the most innovative in logistics, they feel that different conditions in the Netherlands lend themselves to different solutions. In particular, Dutch retailers are much less profitable than their UK counterparts, which removes one strong motive for concentrating on the core retail business. However, the key point for the future may have less to do with the comparative profitability of retailers and logistics contractors. The coordination of logistics information, which becomes more difficult when dealing with a wide variety of suppliers, may be much more crucial. As information systems used by retailers become ever more complex and sophisticated, this places extra demands on their suppliers, not just of products, but also of services such as logistics. Only those suppliers of logistics services who are able to adapt to the new demands of IT may have a future with retailers such as Albert Heijn.

# 7
# Improving Logistics Efficiency

## The Need for a Survey

The preceding chapters gave a broad overview of developments in the European manufacturing and retailing sectors, together with an appraisal of logistics innovation in each sector. This helps to establish the sheer diversity of industry structures, legal restrictions and approaches to business development within Europe; evidently there is considerably more variety than in other economies of comparable size, notably the USA, mainly because European countries have substantial differences between them in language, culture, law and economic development.

As has been already noted in this book, there is bound to be some convergence in both business style and content within Europe as it assumes a more federal structure during the 1990s, but it would be wrong to suggest that new similarities will become more important than old differences. However, logistics will be a key area for change as the process of European integration consolidates, not least because, by its very nature, logistics is critically concerned with the development of links between countries to facilitate the efficient movement of traded goods. Here the experience of multinational companies operating within Europe is instructive, since they have learned to overcome or accommodate trading barriers within the European Community (EC). But in a trading and logistics environment which is undergoing rapid change, some will find themselves better placed than others.

In this chapter we report the results of a major survey we carried out during 1988 and 1989 on logistics within multinational companies based in Europe. Above all, the key objective is to highlight the overall logistics efficiency of companies trading within the EC, so that we are able to find out what scope there is for improvement, and in what areas of logistics activity. In effect, this helps us to move on from the present to the future of logistics in Europe; having established how logistics in manufacturing and retailing has developed, the survey enables us to indicate where there will be changes in logistics demand, as users of logistics services aim to improve upon areas of current inefficiency.

# Background to the Survey

As our study of multinational companies in Europe was primarily intended to be comparative, there was a clear need to establish a common database. This requirement is not without its difficulties, since company data relative to logistics performance are not standardized between companies. Consequently, it was not possible to approach companies for a set of logistics data which could then be directly compared with similar data from other companies.

This is not just a current difficulty, but is likely to be a persistent one, simply because of the variable characteristics of products in supply chains. Products are often subject to value-added processes in manufacture which will result in, say, an expansion of volume (expanded polystyrene) or different handling requirements (frozen foods). Unless an extensive audit is undertaken of the supply chain for each company, it is extremely difficult to make a detailed assessment of logistics performance in relation to, say, the price paid for logistics services.

Given the difficulties of establishing precise measures of performance in logistics, we had to take an entirely different, and more open-ended, approach for the purpose of comparing companies. We felt that it was important to assess companies according to five key areas of logistics performance, namely logistics planning, holdings of inventory, number of logistics services suppliers, performance in customer service, and prices paid for logistics services. In making our assessment of performance in the areas, we conducted personal interviews with senior executives who had major logistics responsibilities within companies. We asked a series of questions relating to the performance of the company in each of the five areas of logistics efficiency, and gave a rating in each area based on the executive's responses.

It is important to stress at this point that our rating often corresponded to the executive's own rating. As our survey guaranteed anonymity for participating companies, executives were mostly prepared to give a frank appraisal of their companies' logistics performance. However, if we felt that an executive was being too critical of his own achievements we reserved the right to upgrade the performance rating from the executive's own assessment. Similarly, if too much credit was sought for performance that was clearly unimpressive, we were prepared to downgrade the rating.

Given the subjective element of performance rating and the lack of supporting data, we felt it inappropriate to 'fine-tune' the ratings on, say, a scale of one to ten: rather, we elected to give companies a strong, weak or neutral rating for each performance indicator (see the appendix at the end of this chapter). These simple ratings form the basis for the results of the survey presented in the next section.

It remains here to outline the main trading interests of the companies (all of them trading in more than one country of the EC) and the size of the sample in relation to the size of the EC economy, and to give examples of the questions asked at interview.

The 57 companies participating in the survey can be divided into two broad groupings; namely, *consumer logistics* and *industrial logistics*. Those in the former category are wholesalers and retailers, together with those manufacturers whose logistics activities are closely tied to retail markets. Producers of brown and white goods clearly fit into this category. In the second category are manufacturers which are mainly concerned with the flow of materials and components, both into their own production plants and the plants of their major customers. A breakdown of the companies, according to these logistics classifications and to the specific market sectors in which they trade, is given in table 7.1.

The size of the sample is, of course, small in comparison to the total number of companies based in Europe. However, it is mainly large companies that are represented in the sample; they have a combined annual turnover in Europe in excess of 150 billion ecu, representing some 9 per cent of the EC's gross domestic product.

During the course of the personal interviews with the representatives of the companies (usually directors or senior managers), information was sought which relates to key indicators for logistics performance, namely:

**Table 7.1**  Classification of surveyed companies

|  | Number of companies surveyed |
|---|---|
| *Consumer logistics* | |
| Food | 7 |
| Non-food | 2 |
| Food and non-food | 9 |
| White/brown goods (electrical and electronic consumer goods) | 7 |
| Sub-total | 25 |
| | |
| *Industrial logistics* | |
| Petrochemicals | 6 |
| Chemicals/industrial gases | 18 |
| Pharmaceuticals/biochemicals | 2 |
| Engineering (including cars and car parts) | 4 |
| Other | 2 |
| Sub-total | 32 |
| Total | 57 |

- *Systematic logistics planning.* Does the company have a systematic and ordered approach to its logistics planning in Europe? Or is there a fragmented, uncoordinated approach that can lead to sub-optimal logistics systems at the Europe-wide level?
- *Optimized holdings of inventory.* Has the company acted upon an analysis of logistics trade-offs to ensure that holdings of inventory are optimized? Or does it hold excessive levels of inventory, possibly as a result of fragmentation in logistics planning?
- *Rationalized number of logistics service suppliers.* Has the company reduced the number of its suppliers, commensurate with the level necessary to make comparisons on service quality and price? Or does it incur unnecessary administration costs by using the services of too many logistics suppliers?
- *Good performance in customer service.* Does the company pay sufficient attention to customer service by consulting consumers on their needs, setting appropriate performance standards and ensuring that these standards are met?
- *Appropriate prices paid for logistics services.* Is there evidence that the company pays no more than it should for logistics services? Or does it pay more than it should by, say, making inadequate comparisons

between alternative suppliers or showing excessive loyalty to longstanding suppliers.

The following section summarizes the outcome of the analysis followed by a more detailed discussion of the results.[4]

# Analysis of the Results
## An overview

From the appendix, the results can be summarized according to the two logistics classifications and the five performance indicators described above. The inefficiencies that currently exist in European logistics are highlighted in table 7.2.

Overall, table 7.2 indicates through the unweighted averages that there is some difference between the efficiency of consumer and industrial logistics. However, there are striking differences among the scores for the five performance indicators.

In rank order, there was most inefficiency in 'Use of Logistics Service Suppliers' (62 per cent), followed by 'Price Paid for Logistics Services' (44 per cent), 'Inventory Holdings' (40 per cent), 'Logistics Planning' (28 per cent) and 'Customer Service' (24 per cent).

These results are discussed in more detail below. To continue the broader overview of the results we can now turn to the issue of company ownership and logistical efficiency. In particular, we ask the question 'Is there any relationship between the degree of logistical efficiency displayed by a company and the geographical origin of that company?' The analysis of the appendix according to each company's country of origin is summarized in table 7.3.

There are two main surprises in table 7.3, the first being Spain's high ranking. Spain is not usually regarded as being in the forefront of logistics development; the haulage sector is extremely fragmented and offers little in the way of specialized services, making it difficult to achieve excellence in logistics, even for multinational companies aware of the potential benefits of good logistics from operations elsewhere. The main reason for the high ranking of Spanish companies probably relates to two key factors. Only the very best Spanish companies will be able to compete on a multinational basis (and therefore be included in our survey). These companies must be judged by their logistics, not just in Spain, but elsewhere in Europe where the supply of logistics services will usually be better.

**Table 7.2** Percentage of companies with logistical inefficiencies[a]

| | | | Inefficiencies in | | | |
|---|---|---|---|---|---|---|
| | Logistics planning | Inventory holdings | Use of logistics services suppliers | Customer service | Price paid for logistics services | Unweighted average |
| Consumer logistics | 17 | 60 | 59 | 29 | 50 | 42 |
| Industrial logistics | 34 | 30 | 64 | 22 | 41 | 39 |
| All logistics | 28 | 40 | 62 | 24 | 44 | 41 |

[a] Logistical inefficiency is calculated under each performance indicator column in the Appendix according to the formula $\Sigma W / \Sigma S + \Sigma W) \times 100$ = logistical inefficiency score (per cent).

**Table 7.3** Logistical efficiency scores for companies according to country of origin

| Country[a] | Logistical Efficiency Score (LES)[b] | Rank order (1 = most efficient) |
|---|---|---|
| Netherlands | 2.7 | 1 |
| UK | 1.8 | 2 |
| Spain | 1.6 | 3 |
| France | 1.4 | 4 |
| West Germany | 1.1 | 5 |
| USA | 0.8 | 6 |

[a] Only countries with five or more companies represented in the sample were included in the analysis.
[b] The Logistical Efficiency Score (LES) is calculated for each country according to LES = $\Sigma S/\Sigma W$ (see the Appendix).

The second reason for the good showing of Spanish companies relates to the market sectors in which they operate. Our survey contains three companies in the petrochemicals sector. For reasons of safety, high standards of operation are usually insisted upon by government, not least in transport. This need for excellence in some areas of logistics probably leads to a knock-on effect in other areas.

However, the even greater surprise from the analysis in table 7.3 is the poor performance of US-owned companies. Given the importance attached to logistics within the USA, a better showing could have been expected. There are again two main factors which might account for this result.

First, in a number of cases, the company may be US-owned but logistics control is exercised from within Europe. The quality of logistics management in these circumstances may clearly not match the standards achieved by, say, the parent company operating in the USA.

Second, there may be a failure among a number of US-owned companies sufficiently to appreciate the different logistics climate in Europe. Not only are there nine working languages within the EC, but vastly different regulations affecting, among other things, transport operations, conditions of employment and company law. It is possible that attempts to impose US-style logistics management in Europe has led to serious inefficiencies in some companies.

Less surprising is the strong performance of Dutch-owned companies. The Netherlands has a strong trading tradition and Rotterdam, its premier port, serves as a gateway to Europe. Furthermore, its international haulage sector has long been recognized as one of the strongest in Europe (Cooper, Browne and Gretton, 1987).

Table 7.3 also serves as a useful reminder that there can be a large gulf between what companies say they do and what they actually do. A study by A. T. Kearney (1987b) produced figures (reproduced here in table 7.4) which show that German companies are the most likely to have a logistics department. Yet according to table 7.3, the logistics *performance* of Germany is relatively weak.

**Table 7.4**  Existence of logistics department

| Country | | Percentage of respondents |
|---|---|---|
| Germany | | 75 |
| Netherlands | | 65 |
| Italy | | 61 |
| UK | | 55 |
| France | | 48 |
| Belgium | | 46 |
| | Overall Europe | 64 |

*Source*: A. T. Kearney (1987b), A. T. Kearney Ltd, London

## *Performance indicator: logistics planning*

Nearly one third of companies in the sample showed significant signs of inefficiency in planning European logistics. In many respects, this is a key performance indicator, in that inefficiencies elsewhere (for example, in inventory planning) may result from not following a coordinated approach to European logistics.

However, given the circumstances of logistics development in Europe, it is not at all surprising to find an inadequate approach to planning. Arguably, the regulation of transport services has been a key factor in stifling new initiatives in logistics planning. Until recently, the typical pattern for European countries was to have strict regulation of haulage capacity and, sometimes, control over prices. This did not make the suppliers of logistics services (such as the hauliers) inclined to be very innovative. Furthermore, there were major differences in the extent to which strict regulations were applied; in Germany there are, even now, extremely tight regulations on haulage capacity and price, whereas in Italy there seems to be some circumvention of apparently rigid rules.

The position is now changing quickly. Deregulation is taking place in international freight markets, and formerly controlled haulage markets (such as France and the Netherlands) are being transformed by recent decisions on deregulation taken by national governments. Even so, there is a lag in the response rate to deregulation by companies which have Europe-wide trading interests. Strict regulation has persisted in many countries for around half a century, conditioning the thinking of management in terms of what can or cannot be done. A number of companies deliberately set up fragmented systems of goods distribution across Europe, with planning responsibility devolved to each country, on the grounds that it was the only way to understand how goods were actually allowed to be moved (Cooper and Browne, 1989). This can now change as liberalization of freight transport markets takes effect, and there were signs among a number of the surveyed companies that they were about to undertake a radical redesign of logistics responsibilities and systems within Europe.

Yet it would be wrong to neglect the human factor which can obstruct the drive for change in logistics. Local departments responsible for planning and organizing logistics in a single country will often be reluctant to give up long-cherished responsibilities to a centralized department responsible for Europe-wide planning. The change could be slower than many senior company managers would like.

Lastly, referring to table 7.2, it is clear that much more action is required to improve logistics planning in the area of industrial logistics, compared with consumer logistics. This is because the process of internationalizing retailing is only just beginning to happen on a significant scale. Many retailers in the sample were restricted to having mainly national interests and, in this context, they were able to bring coherence to their logistics planning activities. In addition, since their international expansion is coinciding with progress towards transport deregulation, retailers will be free to plan efficient logistics systems. In this respect, they have a considerable advantage over companies in the industrial logistics sector which have the more difficult task of dismantling inefficient, traditionally based logistics systems, and replacing them with something rather better.

## Performance indicator: inventory holdings

Complexity in transport operations, as a consequence of strict regulation, is a major factor affecting decisions on where to hold inventory. Too many companies have been operating with too many depots and too much inventory as a result of rigidities in the transport market. Figure 7.1 illustrates the point that many European companies could not only reduce inventory costs by rationalizing their depot network, but could also achieve savings in total logistics costs.

As deregulation of freight transport takes effect within Europe, companies clearly are using the opportunity to rationalize their inventory. Sharman (1989) quotes a good example, together with estimates of the expected savings:

> One automotive manufacturer, for example, is reducing a dozen or more national European product specifications to three or four regional variations. This assists its consolidation of 13 European stockpoints into three – with no ill effect on order response times. In fact, this consolidation will raise the numbers and colours of models available for immediate delivery while cutting inventory levels by more that 45 per cent and overall logistics costs by 20 per cent.

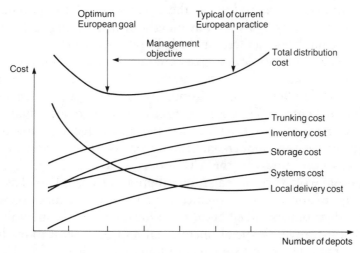

**Figure 7.1**   Achieving reductions in total logistics costs by reducing the depot network.
*Source*: adapted from Rushton and Oxley (1989), *Handbook of Logistics and Distribution Management*, Kogan Page, London.

Note also the importance that Sharman attaches to rationalization of the product range. This is, of course, an important consequence of the completion of the Single European Market (SEM), with more ready recognition of type approval between countries.

Yet although table 7.2 shows that excessive inventory holdings are a problem for 30 per cent of manufacturers, it is a considerably greater problem for retailers, 60 per cent of whom have an excess of inventory. This arises because there has been a very uneven development of efficient logistics management in retailing across Europe. Many European retailers have yet to abandon the practice of keeping goods in storerooms, at the rear of shops, prior to sales display on the shelves. Efficient retailing logistics as practised in, say, the UK has yet to spread throughout Europe (see chapter 6). The increasing internationalization of retailing should do much to promote this much-needed change.

## *Performance indicator: use of logistics services suppliers*

Overall, the sample survey showed that many companies were inefficient in their use of logistics suppliers. In essence, there were too many being used by the companies, and this was costly in administration time. Adding to the complexity of the purchasing decision often outweighs the advantages of negotiating lower rates among the hauliers, so there can be little prospect of overall logistics savings when all the relevant costs are taken into account.

Another example is from the Netherlands, where a retailer uses four or five hauliers to move goods to its shops from each of its distribution centres. While it is quite clear that there are advantages in using more than one haulier for purposes of comparison, this arrangement is too cumbersome and expensive. The retailer expects to move more towards the UK model where a single haulier/distributor works from each distribution centre. This has the advantage of allowing performance comparisons to be made between hauliers/distributors (albeit at different locations) while streamlining the administrative, financial operational and communications links between the retailer and suppliers of logistics services.

This process of using fewer suppliers of logistics services is, to some extent, dependent on the *size* of companies existing on the supply side. The Dutch retailer mentioned above, for example, was unwilling to contract out large amounts of work to small suppliers because it felt that they would become too dependent on the custom of the retailer. Ending the contract could mean bankruptcy for some hauliers and this was thought to be an undesirable risk to the retailer's good image.

To some extent, deregulation of freight transport seems likely to bring changes on the supply side which will make it rather easier to reduce the number of hauliers. Deregulation appears to lead to some concentration of ownership in freight transport and logistics companies (see chapters 8 and 10). Tendencies to this effect have been noted in both Australia and the USA (Joy, 1964; US General Accounting Office, 1987; Thomas, 1988). As a result, large users of logistics services should soon be better able to pair up with larger suppliers, as deregulation in Europe takes effect.

However, it is also important to understand some fundamental changes that are now taking place in the relationship between logistics user and supplier. Take, for example, the case of the Netherlands, where there has been a rise in the average size of the haulage company (table 7.5), particularly in recent years.

**Table 7.5**  Concentration of ownership in the Dutch haulage sector

| Year | Number of haulage companies (national and international) | Average fleet capacity per company (payload tonnes) |
| --- | --- | --- |
| 1978 | 8412 | 88.9 |
| 1981 | 7654 | 99.1 |
| 1984 | 7448 | 107.1 |
| 1987 | 7469 | 144.8 |

*Source*: NOB Wegtransport, 1988

This may suggest that there is a gradual change in the relationships between user and supplier of logistics services when the change can, in fact, be much more abrupt. In particular, it is extremely important to recognize the potential for the change in logistics *control*. Consider the hypothetical example of a retailer who directly employs eight hauliers, as in figure 7.2a.

In order to reduce the burden of dealing directly with so many suppliers of haulage services, an alternative is to nominate two of them as prime contractors, leaving them free to subcontract to the

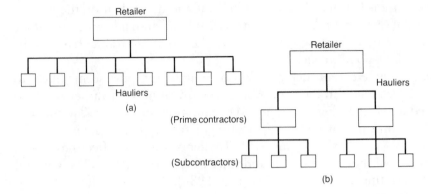

**Figure 7.2**  Changing control in the relationship between logistics users and suppliers: a hypothetical example. (a) Wide span of retailer control; (b) narrow span of retailer control.

other six (figure 7.2b). With information technology (IT) being used to effect control (Quarmby, 1985), the retailer can reduce direct contact with a number of haulage suppliers, yet receive the same level of service. Such an arrangement can be very cost-effective, and is likely to develop to a greater degree in Europe as better computer software becomes available. But the crucial point is that there need be little change in the *size* of haulage companies for retailers to streamline their purchases from logistics suppliers. In the hypothetical example, the eight hauliers in figure 7.2b may be much the same size as they are in figure 7.2a; so there can be considerable scope for improving logistics efficiency without waiting for some fundamental changes on the service supply side.

## *Performance indicator: customer service*

Customer service is clearly multidimensional in nature, embracing a number of factors, including stock availability, order cycle time, frequency of delivery, on-schedule delivery and reliability of delivery. In our assessment of customer service, as a logistics performance indicator, we have rated companies not on the specifics of customer service, but rather on their overall approach to the needs of customers and the satisfaction of these needs.

According to this assessment of customer service, most industrial logistics companies scored well, perhaps reflecting the fierce competition that European-based producers face, not only from the USA and

Japan, but from newly industrialized countries such as Taiwan and South Korea.

Performance was less impressive in the consumer logistics sector. This is most probably because of the reason identified earlier, namely lack of exposure of many European retailers to new ideas and concepts in the area of logistics: too many lead an insular existence in national markets, remaining relatively unaffected by retailing innovations taking place in other countries. Yet, with the approach of the SEM and the increasing internationalization of retailing this must change.

## Performance indicator: price paid for logistics services

The price paid for logistics services, especially in transport, is of key interest; so it is important for us to state clearly the basis for our assessment of whether companies pay excessive amounts for logistics services.

Essentially, what we assessed was whether companies paid more than they should have done for the logistical services requested. This means that we could come to the conclusion that a German retailer, say, was not paying excessive prices, even though a Dutch retailer could be paying less. The considerable differences between freight markets in the two countries could even result in our concluding that the German retailer was paying the right price, whereas the Dutch retailer was paying too much – the national circumstances are all important.

This is not, however, to ignore the point that deregulation in freight transport could help reduce prices for logistics services. Estimates from Germany suggest that the road freight tariff would fall by about 20 per cent if a free market for services were introduced (Kandler, 1989). Similarly, there are substantial savings to be made on the cost of international freight movements if customs delays between the European countries could be eliminated. Cecchini (1988) calculated that the cost of these delays to hauliers amounts to 415–830 million ecu annually.

The key reason for not including these potential savings in our logistics price assessment of companies is that they would lead us to the inescapable conclusion that *all* companies in Europe pay too much. This is not a particularly helpful conclusion when the main emphasis of the analysis is to examine the relationship that exists between the users and providers of logistics services.

Focusing exclusively on that relationship highlights the scope for improvement by the purchasers of logistics services in the area of price. Overall, almost half were assessed as paying too much, with the poorer performance being in consumer logistics. The main causes of overpayment appeared to be excessive loyalty to longstanding providers of logistics services, inadequate comparisons between alternative providers and poor monitoring of the service quality delivered against that which was promised.

## Conclusions from the survey

A number of important points emerge from the analysis of logistics efficiency presented above. First, it is apparent that there are significant differences between the performances of companies from different countries. Furthermore, as the appendix shows, companies originating from any country often range from excellent to poor in their overall logistics performance. No country has a monopoly on logistics excellence.

Second, logistics efficiency varies considerably according to the use of any one performance indicator. It is encouraging that only about one-quarter of the companies in the survey had identifiable customer service inefficiencies (in terms of their approach to identifying and satisfying their customer needs). By contrast, analysis of the performance indicator 'use of logistics service suppliers' shows that 62 per cent of companies have inefficiencies in this field. The message here is that companies may be doing well in one area but that other aspects of logistics performance should also be evaluated and improved. In addition, companies should be wary of using too narrow a range of indicators when assessing their logistics perform-ance – good scores in one may be undermined by poor scores in another. Understanding the exact source of logistics inefficiency is vital management information.

Third, the point must be made that the price paid for logistics services must never be used as the sole criterion for logistics efficiency – it is far too simplistic a measure. What matters is the value obtained from the service. This is of special importance as logistics services providers and users move into closer, more co-operative relationships (Browne and Cooper, 1989). When this happens, aspects of perform-ance and service quality are likely to assume far greater importance than the price alone. For this reason it must be emphasized that, although price can be a useful indicator, it must be interpreted with care; the survey sought only to identify whether users paid more than they *should* have done in a particular market compared with similar companies.

Finally, it must be stressed that many of the inefficiencies identified among logistics services users are partly a product of the complexities and distortions of highly regulated European markets, particularly in transport. As a consequence, complicated, sub-optimal logistics systems have developed in a rather haphazard way, leading in many cases to both poor performance and high costs. However, it is clear that the proposed changes forming part of the SEM transformation in Europe can be used by companies as a strategic spur. Now is the time for companies to effect changes. The first step must be to carry out a logistics audit to identify inefficiencies. For many companies, the results could well be both surprising and challenging.

# Towards More Efficient Logistics

Our survey shows considerable scope for improvement in both the planning and practice of logistics in European companies. We consider possible improvements to planning as part of the discussion on future strategies in chapter 14. Here we concentrate on the practice with respect to inventory holdings, use of logistics services suppliers, customer service and prices paid for logistics services.

The survey of companies showed that there remains considerable scope for inventory reduction, especially in retailing (see table 7.2). There are also parts of manufacturing industry where inventory holdings are too high, although many companies, by already embracing logistics concepts such as JIT and MRP, have done much to reduce excessive levels of inventory. Some further reductions can be achieved relatively easily, just by adjusting the organization of the supply chain (for example, small retailers may purchase from wholesalers when the minimum order quantity for direct delivery from producers is set at a high level). Other benefits, which require investment in the physical infrastructure of the company (such as a revised network of warehouses) will take longer to achieve. Overall, the aim must be to bring down European inventory towards the levels achieved in Japan and the USA: as Waters (1990) has already noted, inventory holdings in European countries are generally higher, and there is good scope for improvement.

Improvements in logistics practice are also certain to change the way in which logistics services suppliers are used by retailers and manufacturers. The carriers of goods (such as hauliers and railways) are major providers of logistics services, and new practices in logistics are likely to have a dramatic impact on their activities. For example, Garreau, Lieb and Millen (1991), in comparing logistics in France and the USA, show that JIT users are putting considerable emphasis on factors which are mainly provided by *larger* carriers, notably the ability to provide a route network and a tracing capability (see table 7.6).

**Table 7.6**  User rating of criteria important in carrier selection since JIT implementation

| | Less important | | Some importance | | More important | |
|---|---|---|---|---|---|---|
| Criteria | USA | France | USA | France | USA | France |
| Terminal proximity | 3 | 0 | 53 | 53 | 44 | 47 |
| Route network | 3 | 0 | 41 | 44 | 56 | 56 |
| Price | 8 | 6 | 45 | 72 | 47 | 22 |
| On-time performance | 0 | 0 | 10 | 0 | 90 | 100 |
| Tracing capability | 3 | 0 | 21 | 25 | 76 | 75 |
| Responsiveness | 3 | 5 | 7 | 5 | 90 | 90 |
| Special equipment | 5 | 12 | 60 | 65 | 35 | 23 |

*Source*: Garreau *et al.*, 1991

Moreover, using *fewer* suppliers of logistics services, which is implied by the tendency to use larger ones, means that there is the opportunity for users to cut the cost of logistics administration. Many companies simply fail to appreciate the full cost of logistics administration, which includes the cost of service selection, the drawing up of contracts and multiple invoicing. All too often these costs are absorbed into 'overheads', with too little thought being given to their magnitude.

As our survey shows (table 7.2), many managers recognize the scope for reducing the number of logistics services suppliers.

Furthermore, this is already taking place as deregulation of the road freight transport sector within Europe takes effect. No longer are users of logistics services so restricted in their use of hauliers, with limited scope to increase capacity or negotiate on price. Increasingly, logistics services users can select the hauliers they want, rather than those they are almost obliged to have because of regulation. In their turn, hauliers can now grow as their businesses grow, and this gives them better opportunities to provide more in the way of added value services in logistics to meet the changing needs of users.

Customer service has been given substantial prominence in the logistics literature as a way of achieving competitive advantage. It is therefore not surprising that good levels of performance in customer service has been sought by many companies.

Indeed, the results of our survey seem to reflect the endeavours of companies to improve levels of customer service. However, there is still some way to go, and part of the problem may be found in the quality of logistics services being provided by third parties. A European survey by GE Information Services, for example, showed that no provider of logistics services achieved an 'excellent' rating by users (Byrne, 1990).

The price paid for logistics services remains a crucial consideration for companies. There are two ways in which real prices for logistics services will fall in Europe by the end of the 1990s. First there are the effects of deregulation, which will be spread unevenly across Europe (see chapter 8). Second, prices will fall as a result of changing purchasing practices. As our survey reveals in table 7.2, many companies currently pay too much for logistics services, often because comparisons between suppliers are made too infrequently.

There is much merit in introducing management systems for logistics which incorporate a process of making comparisons between suppliers of logistics services. This would provide the framework for establishing that the prices paid by a user are not, over time, getting out of line with the prices prevailing in the marketplace for logistics services.

In conclusion, our survey does indicate that there is considerable scope for improved logistics efficiency in Europe which makes it a particularly important area for management attention. Action aimed at improving efficiency would bring substantial benefits to users of logistics services. Apart from the obvious advantages, such as reductions in price, there are some far-reaching possibilities. For example, improved logistics can mean that companies can reduce lead times for product development, possibly yielding important competitive advantages.

Although there is great scope for improved logistics efficiency, it would be unrealistic to expect European companies to reach some kind of orchestrated perfection. There are always innovative companies that will establish new standards of excellence in logistics. In so doing, they provide a benchmark for the others to measure up to. Excellence in logistics is therefore a moving target and perfection is elusive. A more appropriate aim should be for European companies to become more innovative, to produce world leaders in logistics from among their ranks. Increasingly, it is being understood that it is not sufficient to be the best in the European class; world class must be the goal.

# Appendix

There follows a summary of the ratings of each of the 54 companies in the survey, according to the five logistics performance indicators used.

| Performance indicator and company's country of ownership | Planning | Inventory | Logistics suppliers | Customer service | Price |
|---|---|---|---|---|---|
| (a)  Consumer logistics | | | | | |
| *Food* | | | | | |
| 1   Netherlands | S | W | ? | ? | W |
| 2   France | W | W | W | S | W |
| 3   UK | S | S | S | S | S |
| 4   UK | W | S | W | W | S |
| 5   UK | S | W | S | ? | ? |
| 6   UK | S | ? | W | S | ? |
| 7   UK/USA | S | ? | W | S | S |
| | | | | | |
| *Non-food* | | | | | |
| 8   Germany | S | S | W | W | W |
| 9   Netherlands | S | W | S | S | W |

| Performance indicator and company's country of ownership | Planning | Inventory | Logistics suppliers | Customer service | Price |
|---|---|---|---|---|---|
| *Food and non-food* | | | | | |
| 10  France | S | W | S | S | W |
| 11  Germany | S | W | W | S | W |
| 12  Switzerland | S | W | W | S | W |
| 13  Switzerland | S | S | S | W | ? |
| 14  Belgium | W | W | W | ? | S |
| 15  Belgium | S | W | W | ? | S |
| 16  Netherlands | S | S | W | S | S |
| 17  Spain | S | ? | S | W | ? |
| 18  UK | S | S | S | S | S |
| | | | | | |
| *White/brown goods* | | | | | |
| 19  France | W | S | W | ? | ? |
| 20  France | W | S | W | W | W |
| 21  Germany | S | S | S | S | S |
| 22  USA | S | ? | W | W | ? |
| 23  UK | S | W | W | S | S |
| 24  Netherlands | S | W | W | S | S |
| 25  Spain | S | W | W | S | W |
| (b)  Industrial logistics | | | | | |
| | | | | | |
| *Petrochemicals* | | | | | |
| 26  France | S | S | S | S | S |
| 27  France | S | S | W | S | S |
| 28  USA | W | ? | W | ? | ? |
| 29  Spain | S | S | W | S | ? |
| 30  Spain | S | S | W | ? | ? |
| 31  Spain | S | S | W | ? | ? |
| | | | | | |
| *Chemicals/industrial gases* | | | | | |
| 32  France | ? | W | S | S | S |
| 33  France | W | S | W | S | W |
| 34  France | S | S | S | S | W |
| 35  France | S | S | W | S | S |
| 36  Germany | ? | ? | W | S | W |
| 37  Germany | ? | ? | W | S | W |

| Performance indicator and company's country of ownership | Planning | Inventory | Logistics suppliers | Customer service | Price |
|---|---|---|---|---|---|
| 38 Germany | W | S | S | S | W |
| 39 USA | S | ? | W | S | W |
| 40 USA | S | S | W | S | S |
| 41 USA | S | ? | W | ? | W |
| 42 USA | ? | W | W | W | W |
| 43 Canada | S | S | S | S | S |
| 44 Spain | ? | ? | ? | ? | S |
| 45 UK | ? | ? | S | S | S |
| 46 UK | S | S | S | S | ? |
| 47 UK | W | W | ? | ? | S |
| 48 UK | W | W | W | W | S |
| 49 UK | W | W | ? | W | S |
| *Pharmaceuticals/biochemicals* | | | | | |
| 50 France | W | S | S | S | S |
| 51 UK | S | S | S | S | W |
| *Engineering industry (cars and car parts)* | | | | | |
| 52 France | S | S | S | W | ? |
| 53 France | ? | ? | W | W | ? |
| 54 Germany | W | W | S | S | ? |
| 55 Sweden | S | S | W | S | S |
| *Other* | | | | | |
| 56 Germany | W | S | W | S | W |
| 57 Netherlands | S | S | S | S | S |

S, company performing strongly under a particular indicator; W, significant weaknesses exhibited by a company; ?, assessment not possible or neutral rating.

# Case Study   An American multinational

This case study provides a good illustration of a company which is taking important steps to improve the effectiveness and efficiency of its logistics operations in Europe. The company is a leading world brand, and in Europe has long-established production facilities in

France, Germany and the UK. These facilities supply products to 16 European countries, including those of the EC.

As with many other multinational companies operating in Europe, each national market was, in the past, given a considerable amount of autonomy to decide how the local distribution of products should best be handled. However, in recent years, there has been an acceptance by management that this approach has its limitations and that a more coordinated logistics strategy is required.

A key instrument for change within the company's organizational structure is its Management Group for European Distribution (MGED). This was originally set up some 15 years ago to provide a forum for the exchange of information between national distribution managers. More recently, the emphasis has changed to one of strategy/ direction-setting and the initiation of pan-European projects.

In part, this change of emphasis is attributable to the new demands of the SEM after 1992. Through the MGED, the company could readily assess the implications of 1992 and refocus its strategy accordingly. Others have not been so well placed, especially those whose first step in logistics coordination was to set up a 1992 committee. For the company, there has been a relatively seamless absorption of the logistics implications of 1992 into the decision-making structure. The MGED's logistics strategy programme for the 1990s comprises four main elements:

- distribution networks
- demand management
- transport leveraging
- portfolio management

We now examine each of these in turn.

## Distribution networks

The company effectively operates a two-tier distribution system within Europe. In the first tier, the production sites send supplies to central distribution warehouses, often located adjacent to the factories. In the second tier operation, these central warehouses supply regional distribution centres, from where products are delivered to customers.

In the mid-1980s a rationalization programme for warehouses was begun. Between 1985 and 1990 the number of sites holding inventory was reduced from 21 to 17. By 1993 the figure will be 12, and in the longer term there may be just five or six sites to serve the European market.

As a result of this rationalization, there are now many more deliveries to final customers across borders; in the earlier, national, framework for delivery it was much rarer. Customers in Belgium are now served from the Paris warehouse, while customers in Denmark receive goods from Mannheim. Although lead times have in some cases, become longer, the delivery service is more consistent, with fewer unfulfilled orders; and surveys have shown that customers are satisfied with the new delivery arrangements. The direct benefit to the company has, of course, been reduced levels of inventory within the European distribution network.

## Demand management

Traditionally, the company used a re-order point system for inventory replenishment at its warehouses. When the inventory for a given product line fell to a predetermined number of items, this triggered a re-order mechanism. Following a known lead time, replenishment inventory (again a predetermined quantity) would reach the warehouse. However, for the many product lines subject to seasonal demand, this practice required considerable manual intervention to avoid either overstocking or customer service problems.

As a consequence, the company has implemented a Distribution Resource Planning (DRP) system to plan the inventory levels and movements along the supply chain (from final customer demand through to requirements on manufacturing). To do this DRP calculates an inventory plan and requirements per item per week for each location, using estimated customer demand as well as actual inventory and inventory policy. Each week the plans are restated, to take into account changes in activity, and current week recommendations are executed. By this means the company can link inventory requirements directly to customer needs, and thus achieve the optimum deployment of inventory throughout Europe.

## Transport leveraging

The company is a large purchaser of transport services in Europe. Just as its customers secure discounts for bulk purchases of its products, so the company wants a similar arrangement from its suppliers of transport services.

However, at present, transport services are purchased on a national basis within Europe. It is therefore not possible to achieve economies of scale in purchasing and so reduce unit transport costs. The company is now seeking to negotiate regional European contracts with a selected number of transport companies.

In many cases, these regional contracts will be negotiated with transport companies which have a pan-European capability. While there are few that meet this description at present, the company anticipates that more will emerge after 1992 (see also chapters 8 and 10).

## *Portfolio management*

The company recognizes the need to manage both products and customer accounts in a more profitable fashion. This responsibility is delegated to business unit managers in Europe, but there are important implications for logistics and distribution. For example, distribution managers are given little say in which product lines should be sold to which customers; yet there are occasions on which some deliveries might be uneconomic. The aim is to make business unit managers more aware of the distribution costs that they incur in serving customers. Ultimately, this rests on turning the European distribution function into a cost centre where each product's distribution cost is made fully visible to all business managers.

In summary, the company has had to confront a major logistics challenge. Its strength is that its products are already well established in the marketplace, the result of a long European presence. Yet, ironically, this long presence has been largely responsible for the need to improve logistics efficiency. No rival setting up in Europe would use the company's current distribution system – based on national markets – as a model. With the prospect of the SEM, a new entrant would – from the outset – need to have its sights set on a pan-European system. For the company, the immediate task is to dismantle its distribution inheritance, and substitute systems and networks that are appropriate for the 1990s. This is a task which the company is approaching energetically, with a high level of commitment.

# Part II
# Supply-side Logistics

# 8

# Logistics as a Business

## The Suppliers of Logistics Services

Logistics is frequently discussed very much in conceptual terms. This gives the context for valuable discussions such as trade-offs within logistics innovation or the superiority of achieving effectiveness as against efficiency in logistics.

Theoretical considerations of this kind have been amply covered already in the logistics literature and we have no wish to add to it. Rather, in this book, we are mainly concerned with the marketplace for logistics services, and how it is developing. Many developments will spring from interactions between the users and providers of logistics services. In this chapter we begin a discussion of developments on the supply side in logistics services, to complement the demand-side discussions in the five previous chapters.

In broad terms, the *users* of logistics services, such as those manufacturers and retailers discussed in earlier chapters, have two choices. Either they can service their own logistics requirement by having an in-house capability, or they can buy in specialist suppliers of logistics services. Transport and, increasingly, information technology (IT) are two crucial services in logistics. Users can choose to operate their own fleets of vehicles or even railway trains. In Australia, for example, there are a number of private railway lines (Rimmer, 1987). Users can also establish private telecommunications links between different parts of the organization. Alternatively, they can hire carriers to transport goods on their behalf, or use value-added networks (VANs) operated by the likes of GEIS or IBM to meet some of their IT needs. Warehousing too can be part of a user's responsibilities or contracted out to a specialist.

Clearly, then, there are various kinds of specialist company which provide logistics services to users. Among others, transporters, warehousing companies and IT organizations all do this. Increasingly, however, there is a growth of *multiservice* companies in logistics, reflecting the need for integration within the logistics function and the signals from users about their future requirements.

Integration in logistics services is often required simply because of the scale of the interfacing problem. Trucks carry goods from warehouses, and IT systems help to plan which consignments should be carried by which truck; but goods returned by customers need to be put back in the warehouse. Considerations such as these mean that it is not always helpful to have a multitude of suppliers of logistics services working for one company. It is often preferable to use a single supplier who has a capability in a number of logistics functions, say transport, warehousing and IT systems.

Indeed, the emergence of multiservice companies in logistics has been a key development not just in Europe, but also elsewhere in the world. The purpose of this chapter, however, is to outline principal points which relate to the suppliers of logistics services in the European Community (EC). We believe that there are two powerful influences at work:

- the increasingly 'corporate' approach to business by companies offering road freight transport services
- deregulation of road freight transport sectors in Europe, both at the international and national levels

These developments are likely to have a critical impact on the future supply of logistics services in Europe.

It could be argued that innovation in logistics will come as much from, say, railways or the IT industry – after all, the movement of information is often as crucial to the success of a logistics strategy as the movement of goods. But while we recognize the importance of other modes of transport and other sectors which directly influence logistics, the sheer scale and dominance of road freight within Europe means that it will be the main engine for change, and therefore the focal point for this chapter.

# Corporatism in the Road Freight Sector

Entry costs to the road freight sector have always been low. If an individual can raise the price of a truck, often under a leasing or hire-purchase agreement, then that person is in business. Indeed, this represents a common origin for many large carriers; the head of a haulage company will often be a former truck driver who has built up business from small beginnings.

As a result, many companies in the freight sector have a distinctive style of management, reflecting the entrepreneurial origins of the owner. For example, the owner will often be reluctant to delegate decision-making to others; and as the company grows, this can become highly damaging. Furthermore, the owner will often have an affinity with the operating aspects of the business rather than the strategic ones. As a consequence, great consideration will be given to the specification of new trucks being purchased, but rather less to, say, market research. Management of this kind is essentially *proprietorial*, and its days are numbered in all but the smallest companies.

Freight companies with a more recognizably *corporate* approach to business are now in the ascendancy. These companies will reflect many of the business attributes adopted long ago by companies in other sectors of the economy, not least in manufacturing and retailing, who are major users of freight services. Providers of freight services too now undertake strategic planning, marketing, market research and R&D activities, innovations that will give companies a competitive edge over rivals that persevere with a proprietorial approach. There are six important indicators which signal the age of the corporate provider of logistics services:

1  *A multiservice portfolio.* The need for freight companies to develop a multiservice portfolio to integrate many logistics activities has already been touched upon. Thus companies such as Nedlloyd have developed substantial interests in shipping, express parcels, road freight and warehousing (through the Districenter network). Similarly, the Japanese freight company NYK has extended its services within Europe beyond the provision of liner shipping by acquiring an inland freight company.

2  *One-stop shopping for logistics services.* The development of a multiservice portfolio gives logistics users the opportunity of one-stop shopping for their logistics needs. As their logistics needs become ever more complex, many users realize that it is cumbersome and expensive

to use a large number of service providers (see also chapter 7); in some cases this can result in a preference for one-stop shopping, where one provider of logistics services can meet *all* the needs of a user, even when those needs are complex. A global user of logistics services, say, may wish to send bulk products by ship but valuable items by air. Rather than going to separate freight companies, a single logistics specialist with a multiservice portfolio can meet all the needs of the user. While a user may only rarely wish to commit *all* of its business to a single service provider on, say, a global scale, there is a strong motivation for one-stop shopping on a regional basis. European logistics needs may increasingly be handled by a single service provider, especially for users with a relatively small throughput of products within their supply chains.

3  *Formal business-to-business links.*  Both one-stop shopping and the development of multiservice portfolios mean increased formality in business-to-business links; for example, the proprietorial approach will simply be unable to accommodate the complex trade-offs in logistics decision-making. Furthermore, the skill base has to be widened. In particular, marketing staff in the logistics service company will need to be alert to the markets in which clients' companies operate: only then can a proactive approach be adopted in deciding logistics services needs.

4  *Marketing and branding.*  At present, marketing and branding in the logistics services sector is way behind that of manufacturing and retailing. This cannot last. It will be unacceptable to say to potential customers 'tell us what you want and we will do it for you'. Marketing has to be more positive than that. Similarly, branding is poor in logistics services, both at the company level and at the service level. Too few freight companies have an identity with particular service products, with the possible exception of express, where Federal Express, United Parcel Service, TNT and DHL have become established names. But there is a growing awareness of company branding; NFC, for example, recently undertook a major market research exercise to determine a new brand name for one of its divisions which was targeted to grow globally. The result, Exel Logistics, is culturally neutral and designed to reflect 'high-tech' capabilities in logistics. This will increasingly be the pattern for freight companies.

5  *Increased professionalism.*  There is a clear need for increased profession-alism within companies specializing in the provision of logistics services. It is important for staff in these specialist companies to appreciate logistics concepts and applications as much as their customers do. Only in this way can new services be effectively developed to meet the changing needs of client companies.

6  *Investment in logistics companies.*  For many years freight companies were shunned by investment institutions; better returns were often to be

had more easily from investment in other kinds of company. Now this is changing, and for a variety of reasons. First, there is a saturation of investment in what have been considered mainstream or blue chip sectors. Second, there is the realization that the freight sector and its associated logistics activities represents an unrealized investment opportunity. As freight companies become more corporate, they are a better prospect for investment institutions. By degrees, increased investment through institutions helps companies both to grow and become more corporate in their approach to business. In effect, investment institutions have, perhaps unwittingly, enabled many freight companies to distance themselves from their proprietorial origins.

These, then, are the main driving forces behind the increasingly *corporate* approach of many suppliers of logistics services. In parallel, and complementing these changes, the deregulation of freight markets in Europe is profoundly affecting the supply side of logistics.

# Deregulation of the Road Freight Transport Sector

For many decades, markets for road freight services in the EC have been characterized by strong economic regulation, affecting haulage capacity and/or the prices charged for services (tariffs). However, important changes in economic regulation are now taking place, which will have a significant impact on road freight markets and the supply of logistics services.

To a great extent these changes have been initiated by the European Commission as part of its plan to complete the Single European Market (SEM) by the end of 1992. So, in effect, the late 1980s and early 1990s represents an interregnum – a period of change from strict regulation to a more liberal approach. Before 1985 the position on economic regulation in EC freight markets can be summarized as shown in table 8.1.

The important point illustrated in table 8.1 is the extent to which haulage markets were controlled by government before 1985, both with respect to haulage capacity and prices charged. Only in Luxembourg and the UK could free-market conditions be said to apply, with hauliers deciding how many trucks they should operate

Supply-side Logistics

**Table 8.1** Economic regulation of road haulage in the EC before 1985

| Road freight market | Economic regulatory provisions | Comments |
|---|---|---|
| (1) International haulage (that is, the transport of goods by a third-party haulier between member states of the Community) | Bilateral and multilateral permits, reference tariffs | Permits frequently in short supply; prices mostly market-driven |
| (2) Cabotage (that is, the transport of goods within a country by a non-resident international haulier) | Forbidden in all member states | Some illegal cabotage undertaken |
| (3) Domestic haulage | Permit and/or tariff control in Germany, France, Italy, Eire, Spain,[a] Portugal,[a] Denmark, Netherlands, Belgium, Greece;[b] liberal markets in Luxembourg and the UK | Severity of control over haulage markets, particularly enforcement, very variable |

[a] Not a full member of the EC until 1986.
[b] Not a full member of the EC until 1981.

(subject to satisfying safety standards), and hauliers and their customers together deciding the prices for services.

However, in the 1980s, the position began to change dramatically. First, deregulation for *international haulage* was agreed by the Council of Ministers in 1987, and will be fully implemented by 1993. The provisions of the agreement were for a substantial rise in the number of permits up to the end of 1992, followed by free-market conditions thereafter. This means that, from 1993, international hauliers will be free to adjust their fleet capacity in line with market demands and set prices appropriately. (In effect, the international haulage market will approximate the already liberalized haulage markets of the UK and Luxembourg.)

The second change initiated by the Council of Ministers was in respect of *cabotage*. In late 1989 agreement was reached for a permit system to become operative in 1990, with liberalization from 1993. This means that, for the first time, international hauliers will be able to compete in the domestic markets of countries where they are not resident.

A third change in the marketplace for road freight services in Europe relates to *domestic freight markets*. The European Commission has no authority to change the rules of domestic freight operation in any member state, except if they are in breach of the Treaty of Rome. However, it is clear that the Commission has had an *indirect* impact on domestic regulation as a result of successfully promoting change in regulations governing international haulage and cabotage. In effect, many national governments have seen a tide of liberalization sweeping European freight markets and, indeed, markets elsewhere, notably in the USA. Governments have had to consider the future of haulage sectors in their own countries, particularly with respect to future competition. Clearly, many governments have reached the conclusion that it is better to deregulate than not. As table 8.2 shows, only Germany, Italy and Greece have no stated plans for deregulation. Seven other countries have either already deregulated or plan to do so in the near future.

**Table 8.2** The current position on economic regulation in EC member states

| | |
|---|---|
| Long deregulated or never regulated | Luxembourg |
| | UK |
| | |
| Recently deregulated or about to deregulate | France |
| | Netherlands |
| | Belgium |
| | Portugal |
| | Denmark |
| | Eire |
| | Spain |
| | |
| No apparent plans for deregulation | Germany |
| | Italy |
| | Greece |

The economic regulation of road freight markets is certain to mean that they will be significantly different in character in 1995 compared with the position in 1985. There are, however, some continuing uncertainties. Certain decisions have yet to be realized, such as the future abandonment of permits for cabotage and international haulage. In important markets for haulage services, notably Germany, it remains unclear whether strict control over capacity and tariffs, strongly enforced, will remain in the 1990s. It is against this background that the future shape of haulage markets in Europe, and the provision of logistics services, has to be assessed.

## Survey of Key Deregulation Impacts[5]

In assessing how economic deregulation will affect road freight markets in Europe, it is helpful to consider the experience of countries such as Australia, the UK, the USA and France. These are, of course, not the only countries to have deregulated their freight markets. Sweden, for example, could be added to the list. It is simply that deregulation in the chosen countries has been very well documented in official reports, articles in journals and conference papers, making it possible to make comparisons and to draw meaningful conclusions.

Australia deregulated inter-state freight transport as long ago as 1954, as a result of a legal ruling (Hughes and Vale Pty Ltd *vs*. The State of New South Wales) which found that control of inter-state road freight movements was in violation of Section 92 of the Constitution. Deregulation then took the form of removing licence and permit fees and ton-mile taxes on inter-state road movements, which had previously been imposed mainly to reduce competition with the railways.

The legal ruling in 1954 did not apply to *intra-state* road freight and there remained considerable differences in regulation between the states in Australia. In the Northern Territory, for example, there has never been extensive economic regulation of road freight because the state has always been heavily dependent on road freight and has a limited rail system. By contrast, many other states remained highly regulated. But in 1965, with South Australia removing *all* economic controls, a process of deregulation began throughout Australia. Now there is little *economic* regulation (for example, the licence fees, permits and ton-mile taxes mentioned above). Both state and federal government controls are mainly directed at *social* regulation (such as drivers' hours, and safety).

The second of the four countries to deregulate was the UK, through the 1968 Transport Act. The provisions of the Act applied, of course, to *all* freight transport within the UK, which does not have a federal system of government. Deregulation was prompted by the findings of the Geddes Committee in 1965, which concluded that the systems of road freight licensing then in operation did not serve the public interest, particularly in the area of safety. Under the 1968 Transport Act, action was therefore taken to remove capacity restrictions applied to the haulage sector and to introduce new safety controls on road freight operation.

Deregulation in the USA was brought into effect in 1980, under the Motor Carrier Act. It was designed to remove a variety of economic controls on inter-state trucking, applied through the Interstate Commerce Commission (ICC). The powers of the ICC were considerable prior to 1980. Applicants wishing to enter the inter-state trucking sector had to justify their services on the grounds of 'public convenience and necessity'. The ICC would then routinely restrict carriers according to the geographical area of their operation and the types of commodity that they could carry. But, once established, carriers could organize themselves into rate bureaux which would formulate freight rates, then publish and file them with the ICC. The additional role of the ICC, once it had accepted the rates, would be to ensure strict adherence to them.

Deregulation through the Motor Carrier Act removed many of the powers of the rate bureaux and the ICC, particularly with respect to market entry and rates control. However, the Act did not apply to intra-state trucking, which is still regulated at the state level; attempts to impose federal controls failed in the last three Congresses. As a result, there is considerable variability between states in their freight regulation. Two of the larger states, California and Texas, have stricter regulation than elsewhere. Texas limits both haulage capacity and rates, while California controls only rates and is currently leaning towards a degree of deregulation. One study estimates rates within Texas to be 30 per cent higher than inter-state rates for comparable distances (Canny and Rastatter, 1988).

In theory, until the mid-1980s France exercised strict control over the road haulage sector. Tariffs were controlled by means of an obligatory tariff, the TRO (Tarification Routière Obligatoire). Capacity was limited by means of vehicle permits for long- and short-distance work. In addition, cargo was allocated to hauliers through a network of freight bureaux (Bureau de Fret, BdF) and shippers had to advise the BdF of any consignments over 3 tonnes travelling further than 150 km. The rules applied on a national basis and subsequent deregulation has also been national in scope.

By the mid-1980s a number of developments had made it clear to the French government that continued regulation was no longer in the national interest. For example, national regulation and high domestic rates led to French exports being shipped from Antwerp instead of, say, Le Havre (because a domestic journey could be more expensive than the equivalent or longer international movement). Moreover, the impending Europe-wide deregulation of cabotage and international haulage would in any event expose French hauliers to much greater competition, for which it was felt they were ill-prepared.

As a result, the decision was made to relax progressively the TRO from 1987 until it was finally abolished in 1989; the removal of the rules on cargo reservation via the BdF occurred in parallel. This steady deregulation was intended to cushion the blow for the French haulage sector.

Nevertheless, there has been a fall in freight rates of 5.3 per cent in 1987, 7.4 per cent in 1988 and 3.5 per cent in 1989. Not surprisingly, many road hauliers have ascribed this to deregulation. However, it must be remembered that large contracts between shippers and hauliers had been outside the scope of the TRO for some time; and falls in transport prices are also influenced by improved productivity through, say, infrastructure development and better management.

In conclusion to this brief discussion on the origins of deregulation in the four countries, an important (if rather obvious) point needs to be made; namely, that the word 'deregulation' has no precise or unambiguous meaning. In the UK and France it refers to all freight operation within the country, whereas in the USA and Australia it refers to *either* inter-state or intra-state operation. Additionally, in the USA and France, deregulation embraces decontrol of freight rates. This is not the case in the UK where there is no history of price control (except under the general provisions of prices and incomes policies, applied from time to time by governments in the 1960s and 1970s). Nor is it the case in Australia where rates have not so much been controlled, but subject instead to special taxes.

It follows that the meaning of deregulation in any one country is highly dependent upon both the *characteristics of past regulations* and the *aims of new policy measures* designed to affect the operation of freight markets. It is particularly important to establish this point before going on later to consider the likely consequences of 'European deregulation', in the late 1980s and 1990s.

With economic deregulation of haulage markets, a number of consequences may arise, depending on the circumstances. The following list represents the potential effects within any one country:

- reduction in freight rates
- greater efficiency of freight transport operation
- loss of rail traffic
- increasing concentration of ownership in the haulage sector
- worse services for rural areas
- increases in haulage bankruptcy
- lower wages for haulage employees
- poorer safety record in road freight operation

It is sometimes difficult to prove that economic deregulation is directly and solely responsible for subsequent events in the haulage sector. This is because separate but related action (such as enforcement of safety regulations) can be used to prevent unwanted events arising from deregulation.

However, on the basis of the available evidence, it is possible to make an impact assessment for freight deregulation in each of the four countries. In table 8.3 a plus sign (+) is used to indicate that deregulation could be considered responsible (either fully or in part) for some subsequent event. The crosses (×) indicate that deregulation was not a cause of the event, even if it did occur after deregulation.

The most striking feature of table 8.3 is that deregulation appears to have had very different consequences in each of the four countries studied. However, this can perhaps be best explained when the *circumstances* of deregulation are examined in each country.

In the UK, by the 1960s, the machinery of regulation set up in the 1930s had become almost irrelevant, because periodic reforms of the regulations had already amounted to a process of liberalization. For example, the 1953 Transport Act changed the burden of 'proof of need' for haulage services from the applicant to the objectors. What the 1968 Transport Act effectively did was to dismantle a redundant administration for regulation and refocus new regulations towards achieving safety objectives. As a result, deregulation in the UK apparently produced no major achievements but brought no major

**Table 8.3** The impact of deregulation in the UK, the USA, Australia and France

| Potential consequences of deregulation | UK (national) | USA (inter-state) | Australia (inter-state) | France (national) |
|---|---|---|---|---|
| (a) Reduction in freight rates | × | + | + | + |
| (b) Increased efficiency of road transport operation (reduced empty running) | × | + | ? | ? |
| (c) Loss of rail traffic | × | + | + | × |
| (d) Increasing concentration in haulage sector | × | + (slight) | + | ? |
| (e) Worse service to rural areas | × | × | × | × |
| (f) Increasing haulage bankruptcy | × | + | × | + |
| (g) Lower wages for haulage employees | × | + | × | ? |
| (h) Adverse effects on safety | × | × | × (short-term only) | × |

+, significant impact as a direct result of deregulation; ×, no significant impact as a direct result of deregulation; ?, inconclusive results/insufficient information.

upsets either. In effect, deregulation in the UK amounted to a *tidying up operation.*

By contrast, in the USA, government had recognized by the late 1970s that inter-state regulation, coupled with strong trucking unions, was impairing the efficiency of the US economy. Deregulation in 1980 was used to remove unnecessary economic privileges that had reduced competitiveness in trucking. It is shown in table 8.3 that deregulation has benefited the US economy, but at a social price; lower wages and an increase in bankruptcies were the result. Deregulation in the USA can perhaps be summarized as an *economic imperative* in view of the unwanted consequences of regulation prior to 1980.

In Australia, deregulation came about almost by accident. Since the 1930s the legality of control over inter-state haulage had been tested and found to be constitutionally correct, so the outcome of the Hughes and Vale case came as a surprise to government. Deregulation clearly had a significant impact on the operation of the Australian freight market, but *more by accident than design.*

French deregulation has been an attempt to achieve the best of both worlds – a more efficient and competitive transport sector but without the hard landing of bankruptcies and industrial disruption. Deregulation has had an impact on the French market, but in spirit it has been an *economic response* to Europe-wide changes rather than the more politically inspired and dogmatic approach of the USA.


# The USA: a Model for European Deregulation?

Parallels are frequently drawn between the experience of freight deregulation in the USA and what will occur in the EC, as deregulatory policies are pursued. Many simply see the USA as providing a blueprint for Europe and it is easy to see why.

First, the EC is increasingly assuming a federal structure, becoming rather more like the USA than before. Institutional changes such as deregulation may therefore be expected to have a similar impact in both the USA and the EC. Second, the economy of the EC is in many ways similar to that of the USA. Both are market, rather than command, economies and contain a mix of both manufacturing and agricultural businesses. The demand for freight services is likely to exhibit similar characteristics in both the EC and the USA. However, these similarities at the macro-level are not reflected in the processes of freight deregulation. Crucially, the *objectives* of freight deregulation are dissimilar in the EC and the USA.

As discussed in the preceding section, by the late 1970s, the US government had recognized that inter-state freight regulation, in conjunction with powerful trucking unions, had made US inter-state trucking very expensive. In particular, wages for union truck drivers were very high, at about 50 per cent more than for non-unionized truckers in the non-regulated haulage sector (*Journal of Law and Economics*, 1978). The Motor Carrier Act of 1980 is widely seen as a move by the US government to reduce the influence of the Teamster's union and so reduce real wages and, ultimately, the prices of trucking services to business users. In table 8.3 it is shown that both these consequences did, indeed, result from the Motor Carrier Act, along with less empty running of vehicles and the above-mentioned increase in bankruptcies in the trucking sector, among other things.

The driving force behind deregulation in the EC is different. In the first place it relates to the Treaty of Rome, and the right of an individual from any member state to provide goods and services elsewhere within the Community. The European Commission rightly observed that the system of bilateral permits which controlled international haulage in the Community in the mid-1980s amounted to cargo reservation. If a cargo needed to be moved from, say, France to Italy, the bilateral permit system made the cargo *more* available to a French or Italian international haulier than to one from, say, Belgium. This was contrary to the Treaty of Rome, and deregulation was seen as a way of making sure that international hauliers from any EC country would not be discriminated against on the grounds of nationality.

A crucial point in respect of comparisons between Europe and the USA relates to transport price. Although international permits of all kinds were often in short supply in some EC countries at various times, there is little evidence that this caused any substantial rise in the price level. Furthermore, there is no suggestion that union activity in international haulage led to excessively high wages and hence prices: the fragmented structure of trade unionism within the EC has simply not allowed this to happen.

It follows that, in *international* haulage within the EC, a substantial price fall in direct response to deregulation is unlikely to occur. It would certainly be wholly unrealistic to expect the 25 per cent decline in real rates which occurred between 1980 and 1982 for inter-state FTL trucking in the USA. Any falls in international haulage rates within the EC are less likely to be on account of deregulation and more to do with other '1992 factors', notably the elimination of border delays, and the harmonization of operating conditions (for example, vehicle weights) and more efficient network planning by freight companies. Yet, counterbalanced against any prospective falls in rates must be the possibility that improved enforcement of the 'social' regulations (mainly driver's hours) will add to rates. (In chapter 12 we discuss in more detail how prices are likely to change in the 1990s, not just in relation to deregulation but also in response to these other factors.)

Clearly then, the simple proposition that rates for international haulage within the EC will fall dramatically, just as they did in the USA following inter-state deregulation, does not stand up to close scrutiny. There may be changes to rates, but these will result more from various institutional and commercial changes taking place within the EC than from deregulation itself.

Given the circumstances of deregulation of international haulage in the EC, the *likely* consequences can be summarized in table 8.4, which also provides a comparison with the *actual* consequences of deregulation in the USA.

**Table 8.4** The likely consequences of deregulation in international haulage

| Potential consequences of deregulation | EC (prospects for international haulage) | USA (observed occurrences in inter-state trucking) |
|---|---|---|
| (a) Reduction in freight rates | + (slight) | + (substantial) |
| (b) Increased efficiency of road transport operation (reduced empty running) | + (slight) | + (substantial) |
| (c) Loss of rail traffic | + | + |
| (d) Increasing concentration in haulage sector | + | + (slight) |
| (e) Worse service to rural areas | × | × |
| (f) Increasing haulage bankruptcy | × | + |
| (g) Lower wages for haulage employees | × | + |
| (h) Adverse effects on safety | × | × |

+, significant impact as a direct result of deregulation; ×, no significant impact as a direct result of deregulation.

To conclude, it is important to consider briefly the impact of deregulation in the context of *cabotage* and *national freight markets*. Cabotage may be defined as domestic work performed wholly within one country by an international haulier from another country after completing an international journey. So, if an international haulier from Milan were to take freight to Paris and then pick up in Paris a consignment bound for Lyon, the Paris–Lyon work would be termed cabotage. Cabotage has been prohibited for many years in EC member states. With partial deregulation allowing cabotage under a newly introduced permit system, a new market for freight services is created. However, the impact of cabotage is likely to be very small; in many ways the high-profile political debate over its introduction has tended to obscure the fact that cabotage is likely to be a very restricted activity. (For full details of the likely impact, see chapter 12.)

The main impact of cabotage may be most apparent in countries with strict regulation, notably Germany, leading to a softening of domestic rules. Indeed, Germany is probably the one national market in which the combined effects of cabotage and future deregulation may be important. Hauliers in other countries which still have regulated freight markets, especially Italy, appear to have found ways to circumvent apparently strict rules. This means that there may be a better approximation to free-market conditions in these countries than might at first seem to be the case; future deregulation is therefore unlikely to affect the operation of these road freight markets dramatically.

However, for all countries there is the prospect of a hidden agenda when considering the impact of freight market deregulation. In particular, there is the subtle, but powerful, influence of deregulation on the way in which freight companies are managed. Three quotations, from Australia, the UK and USA, respectively, make the same point about companies on the supply side of freight markets being invigorated following deregulation:

Freedom of entry imparts to [haulage] a dynamism not found under regulation.

(Joy, 1964)

General haulage, which is work of all kinds carried out by a non-specialist contractor, has declined significantly. In its place have emerged highly specialized services, tailored to the exact requirements of individual customers. Many of these services offer a complete distribution package rather than just a transport operation and embraces concepts such as logistics and supply chain management.

(Cooper, 1990a)

The relaxed regulatory climate has also spawned new concepts in trucking and logistics management. Shippers may now use dedicated contract carriage, in one of its many forms, as an alternative to trucking services controlled either by the shipper or entirely by the carrier. There is now a range of for-hire trucking services beyond the traditional common and contract carriage, which can be tailored to the needs of a particular shipper.

(Schweitzer, 1988)

# 9

# Patterns of Logistics Services

## The Nature of Logistics Services

Logistics, when spoken of simply as a concept, assumes a singularity which can never be realized in practice. At the practical level, supply chains take on many different forms, and management priorities within the supply chain can vary considerably from company to company; one may manufacture products which demand high levels of customer service with, perhaps, daily delivery. Another will find that a lower level of customer service will be sufficient.

Logistics services are essentially multidimensional and any given service has a combination of service attributes. A description of a service could be constructed to read as a 'national, third-party, customer-dedicated, premium-quality transport operation for the complete supply chain, embracing computer-integrated logistics'. But neither our memories nor our inclinations encourage the discussion of logistics services in this way, although it is both comprehensive and unambiguous. Users of language usually choose to simplify, with the result that there is a loss of precision.

This is a condition which will inevitably affect the discussion of logistics services in this chapter, because we need to concentrate on a limited number of service attributes in logistics, just to make ourselves understood. Consider the full range of service attributes as illustrated in figure 9.1.

The Logistics Service Heptagon comprises seven *vector sectors*. Each vector represents an *attribute class* in logistics services. The attribute classes are space, capacity, management, activity, customer service, information technology (IT) and logistics function. Each

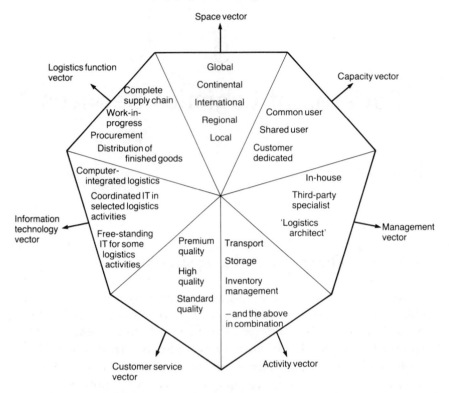

**Figure 9.1**   The Logistics Service Heptagon.

class has, in its turn, a number of *attribute options*. So, for the capacity vector, for example, the options are:

- 'customer-dedicated', where some given capacity (for example, in transport) is used exclusively for one customer
- 'shared user', where capacity is used on behalf of a selected number of clients whose needs are similar – the logistics service will have been developed to reflect those shared needs
- 'common user', where capacity is used for a variety of customers and where the logistics service is not designed to reflect the special needs of one or several of them

A description of any given logistics service can be generated by reference to the vector sectors in the Logistics Service Heptagon. Selection of one option from each of the vector sectors gives a comprehensive account of the attributes of the logistics service as a whole; the precise but wordy description of a service that we used at the beginning of the chapter was generated from the Logistics Service Heptagon.

# Segmenting the European Logistics Market

Devices such as the Logistics Service Heptagon can be readily used in management consultancy when a particular company is unsure of its logistics strategy; it is a useful basis for constructing a full range of 'what if. . . ?' questions. It would also be the preferred basis upon which to examine and segment the market for logistics services in Europe but, unfortunately, it is far too complicated. There are problems of definition (for example, would a premium service be the same thing in, say, Portugal and Germany?). There are also problems of knowledge. Who would actually *know* whether a service specified in such detail (using the seven attributes) was on offer within a country? It is extremely difficult to find people who are that close to all sectors of the logistics services market.

We felt that it would be appropriate to adopt a more modest approach to achieve a result which would be both fairly reliable and comprehensible. Our approach took three of the vectors (capacity, management and activity) from the Logistics Service Heptagon as the basis for further analysis. A two-dimensional matrix was constructed (figure 9.2) along the following lines:

- The 'management dimension' of the matrix reflects an important aspect of the relationship between the user and provider of logistics services; namely, does the provider organize the work or does the user?
- The 'capacity dimension' represents how capacity can be shared among users.
- The activity vector is represented by making a distinction between the mainstream activities of transport and distribution (transport with storage) within the matrix.

Using the matrix, services on offer in logistics markets can be assigned to a particular cell. This then gives each service a unique identity, which is not compromised by any local description in different countries. So, for example, cell number 4 can be described in English as 'dedicated contract transport'. Exactly the same service is described in German as 'Massgeschneiderte Transporte'. It does not matter in the least that the names are different. What matters is that *exactly the same kind of service* is being referred to in both the UK and Germany.

The matrix therefore offers the opportunity to identify with some clarity the existence of particular logistics market segments. It avoids

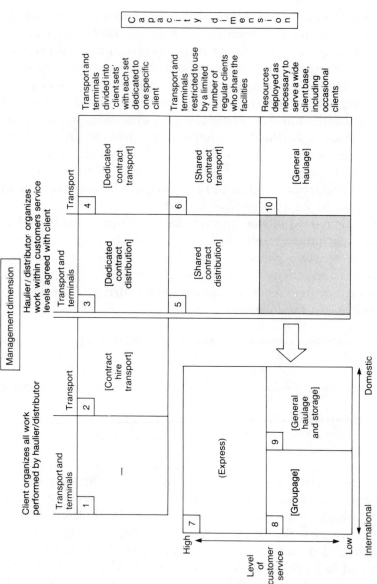

**Figure 9.2** A classification of third-party haulage and distribution services. In this context, 'organizes all work' implies the routeing and scheduling of vehicles, and the day-to-day operation of the terminal. A 'terminal' is a depot, warehouse, parcels sorting centre and so on

having to translate and interpret *names* of services, which invariably leads to considerable misunderstanding and a failure to classify accurately the separate parts of national logistics markets.

In conjunction with the matrix, which allows the identification and naming of logistics services, a questionnaire (not reproduced here) was used to establish both the present *scale* of a particular service, and whether it was growing or declining relative to other services. Both the matrix and the questionnaire were then sent out or taken to correspondents across Europe for completion.

An important point to note about the questionnaire was that it was designed largely for judgemental use. Very little data exists to describe, for example, expenditure on general haulage services in the various European countries. Correspondents (about 10 in most countries) had to use their judgement to say how substantial services were relative to others. Although this is an undeniably imprecise way of judging scale we were impressed by the degree of consensus among correspondents from any given country. Experts in the field of logistics do appear to have an encouragingly similar view of what is going on.

Moreover, the purpose of the exercise was not so much to judge the absolute scale of a logistics service in any one country, but rather to establish a service profile for each country. In broad terms, services 2–7, as represented by the cells in the matrix (see figure 9.2) represented the more advanced services. The remaining services 8–10 (groupage, general haulage and storage, and general haulage) are altogether more traditional. By establishing a service profile, some basic comparisons, appropriate to the precision of the study, could be made between countries.

The study, which fundamentally aims to build up a picture of logistics market segmentation in Europe and then form a view on the future shape of logistics services, was conducted during 1989 and 1990. Other points which relate to the conduct of the study are as follows:

- *Geographical coverage.*   The matrix was used for a selected number of *national* freight markets in Europe, including Germany, the UK, the Netherlands, Greece, France and Sweden (for the purposes of comparison with non-EC countries). The aim was to establish any differences that might exist between particular countries or regions (for example, northern and southern Europe).
- *Validation of matrix cells.*   In addition to respondents providing local descriptions of matrix cells, it was requested that they should also give

examples of companies providing any one service. This helps to validate the existence of a cell in the country for, if a respondent cannot identify a company providing the service, then it is unlikely that the service exists.

- *Analysis of the results.* Completed matrices and questionnaires from respondents in each country were centrally analysed, for the purposes of consistency, at the Logistics Unit of the Polytechnic of Central London. Continuing dialogue with selected respondents helped to clarify potential anomalies and correct prospective errors.

Prior to discussion of the results of the study, there is a need to discuss the kind of freight service that each cell of the matrix represents. Here each service is given an English name. Each service is also identified by a number which corresponds to its cell in the matrix (see figure 9.2):

*Cell 1.* Use of the matrix allows for the existence of a service of this type, where ownership of both transport and warehousing rests with the third party but where all control is exercised by the customer. However, the existence of this theoretical possibility for a service has not been confirmed through the market segmentation study.

*Cell 2: Contract Hire Transport.* Here a haulier/distributor provides vehicles and (usually) drivers, which are put at the disposal of the client. All maintenance and vehicle replacement responsibilities fall to the haulier. However, it is the client that organizes the work of the driver and vehicle. In particular, the client's responsibility will be to allocate consignments for delivery and decide upon routes.

*Cell 3: Dedicated Contract Distribution.* Services of this kind involve both transport and warehousing capacity, which is divided into 'client sets' with each set dedicated to one specific client. This compartmentalization of the contractor's capacity between clients means that the service needs of any one client will not be compromised by the conflicting needs of other clients, such as may occur when capacity is shared. Dedicated contract distribution is, in effect, a third-party replication of own-account operation, and contracts generally have a 2–5 year duration. As a comprehensive, 'tailor-made' service for clients, dedicated contract distribution offers good scope both for the application of logistics concepts and the advanced uses of IT systems.

*Cell 4: Dedicated Contract Transport.* This is directly analogous to dedicated contract distribution (cell 3 above), but involves only a transport service.

*Cell 5: Shared Contract Distribution.* This service arises when several clients of a distributor have specialized needs in common (for example, in packaging, handling, storage, or even common destinations, such as hospitals). The client benefits from the distributor being able to *consolidate* consignments which have these specialized needs in both transport and warehousing.

*Cell 6: Shared Contract Transport.* This type of service is a variant upon shared contract distribution, but involves only transport.

*Cell 7: Express.* Most express services are sophisticated versions of a common user service involving both transport and warehousing (for sorting rather than storage). Companies offering express services accept only relatively small consignment sizes (say, up to 25 kg) but offer a high level of service in return, often with next-day delivery. Tracking and tracing systems often contribute to a high level of customer service.

*Cell 8: Groupage.* The main difference between groupage and express is that groupage services will accept larger consignment sizes, but delivery will invariably be slower. Overall, levels of customer service are not as high as in express.

*Cell 9: General Haulage and Storage.* This is a common user service where the haulier provides not just transport services for a variety of customers but also storage facilities.

*Cell 10: General Haulage.* This is yet another common user service, but the haulier only performs a transport operation. There is no warehousing dimension to the work, unlike cell 9.

# The Results of the Study

The results of the market segmentation study of European logistics services are presented below as figures 9.3–6 and 9.7–8. Also accompanying these results is a short profile of freight transport and logistics markets in a number of European countries. These countries include all those studied as part of the market segmentation exercise, together with others such as Portugal, Spain, Belgium and Italy which, for various reasons, could not be included in the exercise.

## *Benelux countries*

The hauliers from the Benelux countries have received considerable support from their governments because of their important role in intra-EC trade and the consequent revenue from export services. Because the Benelux countries are small the international road haulage market is far more important to hauliers from these countries than is the case with their counterparts in other EC member states. However, the Belgian and Dutch markets both have important national flows and perhaps more complex markets than is sometimes realized.

## Belgium

A number of reports and surveys have identified Belgian hauliers as having low costs and being extremely price competitive. The domestic market is typified by small firms, although the number of operators fell from 10 044 in 1978 to 7 773 in 1988, showing increasing concentration of ownership in road goods transport.

Some Belgian operators suggest that they see themselves lacking some of the more sophisticated distribution and logistics skills of their Dutch neighbours. The majority of the hauliers are engaged in simple haulage operations and frequently work as subcontractors for the numerous freight forwarding companies. The importance of Antwerp as a European gateway port – especially for the steel and chemicals industries – means that Belgian road transporters are well located to obtain international traffic, much of which is controlled by forwarders. The Belgian Ministry of Transport see the removal of cabotage restrictions as beneficial, and expect it to reduce the level of empty running (currently 27 per cent on international work).

In the absence of innovative large transport and distribution companies and/or grocery retailers it appears that the main force for change in the Belgian haulage industry will come from the international freight forwarders. Much emphasis is being placed by them on the use of IT in transport. For example, SEAGHA, an information system for the port community in Antwerp, links together shipping lines, terminal operators, railways, hauliers, customs and shippers.

## The Netherlands

Deregulation of the Dutch domestic freight market in 1985 has clearly encouraged the use of third-party haulage and distribution. Third-party haulage in the Netherlands held 67 per cent of the national goods transport by road 1987 (a 5 per cent increase compared with 1982).

As in Belgium, the international transport market is of vital importance to Dutch hauliers; they have been very successful in capturing a significant share of intra-EC traffic. However, despite the formidable reputation of the Dutch as the hauliers of Europe, there are perhaps surprisingly few large transport companies operating in the domestic market. In addition, the domestic market still lacks integrated storage and transport companies and, in grocery retail distribution, there is a rather 'traditional' feel compared to the UK. There are a number of significant developments in the Dutch transport and logistics industry:

- *Growth of logistics services companies.* A small number of companies (such as Intexo Veghel) appear to have developed advanced logistics approaches to the services they offer customers. The management of these companies is perhaps less entrepreneurial and rather more 'scientific' than is typical of many transport companies in the areas of IT and the development of added-value logistics services (such as assembly) for their customers.
- *Importance of international traders.* Innovation in the Dutch distribution sector is being driven by international companies that are using the Netherlands as their European platform or gateway. For example, Rank Xerox have focused their European distribution through the Netherlands and, in partnership with Frans Maas, have developed a sophisticated JIT-type approach to control of the logistics chain. The innovation by international traders contrasts with the important role played by grocery retailing in the UK and manufacturing in Germany.
- *Environmental influences.* Within the Netherlands there is strong evidence of increasing environmental concern about the impact of road transport, in terms of pollution and congestion. As a consequence there has been a significant shift in the attitude of the government in favour of railways and, in particular, a stated desire to increase the scope for combined transport. Although the railways will never be of special importance for Dutch domestic transport (in view of the small size of the country) it appears likely that combined transport investment will grow, leading – for example – to more terminals and improvements in the information systems used by the combined transport companies.

The market segmentation results for the Netherlands (see figure 9.3) show a large element of common user services (from cells 8, 9 and 10 in the matrix) and a moderate presence of some of the more specialized services (from cells 4, 5 and 6). Perhaps a greater degree of specialization might have been expected, but this may have been inhibited by recent capacity regulation in the haulage sector and the role of the Netherlands as a trading nation, where the possibilities for freight service innovation can be constrained by the attitudes of overseas trading partners.

## Luxembourg

The smallest of the EC countries, Luxembourg has the distinction of having a haulage sector which has never been subject to economic

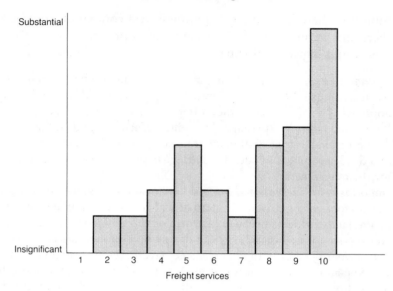

**Figure 9.3**   Freight service segmentation in the Netherlands. Freight service code: 1, –; 2, contract hire transport; 3, dedicated contract distribution; 4, dedicated contract transport; 5, shared contract distribution; 6, shared contract transport; 7, express; 8, groupage; 9, general haulage and storage; 10, general haulage.

regulation. Both price and capacity have been freely determined according to market forces. One result has been a substantial expansion of the international haulage sector. Many of the international hauliers based in Luxembourg are German in origin. Being based in Luxembourg frees them from many of the restrictive operating conditions that would be placed upon them by the German haulage authorities (see the German section below).

## Denmark

For many years, freight regulation was mainly directed at carriers operating scheduled services between locations in Denmark. In effect, these carriers were given concessions for work, and the rights to these concessions could be traded between them. Obligatory tariffs were also in force for the scheduled services.

General hauliers were exempt from this kind of economic regulation until 1973, when Denmark joined the EC. The government, recognizing the need to reorganize the haulage sector, introduced a quota system of permits, originally allowing about 24 000 in number. Since these permits were in short supply, they acquired considerable value when traded between hauliers; the peak price for a single permit in 1984 was DKK 24 000.

One effect of this period of regulation was to freeze the structure of the haulage sector. It is shown in table 9.1 that there was virtually no difference in the holdings of permits, according to size of haulier, between 1979 and 1983.

**Table 9.1**  Permit holdings by size of Danish haulier, 1979–83

| Number of permits per haulier | Percentage share, 1979 | Percentage share, 1983 |
|---|---|---|
| 1 | 52.8 | 51.5 |
| 2 | 18.3 | 19.8 |
| 3 | 9.1 | 9.8 |
| 4 | 5.4 | 4.9 |
| 5 | 3.4 | 3.4 |
| 6–9 | 6.3 | 6.1 |
| 10–19 | 3.4 | 3.2 |
| 19 or more | 1.3 | 1.3 |

However, the Danish government later decided to abolish the permit system, and this was achieved on 1 January 1989. A haulier now needs only to meet EC qualitative conditions to operate vehicles; namely, good repute, sound financial standing and professional competence.

## Eire (Republic of Ireland)

In common with many other European countries, Eire introduced quantitative controls on haulage in the 1930s in order to protect railway traffic. Over the years, it became clear that this objective was not being achieved; the main consequences were a growth in own-account transport and a growing value for scarce permits. By 1973, the National Prices Commission estimated that the value of each permit traded between hauliers was around £5000.

The deregulation of road freight in Northern Ireland (part of the UK) had a significant impact on cross-border traffic. According to Barret (1988), before deregulation in Northern Ireland, hauliers from

Eire held about 50 per cent of the cross-border traffic. Afterwards, this share fell to around only 30 per cent.

Progressive deregulation of the haulage sector in Eire began in 1970, but it was not completed until the end of September 1988. Now all hauliers have to obtain a 'road freight carrier's licence' which is granted to all applicants who can meet the qualitative criteria stipulated by the EC in respect of good repute, financial standing and professional competence.

## *France*

The latter half of the 1980s saw the progressive deregulation of the French road haulage industry. The government-inspired move to deregulate led to the scrapping of the Tarification Routière Obligatoire (TRO) in January 1989. However, the TRO was never as rigid as the German tariff, and large shippers were always able to negotiate discounts. Interestingly, there seems to be a tendency for French shippers to concentrate more on service price than their UK counterparts, and to be less ready to adopt new distribution practices.

A consequence of the relatively recent deregulation has been that the freight market in France feels unsettled. This is reflected in the declining value of permits: they were each worth FF165 000 in 1986, but only FF 70 000 by the end of 1987 (Bonnafous, 1988). By now they are of little, if any, worth. Moreover, power seems to have shifted very strongly to the shippers, who have used it to squeeze rates rather than take the opportunity to enhance service quality. Own-account operations are likely to decline in the next few years as low prices make the contracting out of the distribution function increasingly attractive. Improving logistics skills and IT will be used to integrate the distribution function when using third-party operators.

A feature of the French road haulage sector has been the use of freight brokers known as 'Commissionnaires/Auxiliaires de Transport'. Their skills lie in matching vehicle supply and demand for load space and they operate mainly for domestic traffic. However, the deregulation of the haulage market threatens many of these companies because shippers are now free to fix price and service levels direct with the hauliers. In addition, the widespread use of the Minitel service for load matching diminishes the scope for the Commissionnaires' activity.

The transport market in France is sometimes said to be regional rather than national. This reflects the large size of the country and the spread of economic activity and population. But in many ways this concept of regionalism is slightly dated and is an oversimplification. Some of the major companies (such as Calberson) are clearly national in their coverage. Others (such as Prost in Brittany) have strong regional roots but now offer national coverage. However, a third category of medium-sized companies remains truly regional in nature.

The size and location of France make French road freight traffic an attractive target for hauliers from both northern and southern Europe. The activities of foreign hauliers could continue to erode the share of traffic moved internationally by French operators and, in time, could open up sections of the domestic market (through the mechanism of cabotage). The Netherlands in particular have seen this opportunity, as is clear from the open letter sent by the Dutch Ministry of Transport to French industrial companies, emphasizing the quality of Dutch road haulage firms (Chardin, 1990a).

The spread of population and the pattern of goods flows mean that, for all but the largest carriers, co-operation has always been essential in order to offer national coverage to shippers. Co-operative ventures in France have perhaps been assisted by the scope for forming GIEs (Groupe d'Intérêt Economique). Co-operation between modes is also evident in France and combined transport is well developed. Environmental concerns, continued large-scale rail investment and rising wage rates should boost the use of combined transport systems during the next ten years.

Retailing, particularly grocery retailing, provides a contrast to the UK. In France much of the supply chain management still lies with suppliers (in the UK control is exercised by the retailer or nominated distribution company). As a consequence, there is a much greater emphasis on shared distribution rather than the dedicated approach seen in the UK (this is also influenced by the long-distance nature of some movements). However, there are signs of a growing battle for control of the supply chain between the major grocery retailers (such as Leclerc) and suppliers such as Evian.

The market segmentation results for France (see figure 9.4) show that common user services (from cells 8, 9 and 10) remain strong in France; the more specialized services (from cells 3, 4, 5, 6 and 7) have a moderate presence. Contract hire transport (from cell 2) is shown to be particularly popular in France, perhaps demonstrating the extent to which the users of logistics services like to keep a hands-on approach to operations.

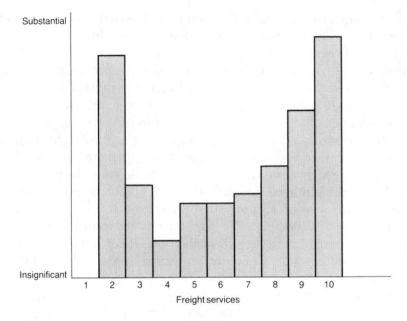

**Figure 9.4** Freight service segmentation in France. Freight service code: 1, –; 2, contract hire transport; 3, dedicated contract distribution; 4, dedicated contract transport; 5, shared contract distribution; 6, shared contract transport; 7, express; 8, groupage; 9, general haulage and storage; 10, general haulage.

## *Germany*[6]

Regulation of freight transport in Germany is still extremely rigid, and many more goods are moved by rail and inland waterway compared with, say, the UK. To a certain degree this extensive use of non-road modes of transport is a consequence of shortages in the supply of haulage services; the federal authorities in Germany exercise strict capacity control in the haulage sector with permits being required for different kinds of operation (see table 9.2). But there are also physical reasons (such as the navigability of the Rhine) and political ones (such as the strength of the Green movement) which favour the extensive use of inland waterways and railways as well as roads.

A distinguishing feature of the domestic freight market in Germany is the importance of the 'spedition' company (such as Rhenus, Kuehne and Nagel). In broad terms, the spedition company acts as a freight forwarder, selecting routes for goods according to

**Table 9.2** Types of authorization in the German haulage sector (1988 totals in brackets – number of authorizations)

---

*National authorizations* (over 150 km)
Red (18,324)   General authorization for all kinds of long-distance work.


New Red      Formerly furniture carriers (both removals and new
(3,170)      furniture) holding now obsolete yellow authorization – can
             undertake general haulage, but are limited to the 15/20
             tonne vehicles they use(d) as furniture carriers.


*Regional* (50–150 km; less than 50 km is unrestricted)
Blue (8,728)   Allowed to undertake general haulage within a restricted
               regional area.


*Maritime*
White (220)    Special quota for hauliers working from ports. It means that
               they can readily move containers/semi-trailers, and keep
               traffic at German ports, rather than have it go to Rotterdam
               or Antwerp.


*International* (controls German part of international journey)
Pink (1,173)   One domestic journey allowed between international
               journeys (such as Paris–Frankfurt–Hamburg–Amsterdam,
               all legs loaded).

New Pink     Does not allow an intermediate domestic journey. Number
(2,652)      to be increased from 2880 (1989) to 3000 by 1990.

---

Note that the authorizations apply to one vehicle at a time, and so hauliers have to carry them with the vehicle at all times: this clearly imposes a rigid upper limit to haulage capacity. Hauliers are able to use the haulier-only road–rail system (Kombiverkehr) to increase their effective capacity.
*Source*: Bundesverband des Deutschen Güterfernverkehrs (BDF) e.V., Frankfurt.

price and service quality, engaging hauliers to move the goods and processing the paperwork. This is, of course, routine work for *international* freight movements throughout the world. Importantly, though, it is prominent in domestic work within Germany, unlike many other countries in Europe in which a direct shipper–haulier relationship is the norm.

A main reason for the existence of spedition companies in Germany is the sheer complication of freight regulation. Tariff rates govern the movement of many goods by product, mode of transport and route. Therefore some skill is needed to select the transport combinations which best meet the needs of the freight users. Whether or not the spedition companies would survive unchanged following deregulation in Germany is debatable. No doubt many freight operators will wish to negotiate directly with the freight users (such as manufacturers) rather than the spedition companies, which they often see as unnecessary middle-men.

The pace of innovation in German freight transport and logistics has not been especially fast for a variety of reasons. First, on the service supply side, hauliers are cushioned from competition and are not forced to innovate. Second, retailers have been slow to use distribution as a competitive weapon. As a consequence, most distribution remains in-house and techniques are weak compared with say, the UK. Third, many German companies are owned either by families or banks, which agitate for change less than, say shareholders. Within this environment, logistics will often receive little development priority.

However, one sector of business in which logistics is relatively advanced is manufacturing. This is partly because German manufacturing, although very strong, is under fierce attack from Japan. Companies such as BMW and Volkswagen are therefore doing as much as they can to stay competitive, and new ideas in logistics are being developed. For example, JIT is being practised by Kuehne and Nagel for BMW although, as elsewhere in Europe, it is unlikely that it conforms to the original Japanese concept. However, techniques in manufacturing logistics are matched by other European countries. In Italy for example, Fiat is a leader in automotive logistics, with extensive use of logistics-based technologies such as automated guided vehicles (AGVs). Arguably, the strength of the German manufacturing sector is founded more on the quality of its products than on any advanced application of logistics.

For many German freight companies the possibility of haulage being deregulated in the near future is a crucial issue. As yet the government has made no formal declaration that deregulation will take place. However, many freight organizations in Germany are given to understand that tariff control will gradually be relaxed and that restrictions on haulage capacity will slowly be lifted, to give a 'soft landing' to German freight companies. There are also concerns about the possible consequences of 'creeping deregulation'.

First, there is widespread worry about poorer standards of operation, not least with an influx of foreign operators, should capacity controls be relaxed. It is greatly feared that high safety standards will be eroded.

Second, operators are unhappy about the prospect of prices for haulage services falling in the wake of deregulation: estimates of a 20 per cent price fall are cited (Kandler, 1989). Indeed, such is the concern about the future of the German haulage sector that many companies are selling up to realize the current high value of haulage permits. It is feared that after deregulation they might lose most, if not all, of their value. With deregulation feared, permits are already losing their value. Long-distance 'red' permits, which were traded at 100 000–120 000 ecu in 1986, only fetched about half that amount by 1990.

Uncertainty among German freight companies, coupled with the impressive performance of the German economy as a whole, has

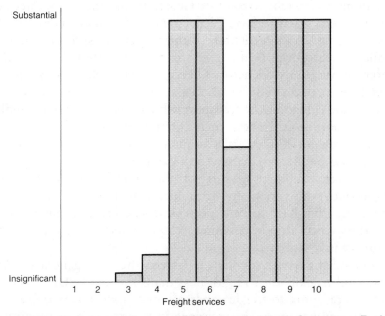

**Figure 9.5**  Freight service segmentation in West Germany. Freight service code: 1, –; 2, contract hire transport; 3, dedicated contract distribution; 4, dedicated contract transport; 5, shared contract distribution; 6, shared contract transport; 7, express; 8, groupage; 9, general haulage and storage; 10, general haulage.

made German freight companies a frequent target for takeover. For example, Nedlloyd has purchased Union Transport and Andreas Christ, Lep has bought Wolfarth, and P & O have added Rhenania to their company portfolio.

The market segmentation results for Germany show a number of services which are well developed (see figure 9.5). Shared services are particularly strong (from cells 5 and 6). Common user services are also well represented. This probably reflects a variety of factors, including the strength of export business (from cell 8), and strict regulation that makes innovation in specialist services unnecessary for many freight service providers (from cells 9 and 10). Finally, it is important to note the complete absence of contract hire transport (from cell 3) in Germany. Confusion over its legality has halted its development.

## Greece

The domestic freight market in Greece is dominated by hire-and-reward operators who have 75 per cent of the road freight market; this is despite strict regulation of their operations. There are three regulatory categories in the domestic market; national, for hauliers who offer their services across Greece; prefectural, for hauliers who offer their services only in particular regions of the country; and special, for categories of transport which have particular handling and transport requirements (such as refrigerated vehicles). Across all of these categories there is a 'tonnage freeze', meaning that it is difficult for hauliers to acquire new capacity.

Moreover, the supply side of the freight market is highly fragmented, with very many small operators. Even the 'co-operative companies' that have recently been established comprise many small operators, with little in common except shared depot facilities and administrative support.

Most freight service suppliers in Greece offer only general haulage, either full-truckload (FTL) or less-than-truckload (LTL). This is partly in response to the demands of Greek industry, which are not yet very sophisticated. The main products, such as cement, alumina and fertilizers, are still relatively low in value and high in bulk. Agricultural production remains equally important to Greece, and the need here is also for relatively unsophisticated transport. However, in the service sector of the economy (such as banking and insurance), there is a growing demand for better freight services, mainly in the form of express transport for parcels and other small packages. Although there is apparently strict regulation of transport capacity, there is fierce competition between hauliers, leading to low rates and poor profitability. One consequence is that when hauliers renew their fleets, they often buy secondhand from other countries. Vehicles are therefore rather old, on average, compared with other European countries.

Perceived weaknesses in transport supply have led to the entry of freight forwarders into Greece. They see an opportunity to provide a better service to freight users through the better coordination of transport supply, the traditional skill of freight forwarding. The forwarders, which include Danzas, Kuehne and Nagel, and Schenker, are now well-established in the marketplace and are expected to control more of the market in the future. Building on existing international links will help to reinforce this trend, given the growth

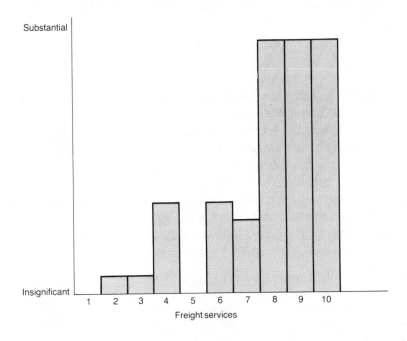

**Figure 9.6** Freight service segmentation in Greece. Freight service code: 1, –; 2, contract hire transport; 3, dedicated contract distribution; 4, dedicated contract transport; 5, shared contract distribution; 6, shared contract transport; 7, express; 8, groupage; 9, general haulage and storage; 10, general haulage.

in trade between member states of the European Community (EC). They are also expected to make a particular impact in specialist areas of the freight market (such as furniture removals and refrigerated transport), possibly providing help with fleet financing. In addition, the development of logistics-based services in Greece, by freight forwarders and others, will depend on better facilities for depots and the establishment of warehouses. Current facilities are either poorly equipped or entirely lacking.

According to the market segmentation study (see figure 9.6), Greece is dominated by common user services (from cells 8, 9 and 10) although two, more specialist, services have some strength, namely dedicated contract transport (from cell 4) and shared contract transport (from cell 6). Express (from cell 7) is also relatively strong, probably on account of it frequently being an international service, and due to the poor performance of the public mail service in Greece. It is noteworthy that shared contract distribution (from cell 5), a service requiring considerable supply-side sophistication, is wholly absent in Greece.

## *Italy*

The road freight transport sector dominates Italian domestic distribution, accounting for 62 per cent of inland movements by weight in 1988. Despite its national importance there has been an absence of a defined national strategy for road transport. This factor, combined with the structure of the industry, has given rise to the strong feeling among many observers that the road freight market is relatively unproductive in comparison to other EC member states, exhibiting high costs and rather poor quality.

Road transport is currently regulated by numerous laws and specific measures, emanating from a variety of ministries:

- Ministry of Transport – authorization for transport for third party or on own account, and for the related rates
- Ministry of Public Works – responsible for road laws
- Ministry of the Interior – driving licences
- Ministry of Labour – working hours

The consequence of this divided responsibility is that, despite apparently extensive regulation, there is practical difficulty with enforcement and the industry operates in a relatively unregulated manner.

There are over 200 000 Italian firms engaged in public haulage, operating some 250 000 vehicles. The supply side is therefore characterized by an extreme fragmentation, with the vast majority of firms being owner–operators. The fragmentation means that profitability tends to be low and this inhibits the development of specialized large-scale Italian transport companies.

Italian transporters, in common – it must be said – with many of their EC counterparts, complain of an excess of competition, underutilized vehicles, non-remunerative rates and too easy access to the profession. The German system of regulation is regarded by some in the industry as a model for the future, rather than the anachronism that many outside observers would view it as.

At present a search is under way for forms of aggregation among companies (such as co-operatives and consortia) in order to achieve economies of scale, and to combat the current tendency for foreign-owned competitors to seize larger parts of the market through takeovers of Italian companies (such as Nedlloyd buying Messageria Emiliana). There is a growing feeling that widespread changes are taking place in logistics and that in some way the industry must respond to this – although the mechanism for producing a coordinated response from such a fragmented industry is far from clear.

Retail distribution developments are also slowed by the fragmented nature of the Italian retailing sector. Grocery retailing is the province of numerous small shops, many of which are members of voluntary chains such as VG or Spar. At present there is little management emphasis on achieving better control of the transport aspects of the supply chain, and far more attention seems aimed at the following:

- opening new, larger, stores (hypermarkets)
- developing better warehouse control
- forming strategic buying and management alliances with foreign-owned retailers (Casino and La Rinascente)

In terms of logistics development within the manufacturing sector, the automotive industry seems well ahead and there is considerable talk of moves towards JIT production. Other sectors which are upgrading their distribution practices and systems include domestic appliances (white goods) and chemicals; both are helped by the multinational nature of the companies dominating these sectors.

## *Portugal*

The structure of the Portuguese economy is fast-changing. Even before accession to the EC in 1986, Portugal was becoming much less dependent upon traditional sectors, such as agriculture, and was developing new interests in manufacturing and services. In the 27 years from 1960, agriculture's contribution to GDP fell from 26 per cent to 9 per cent (Banco de Portugal, annual reports from various years).

The pace of change within the Portuguese economy is, however, unlikely to relent over the next few years. Three factors are likely to be especially important. First, parts of Portuguese industry still remain protected by tariff barriers, even for intra-EC trade. These barriers must disappear by 1993, leaving industry much more exposed to competition from elsewhere in Europe. Second, the influence of foreign-owned companies operating in Portugal is likely to become stronger. This will happen partly because of the takeover of local companies weakened by the removal of trading protection, but also because Portugal is a low-wage economy, attractive to producers able to relocate factories from high-cost countries such as Germany. Third, the role of the state in Portuguese industry is likely to change. While there is a general movement in Europe away from direct state ownership and control of industry, nine of the top ten companies in Portugal are still state-owned (Hudson, 1989). Privatization of some of these is now in prospect.

Change in the structure of the Portuguese economy is bound to have important consequences for the transport sector: yet the ability of the transport sector to respond effectively is much in doubt. Part of the problem is that regulating reform is long overdue. The current licensing system for road freight has failed in its main objective (as enshrined in Basic Law No. 2008 of 1945), which was to protect the railways. Railways now carry only 3 per cent of the freight tonnage in Portugal and perform just 13 per cent of the tonne–kilometres, figures well below the European averages (Eurostat, 1989a). Yet the licensing system is relatively unchanged: it has simply become a self-perpetuating system of rules which are both overcomplicated and inappropriate to the rapidly changing needs of the Portuguese economy.

The main effect of tight control over haulage capacity has been a massive expansion of the own-account sector which, according to the official statistics, carries 86 per cent of the road tonne–kilometres.

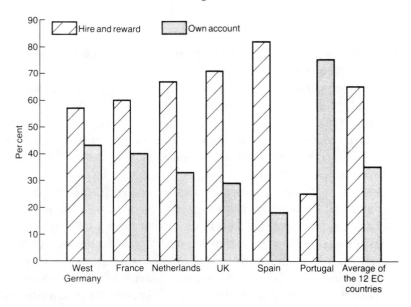

**Figure 9.7** Hire-and-reward and own-account shares of freight markets (by tonne kilometres) in selected countries.
*Source: Basic Statistics*, Eurostat, Commission of the European Communities

This is by far the largest proportion in any EC country. As shown in figure 9.7, the EC average is about 35 per cent.

An unwanted by-product of the restrictions on haulage capacity is that a great deal of illegal operation takes place. Operators will often be unlicensed and carry excessive loads, while some drivers will have been working for too many hours. This causes problems for hauliers trying to run their businesses legally. Not surprisingly, in the circumstances, freight services in Portugal are often unsophisticated and not very profitable.

Fortunately, the Portuguese government understands the need for regulatory reform, and has put forward proposals for a new framework which would do much to modernize the freight sector. Many hauliers fear the outcome; increased competition from foreign freight companies is a frequent worry. However, on balance they will probably be better off competing fairly against outsiders than with local hauliers operating illegally.

## Spain

Upon its entry to the EC in 1986 Spain's haulage sector was highly regulated. It is now committed to deregulation by 1992. At the present time, entry to the haulage market is highly dependent on being able to argue a case successfully with the formidable bureaucracy of the Spanish government. Permits will be made available if an applicant can prove a need for his proposed haulage service, although what constitutes need is very much left to the discretion of local officials.

Spain has a highly fragmented haulage sector, among the most fragmented in Europe, with 98 per cent of operators having fewer than five vehicles (compared with a figure of 86 per cent in the UK). Not surprisingly, the service that is usually on offer is non-specialist haulage. This has been problematic in the retailing sector, in which rapid development has been taking place. French retailers in particular (Carrefour, for example) have begun to transform the face of Spanish retailing, moving trade away from family independents to modern hypermarkets and malls. They have been unable to secure adequate haulage services for merchandising, and some have turned to importing foreign distribution skills (for example, Pryca, owned by Carrefour, use Christian Salvesen).

A further problem for retailers in Spain is that the local suppliers of products are very small in scale. Therefore, typically, a department store will purchase from around 8000 suppliers, compared with about 4000 in the UK. This represents an enormous merchandising problem, and distribution is seen by many retailers as the solution. Retailers such as Galerias wish to use distribution as the means to discipline the delivery practices of suppliers and to ensure a streamlined flow of goods into stores. Most observers of the Spanish economy see problems ahead for Spanish producers, particularly for manufacturers. This is because they are still protected by tariff barriers from competition *within* the EC. When these barriers finally fall, in 1992, many Spanish producers are expected to go out of business. After 1992 Spain is expected to import much more than it does now, and this is certain to have a major impact on the structure of its distribution services sector.

# *Sweden*

Sweden embarked upon a programme of progressive deregulation of its freight markets as early as 1963. By 1972 restrictions on entry to the market were lifted and tariffs abandoned. Permits are still required by operators, but these are issued on a qualitative basis; professional skills and financial standing are the main criteria for permit issue.

The market for long-distance freight services in Sweden is dominated by two forwarding companies, Bilspedition and ASG (Allamna Svenska Godsaktiebolaget), with respective market shares of 47 per cent and 43 per cent in 1988. Neither of these companies owns many trucks: instead, they contract smaller operators to work on their behalf. Many of these operators will be members of haulage co-operatives, a distinctive feature of the Swedish freight market.

When duopolies operate within a market there can either be a cosy relationship or strong competition between the two companies. In the case of Sweden's freight market, the tendency is towards the latter. As a result, profit levels for both Bilspedition and ASG have tended to be poor. The further consequence has been limited investment in service developments by these leading companies.

Local transport is left mainly to independent hauliers, either acting independently or as part of haulage co-operatives. The foci for local transport are truck centres, which are owned by associations of independent operators. In 1988 there were 234 of these centres spread across Sweden; on average, each had 40 operators with 58 trucks between them. However, the strength of the owner–operator is declining. Around 60 per cent of permit holders were owner–drivers in the late 1980s, compared with 70 per cent earlier in the decade.

Several of the largest industrial companies have their own transport companies, notably Volvo Transport, IKEA, Distrolux (for Electrolux), Stora and Sandviken, most of which ship exclusively for their parent companies. However, Sandviken is one exception, selling third-party services to some 100 shippers. In general, these own-account services are regarded as the logistics leaders in Sweden. Many operate JIT systems, often over very long distances, for assembly plants.

Nonetheless, there is increasing competition from specialist services which are now being developed by the larger third-party freight companies. These specialist services are effectively 'tailor-made' to meet the needs of shippers and are superior to general haulage services in respect of quality and reliability. In parallel with this specialization is the rapid development of express service, notably with American involvement. Bilspedition Packet Services has been established in partnership with United Parcel Service, while ASG works with Federal Express to provide an alternative to the Swedish mail service.

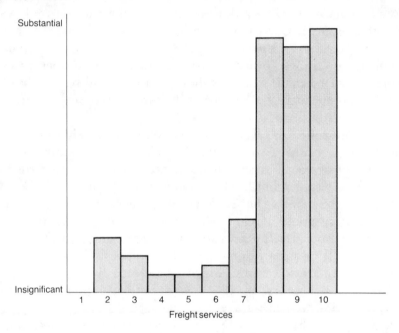

**Figure 9.8**  Freight service segmentation in Sweden. Freight service code: 1, –; 2, contract hire transport; 3, dedicated contract distribution; 4, dedicated contract transport; 5, shared contract distribution; 6, shared contract haulage; 7, express; 8, groupage; 9, general haulage and storage; 10, general haulage.

The market segmentation results for Sweden (see figure 9.8) show a concentration on common user services (from cells 8, 9 and 10). This most probably reflects the limited opportunities for specialist services afforded in a small, but wealthy, economy. Relatively long distances, both within Sweden itself and to major markets overseas, also make common user services the preferred option for many shippers.

# United Kingdom

The UK has had a liberalized haulage market for almost 20 years. Easier market entry had a profound effect on the suppliers of haulage services; fierce competition in general haulage forced many hauliers, especially the larger ones, to specialize much more than they did before deregulation. Companies such as Wincanton, NFC and Christian Salvesen now do very little, if anything, in the way of general haulage. They specialize either by type of service (such as vehicle contract hire or dedicated contract distribution) or by the type of product (such as chilled or bulk liquids).

It is also generally recognized that grocery retailers have been very influential in changing the role of the hauliers within the UK, giving them responsibilities for distribution rather than just transport, making IT an integral part of the distribution process, and using distributors to streamline merchandising (that is, by designating 'nominated carriers' which suppliers have to use, rather than delivering direct to the grocery retailer). This has happened mainly as a result of strong competition between grocery retailers; the five

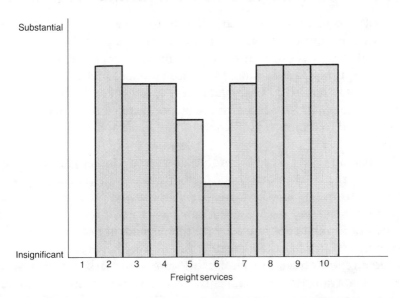

**Figure 9.9**  Freight service segmentation in the UK. Freight service code: 1, –; 2, contract hire transport; 3, dedicated contract distribution; 4, dedicated contract transport; 5, shared contract distribution; 6, shared contract transport; 7, express; 8, groupage; 9, general haulage and storage; 10, general haulage.

majors in the UK together account for about 60 per cent of all grocery sales, and competitive advantage is sought through more effective distribution.

The pioneering developments in distribution by the grocery retailers (see chapters 5 and 6) have, to a certain extent, been copied by the other, non-grocery retailers and manufacturing industry. However, the diffusion process has been slower, and more unevenly spread across these sectors.

Of all the countries surveyed, the UK has the widest developed range of services according to the market segmentation results (see figure 9.9). The weakest is shared contract transport (from cell 6), which seems to have lost its market share to dedicated services (from cells 3 and 4). Reasons which mainly account for this pattern of services are: deregulation in 1968 leading to rapid innovation through increased competition; oligopoly in grocery retailers creating demand-led changes to distribution practice; and a high geographical concentration of economic activity.

## Commentary on the Market Segmentation Results

Overall, the results confirm the important role that common user services continue to play in most European countries. Despite many claims that services are now overwhelmingly specialist, the general haulier continues to dominate the marketplace. Indeed, if anything the study has tended to *understate* the role of general haulage. This is because the *qualitative* responses of respondents with respect to scale have tended to diminish the importance of general haulage relative to other services.

Interestingly, the service profiles between the north European countries (the UK, Germany, the Netherlands and Sweden) were very different from one another. This seems to indicate that the structure of services for any one country will be sensitive to: the scale and concentration of economic activity; the dependence of hauliers upon international trade; the deregulation of the haulage sector; and attitudes of local freight users. But, of course, the market segmentation study is not an appropriate instrument with which to explain the service structure in terms of cause and effect.

Another observation concerns a possible north–south division within Europe. From the limited evidence so far available, it does not seem possible to conclude that southern Europe has a dramatically different structure of services as compared with northern Europe.

There is a preponderance of common user services in, say, Greece, but the same is true for Sweden. That is not to say, however, that services will always be comparable in *quality* between Greece and Sweden. The weight of anecdotal evidence, at the very least, would suggest that levels of customer service in northern Europe are better than in the south, and that quality is a key consideration when assessing the potential for, say, logistics development.

# How is the Market for Freight Services Changing?

As discussed earlier in the chapter, respondents to the market segmentation survey were asked about *change* in services; which ones were growing, which were static and which were in decline. Their responses to the question about change are summarized in figure 9.10, and the key trends identified are discussed in the following list:

- *Growing.* The services most consistently marked out as very strongly 'growing' are dedicated contact distribution (3) and express (7). Groupage (8) is also relatively strong, possibly reflecting the increasing demand for international services with Europe. The trend is also generally upward for dedicated contract transport (4), with the exception of the Netherlands which sees it as static. Contract hire transport (2) is also upwardly mobile except in Germany, where doubts about its legality have restricted its prospects.
- *Static.* Overall, shared contract transport (6) is seen as a 'static' performer. There is no perceived movement in market share in either Germany or the Netherlands. A small rise in Sweden is counterbalanced by decline in the UK. Shared contract distribution (5) is also reasonably static, with growth being confined mainly to the Netherlands.
- *In decline.* Without exception, general haulage (10) is in substantial decline across Europe. The position is similar for another common user service, general haulage and storage (9): only Greece is experiencing growth in this service.

Overall, therefore, it appears that there is a shift in Europe from common user services (such as general haulage, and general haulage and storage) to more specialized freight services, which have enhanced potential for logistics development. Dedicated contract distribution and express seem to be in particular demand. This has special implications for both the size of freight companies providing logistics services and their use of IT. Chapters 10 and 11 concentrate exclusively on these key aspects.

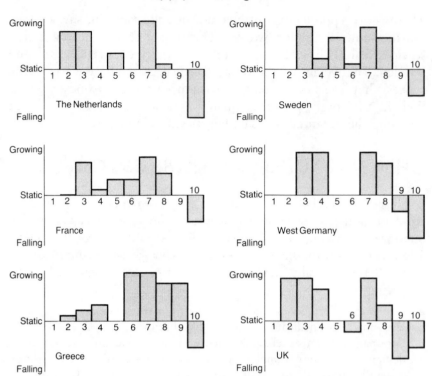

**Figure 9.10**   Changes in market share for freight services. Freight service code: 1, –; 2, contract hire transport; 3, dedicated contract distribution; 4, dedicated contract transport; 5, shared contract distribution; 6, shared contract transport; 7, express; 8, groupage; 9, general haulage and storage; 10, general haulage.

# The Own-account Sector

Not all logistics services are provided by third parties; for example, many manufacturers and retailers have in-house arrangements, especially for transport and warehousing. These 'own-account' arrangements will often be very similar to the kind of work that was described earlier in the chapter as 'dedicated contract distribution'. Indeed, dedicated contract distribution is often designed to mimic own-account operations.

The preference for own-account operations by some companies arises for a number of reasons, including the following:

- it avoids the need to pay the profit that the third-party contractor would expect to earn for providing logistics services
- it means that the needs of the logistics user can be met in a focused way, without the conflict of interest that may arise in, say, shared contract transport
- vehicles can be used as a medium for advertising the companies' products (although many third-party contractors now use their customers' liveries as a matter of course)

Similarly, there are numerous counter-arguments in favour of third-party services, including the following:

- it offers the opportunity to overcome industrial relations problems or peaks in demand, which sometimes occur in in-house transport service departments
- the purchase of third-party services can sometimes be shown 'off balance sheet' (depending on any one country's accountancy laws), which improves profitability ratios and the attractiveness of user companies to potential shareholders (Cooper and Johnstone, 1990)
- contractors providing third-party services are often better exposed to innovation than their in-house counterparts, making their services more cost-effective

Another major factor which has an important bearing on the extent of contracting out is, of course, freight regulation. In countries where regulation is strict this serves to limit haulage capacity, and own-account may be the choice of more logistics services users, compared with countries with deregulated haulage sectors.

The relative merits of contracting out also vary over time. As a result, there may be a shift towards own-account followed by a reverse trend; the pattern is rarely static. Consequently, there are different levels of own-account operation in different European countries, as shown in figure 9.6.

In the future the pattern of own-account transport is likely to change in Europe. Countries which may deregulate in the 1990s, such as Germany, are likely to show a decline in the importance of the own-account sector. By contrast, in the UK, which has long been deregulated, third-party penetration of the road freight market may already have reached saturation. Unless UK operators can successfully introduce new added-value services (such as labelling and packaging, and IT) then there may even be some reversion back to own-account operation. This may be especially true of those manufacturers and retailers which have learned from innovatory logistics practices brought in by third-party operators and then decide to do it themselves.

Perhaps the major challenge facing the own-account operator is the increasingly international nature of trade within Europe. Restrictions on own-account operation mean that they have very limited scope for backloading; this will only be possible when the own-account operator holds title to the goods being carried. As a result, many own-account operators must return empty after making deliveries, and on long international runs this means that it is difficult to remain competitive with international hauliers who are free to backload. Worse still, even fundamental cabotage rights are denied to own-account operators in the EC and elsewhere. Consider, for example, the hypothetical case of a French retailer with stores in both France and Spain. If the retailer runs an own-account fleet based in France, then its vehicles will not be able to carry goods owned by the retailer between any two of its Spanish locations (for example, warehouse to shop). There is a feeling among some trade associations that this restriction is unwarranted, and that it leads to inefficient resource use (Freight Transport Association, 1989). However, while it remains in force, the attractiveness of own-account operations will be reduced as trading grows between European countries.

# 10
# The Rise of the Mega-carrier

## What is All the Mega-fuss About?

Several key developments provide the foundation for the proposition that the 1990s will be the era of the freight mega-carrier, with the future European freight industry coming to be dominated by a few, very large, companies. First, activity in the freight transport and logistics industry has been stimulated by events beyond the freight sector, most notably the rise of mega-carriers in the airline world. This trend has led observers to conclude that there is an inevitable cycle taking place among service providers in which, perhaps, big may be bountiful, if not beautiful. Second, the globalization of manufacturing and the internationalization of retailing have stimulated the suppliers of logistics services to grow in an attempt to offer one-stop shopping to their principal customers. Finally, there is a strong feeling that deregulation in Europe, together with the implementation of the single market, must encourage the rapid move towards mega-carrier status for some freight transport and logistics service companies. Potential mega-carriers have the greatest opportunity to respond to these deregulated markets and new demands for Europe-wide services.

The result is almost certain to be an increasing concentration of ownership within the freight sector, with larger companies dominating more of the marketplace. Indeed, this is exactly what has happened in two other continental countries (the USA and Australia) following deregulation of their freight markets. There is some reason to suppose that Europe will develop along similar lines. Once Europe develops its own mega-carriers in freight transport, the consequences for the organization and marketing of freight services are likely to be dramatic.

The prospect that a small number of mega-carriers will come to play a dominant role in the European freight industry raises important questions:

- What will happen to traditional small and medium-sized companies?
- What will become of predominantly national activities?
- Will mega-carriers and 'one-stop shopping' signal the end for traditional freight forwarders (the architects of transport)?
- Which companies and sectors are ahead in the mega-carrier race?
- Do strategies aimed at achieving mega-carrier status really make sense in Europe?

Before exploring these points in depth it is timely to attempt a definition of a freight mega-carrier. In Europe, a mega-carrier would be a company servicing European distribution requirements at a Europe-wide level, and providing links between Europe and other major trade blocs. As a result we do not consider that large operators engaged mainly in, say, express services constitute freight mega-carriers. Although they may have a Europe-wide or even global capability, their service range is too narrow to allow them to enjoy mega-carrier status.

It is our contention that at present there are, indeed, no mega-carriers in European freight transport. However, there are signs that they are coming, and their development will have a dramatic effect within the freight industry and on relations between the freight industry and their customers. The way in which mega-carriers are evolving, how they are shaping their strategies, and the consequences of their growth go to the heart of understanding the European freight markets of the 1990s.

# The Changing Shape of the Freight Industry

## From fragmentation to concentration?

Considered as a whole, the European freight industry is highly fragmented; but not equally so in all sectors or all markets. In the road haulage sector the extremes within the EC are represented by the UK and Italy. In the UK, hauliers with one or two vehicles control only 25 per cent of the capacity, whereas in Italy the owner–operators (*padroncini*) have 98 per cent of truck capacity. Fragmentation is also apparent in the liner shipping sector more than 20 years after containerization. At the close of 1989 there were just over 200 deep-sea liner operations serving northern Europe (*Lloyd's Shipping Economist*, 1990).

Several reasons can be advanced to explain the phenomenon of fragmentation. One of the most significant is that certain sectors of the freight industry exhibit low entry costs; the road haulage industry is a prime example. As a result, there are always many small firms trying to enter the market. A further contributory cause of fragmentation is that in freight transport many of the present economies of scale are at the level of the individual vehicle (for example, larger trucks and ships), unlike in manufacturing where huge investment is often required in expensive facilities to achieve economies of scale. Therefore, small entrants are often able to compete against larger established operators in many freight sectors.

However, the picture is changing and there are clear signs of growing concentration. In a number of European countries the number of transport companies in the road haulage sector fell significantly in the period from 1970 to 1985 (table 10.1). This trend has continued and we can expect to see an increase in the average number of trucks owned or controlled by each transport company (table 10.2).

**Table 10.1** Changes in the number of road transport companies, 1970–85

| Country | Change (%) |
| --- | --- |
| Belgium | −33 |
| Netherlands | −23 |
| Spain | +31 |
| West Germany (long-distance) | −5 |
| France | +17 |

*Source*: Hambros Bank Ltd, February 1989, *European Road Transport and Distribution: Towards 1992*

At the European level only a small market share is controlled by even the largest transport companies. The top 50 road-based transport companies are listed in table 10.3, together with details of their revenues for the year 1989. The combined revenue for these companies is in excess of £30 billion, representing 37 per cent of the

**Table 10.2** Average number of trucks per transport company

| Country | 1970 | 1985 | Change (%) |
|---|---|---|---|
| Belgium | 2.2 | 4.3 | +95 |
| Netherlands | 2.7 | 6.0 | +118 |
| Spain | 1.6 | 1.5 | −5 |
| West Germany (long-distance) | 2.1 | 3.5 | +66 |
| France | 4.6 | 5.5 | +19 |

*Source*: Hambros Bank Ltd, February 1989, *European Road Transport and Distribution: Towards 1992*

**Table 10.3** Top 50 European road-based transport companies

| | Company | Country | Revenue (£ million) | Market share (%) | Cumulative market share (%) |
|---|---|---|---|---|---|
| 1 | Danzas | CH | 3 552 | 3.9 | 3.9 |
| 2 | Schenker | D | 2 555 | 2.8 | 6.8 |
| 3 | Bilspedition | S | 2 015 | 2.2 | 9.0 |
| 4 | Kuehne & Nagel | D | 1 881 | 2.1 | 11.1 |
| 5 | Nedlloyd | NL | 1 820 | 2.0 | 13.1 |
| 6 | NFC | UK | 1 494 | 1.7 | 14.8 |
| 7 | Sceta | F | 1 466 | 1.6 | 16.4 |
| 8 | LEP | UK | 1 387 | 1.5 | 18.0 |
| 9 | Panalpina | CH | 1 344 | 1.5 | 19.5 |
| 10 | Ocean Group | UK | 930 | 1.0 | 20.5 |
| 11 | ASG | S | 834 | 0.9 | 21.4 |
| 12 | Birkart | D | 805 | 0.9 | 22.3 |
| 13 | Internatio Muller | NL | 802 | 0.9 | 23.2 |
| 14 | Van Ommeren | NL | 729 | 0.8 | 24.0 |
| 15 | TNT | EUR | 722 | 0.8 | 24.8 |
| 16 | Interforward | S | 700 | 0.8 | 25.6 |
| 17 | Wincanton | UK | 652 | 0.7 | 26.3 |
| 18 | SCAC | F | 606 | 0.7 | 27.0 |
| 19 | TDG | UK | 593 | 0.7 | 27.6 |
| 20 | DFDS | DK | 566 | 0.6 | 28.3 |
| 21 | Haniel | D | 545 | 0.6 | 28.9 |
| 22 | P&O | UK | 518 | 0.6 | 29.5 |
| 23 | Mory | F | 506 | 0.6 | 30.0 |
| 24 | Gefco | F | 505 | 0.6 | 30.6 |
| 25 | Securicor | UK | 502 | 0.6 | 31.1 |

**Table 10.3** (*cont.*):

| | Company | Country | Revenue (£ million) | Market share (%) | Cumulative market share (%) |
|---|---|---|---|---|---|
| 26 | United Transport | UK | 365 | 0.4 | 31.5 |
| 27 | Saima SPA | I | 325 | 0.4 | 31.9 |
| 28 | Pakhoed | NL | 316 | 0.4 | 32.3 |
| 29 | Christian Salvesen | UK | 311 | 0.3 | 32.6 |
| 30 | Hays Distribution | UK | 302 | 0.3 | 32.9 |
| 31 | Saga Group | F | 301 | 0.3 | 33.3 |
| 32 | Merzario Group | I | 295 | 0.3 | 33.6 |
| 33 | Sanara | F | 261 | 0.3 | 33.9 |
| 34 | Gondrand | F | 236 | 0.3 | 34.2 |
| 35 | Thyssen Transport Group | D | 230 | 0.3 | 34.4 |
| 36 | Federal Express | EUR | 224 | 0.2 | 34.7 |
| 37 | DHL | EUR | 216 | 0.2 | 34.9 |
| 38 | DPD | D | 202 | 0.2 | 35.1 |
| 39 | Zust Ambrosetti SPA | I | 197 | 0.2 | 35.3 |
| 40 | Italsempione SPA | I | 185 | 0.2 | 35.5 |
| 41 | Frans Maas | NL | 180 | 0.2 | 35.7 |
| 42 | CAT | F | 180 | 0.2 | 35.9 |
| 43 | United Carriers | UK | 173 | 0.2 | 36.1 |
| 44 | Fernandez E Hijos | SP | 171 | 0.2 | 36.3 |
| 45 | Dubois | F | 163 | 0.2 | 36.5 |
| 46 | Frigoscandia | S | 158 | 0.2 | 36.7 |
| 47 | GCA Atrans | F | 158 | 0.2 | 36.9 |
| 48 | TFE | F | 153 | 0.2 | 37.0 |
| 49 | Coldstream | UK | 147 | 0.2 | 37.2 |
| 50 | Causse Walon | F | 134 | 0.1 | 37.3 |
| | Sub-total (Top 50) | | 33 608 | | |
| | European distribution market (estimated total) | | 90 000 | | |

*Source*: adapted from *Motor Transport*, 25 October 1990

total estimated amount spent on distribution in Western Europe (that is, £90 billion). But this exaggerates the apparent dominance of the top 50 companies, since their revenue figures include worldwide earnings. Moreover, when individual companies are considered it is clear that even the largest hold at the very most less than 3 per cent of the total European market.

However, it might be argued that at the European level, as well as nationally and sectorally, severe fragmentation will become a feature of the past as mega-carriers seize the market share held by small and even medium-sized transport companies. But will this really happen? Perhaps a more plausible scenario would suggest that mega-carriers will wish to control their transport networks but not necessarily own or employ all of the network resources; especially the trucks and the drivers. Therefore, the mega-carrier will concentrate on aspects where they can add value – such as inventory management and time-definite delivery – while leaving, say, the full load long-distance transport to owner–operators. For instance, the mega-carrier will choose to provide rather different services in densely populated regions compared with sparsely populated rural areas and may well not wish to do the long-distance trunking. A hypothetical network of services that a mega-carrier may need to offer across a European region is shown in figure 10.1.

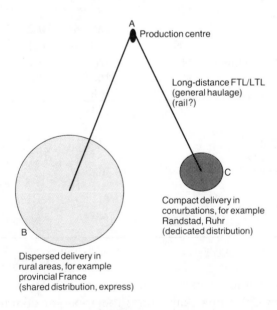

**Figure 10.1** Hypothetical network of services for a mega-carrier, based on logistics services requirements in European regions.

## Growing internationalization

By definition, mega-carriers cannot be confined to national boundaries, as they must be offering a range of services to customers within and between many countries. Yet a key feature of the freight industry is the parochial nature of many carriers, and it is vital to resolve the reason for this. The national service pattern of many operators is, above all, a reflection of the overwhelmingly domestic nature of most freight activity, and not the result of a spectacular lack of adventure on the part of the transport and storage companies.

Despite increased trade among EC member states and overall growth in international trade during the 1980s, most freight movement is still generated by domestic activity. For example, France imported and exported 44 million tonnes by road in 1988, yet domestic road freight traffic accounted for 1.4 billion tonnes. Therefore, it is not surprising that the ambitions of many logistics services providers have stopped at their national borders – no matter what sector they are principally concerned with.

Countries within the EC depend to differing degrees on external trade, and the Netherlands and Belgium play a particularly important gateway role for Europe. Carriers based in these countries can turn this dependence to their advantage, as they are able to offer Europe-wide services based on strong traffic flows from their home territory. The aggressive and successful marketing policy adopted by the Dutch international road haulage community is well known.

However, the complexity of international road movements, involving a variety of permits, delays at frontiers and low margins resulting from intense competition, have deterred many of the larger domestic carriers from exploiting this market sector. For somewhat different reasons small companies find it hard to be anything but parochial. Although they may be content with lower profit margins, small and medium-sized enterprises are frequently daunted by the bureaucratic difficulties of company formation in different countries, and have limited resources available for market research and strategy development.

European deregulation, the abolition of internal frontiers and harmonization of technical and fiscal matters will all help to boost trade among the member states of the EC, and make it simpler for all carriers to participate in that trade. However, we can expect to see not only increased cross-border traffic but also the growing internationalization of carriers' activities, with a company providing full national distribution services in more than one country. This does happen to a limited extent at present, but is in fact sometimes obscured because the carrier chooses to retain a national brand. A good example was the continued use of the name SAVAM in France, even after this large distribution company was bought by a UK company, United Transport.

## Increased specialization and use of third-party logistics services

Deregulation stimulates suppliers to 'add value' to their products (see chapter 8). For example, in a deregulated market general haulage may become too competitive; there are few opportunities for economies of scale and profit margins will fall. A strategy for larger carriers is to provide more specialized services such as contract distribution. Services of this type are complex, and much more integration can be expected between user and provider. Developments along these lines took place in the UK following deregulation of road transport, and there are parallels with the forthcoming liberalized single market.

The use of third-party logistics services will also increase in a deregulated market because manufacturers and traders will seek to replace in-house operations. In-house logistics are often used simply because of excessive control on price and capacity in the haulage sector. In addition, tight regulation stifles innovation and may have prevented or discouraged the development of innovative and large-scale services that manufacturers and traders are demanding from modern third-party logistics services providers, the mega-carriers of the future.

A switch to third-party logistics services can enable a manufacturer or retailer to concentrate on their core business, and while contracting out the entire logistics operation is at present largely a UK phenomenon this can be expected to spread as deregulation develops. As a consequence, opportunities for mega-carriers will grow.

# Directions, Options and Strategies in the Great Mega-carrier Race

## Carrier taxonomy

Given the rationale for the rise of the mega-carriers, a key question that remains is: how do the present large carriers achieve this new status? Put simply, mega-carrier status could be attained by one or more of the following actions; acquisition, organic growth or strategic alliance. Of the three, organic growth has been, and still is, impracticable in some European markets because of restrictions on market access. In response to this barrier to expansion, the main thrust of companies' growth has been by acquisition and, increasingly, by strategic alliance.

It is an obvious, although important, principle of navigation that you cannot sensibly decide which direction to go in if you are not sure where you are. As a result, any decision on the type of acquisition or alliance and where it should be made will clearly depend on where a particular carrier is starting from; and this in turn is dictated by the nature of the carrier. Identifying the starting point for a company (that is, what type of company it is) provides an insight into the service, territory and skills gaps that they need to close.

Moreover, the strategic choices facing the bigger companies are more easily understood when a conceptually simple but robust classification of carriers is considered. We have developed such a classification on the basis of the portfolio of services offered by a carrier together with their geographical presence. At the simplest level, major carriers can be divided among five principal types:

- airlines
- integrated parcels carriers (express operators)
- liner shipping companies
- freight forwarders
- distribution companies (offering haulage and storage)

It must be noted that the European railways are not in a position to achieve mega-carrier status because they are at present all confined to their national markets, controlled and funded as they are by their respective national governments. A classification of the current positioning of the five potential mega-carrier groups is shown in figure 10.2.

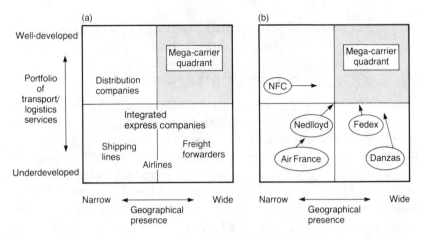

**Figure 10.2** Mega-carrier classification: (a) carrier and logistics services taxonomy; (b) current positioning of selected players.

Reference to the taxonomy suggests that the decision about acquisition depends very much on where the carrier is in the positioning map, and in which direction they must move to reach the mega-carrier quadrant. For instance, a large European freight forwarder may have more than adequate geographical presence but may lack key skills in, say, inventory management and the allied information systems. This will act as a significant brake on their ability to provide a well-defined portfolio of services to key customers, and so the acquisition or alliance need will be for companies with these missing skills. By contrast, major domestic distribution companies often have well-defined service portfolios, but lack Europe-wide presence and skills in cross-border flow control and customs management.

## The extent of merger and acquisition activity

By no means will all large freight companies be able to achieve mega-carrier status; indeed, some will not wish to do so, preferring instead to adopt a niche market strategy. Moreover, few, if any, carriers are able to go straight from being large operators to being mega-carriers. The financial implications of operating a completely 'closed loop' system in which all resources such as trucks, planes, terminals and drivers are employed by the carrier are considerable. Some prospective mega-carriers will seek the benefits of scale and control without the full financial commitment that total operation implies by subcontracting some activities. This highlights the critical role of IT, since some mega-carriers will develop logistics and transport control through information systems rather than control by ownership and 'doing'.

Rather than achieving mega-carrier status in one jump, companies must take a series of steps, building their service portfolios and extending their networks. It is intriguing to assess the direction of the mergers and acquisitions which have been the vehicle for change in this programme of company expansion.

One of the most exciting features of the logistics services sector between 1988 and 1990 was the spate of merger and acquisition activity. At first sight this process seems to provide conclusive proof that companies were responding to the imperatives of the single market. However, relatively little of the activity was cross-border and in the case of the UK the completed deals were mainly domestic (table 10.4).

**Table 10.4** Mergers and acquisitions in the transport sector involving the UK (UK-related deals in and out)

| Deals by UK companies in: | | Deals in UK by companies based in: | |
|---|---|---|---|
| UK | 114 | | |
| Benelux | 21 | Benelux | 2 |
| West Germany | 4 | West Germany | 1 |
| France | 2 | France | 2 |
| Other Europe | 6 | Other Europe | 4 |
| USA/Canada | 10 | USA/Canada | 5 |
| Australia/Pacific | — | Australia/Pacific | 3 |
| Total | 157 | Total | 17 |

*Source: Motor Transport*, 28 February 1990

It is revealing to look in rather more detail at the activity by sector (table 10.5). Clearly, the multi-service operators are leaders in terms of both their desire to expand geographically and their service range. By contrast, freight forwarding companies were relatively inactive as acquirers. Also, there are some doubts about the future role of freight forwarders after 1992, when the SEM will reduce the importance of some of their traditional skills, such as processing trade documentation. For some freight forwarders, inactivity in business development may equate to considerable uncertainty about the future.

**Table 10.5** Acquisition activity by sector

| Principal activity of acquirer | Principal activity of company acquired | | | | | | | | |
|---|---|---|---|---|---|---|---|---|---|
| | A | B | C | D | E | F | G | H | Total |
| A  Haulage and transport | 21 | 1 | 3 | 1 | 2 | — | — | 1 | 29 |
| B  Warehousing | 1 | 1 | — | — | — | — | — | — | 2 |
| C  Distribution | 7 | 3 | 4 | 1 | — | — | — | — | 15 |
| D  Parcels | 2 | — | 1 | 18 | 1 | — | — | — | 22 |
| E  Freight forwarding | 2 | 1 | — | — | — | — | — | — | 3 |
| F  Multi-service road-based | 16 | 3 | 11 | 1 | — | 1 | 1 | 3 | 36 |
| G  Multi-service multi-mode | 10 | 4 | 9 | 1 | 9 | — | 1 | 2 | 36 |
| H  Vehicle/tractor rental | — | — | — | — | — | — | — | 12 | 12 |
| I  Other | 5 | 1 | 4 | 3 | 2 | 1 | — | 3 | 19 |
| Total | 63 | 14 | 32 | 25 | 14 | 2 | 2 | 21 | 174 |

*Source*: adapted from *Motor Transport*, 28 February 1990

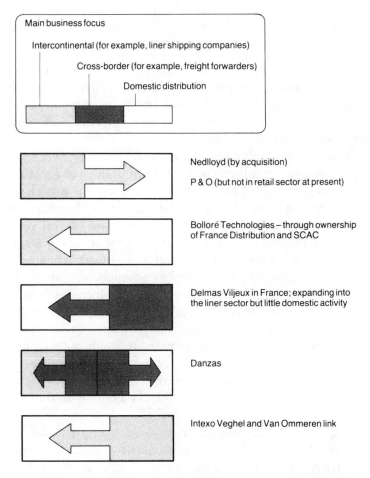

**Figure 10.3**   Directions for freight company growth.

The direction of freight companies' growth is illustrated in figure 10.3, using examples of companies which have chosen to develop in each way. Using the framework, it becomes evident that some growth directions are more common than others. Moreover, some companies may not perceive any logic in adding, say, cross-border skills to their portfolio and may, instead, move straight from domestic to intercontinental operations.

## Service branding: how to stay ahead in the mega-carrier race

Branding is a crucial part of the strategy in the drive for increased market share for a prospective mega-carrier. However, branding needs to be considered at two levels; namely, the company brand and the service brand. It is certain that large carriers will search for branding opportunities at both levels.

The influence of corporate fashion should never be underestimated. When millions of pounds can be spent to re-brand a chocolate bar (as was the case when the UK brand name 'Marathon' was changed to 'Snickers') then it is no surprise that transport and logistics directors get bitten by the same bug. However, there are several very good reasons for adopting branding as part of a mega-carrier strategy.

First, branding at the company level is important when selling the concept of one-stop shopping to large customers who are themselves global and have strong brand images (such as Mercedes Benz, Philips and Toyota). The action of Nedlloyd in re-branding all road-based activity as 'Nedlloyd Road Cargo' is in part a response to this need.

Second, the rapid rate of growth through acquisition puts considerable pressure on the prospective mega-carrier in terms of staff commitment and quality control; having a strong company image can play a key part in ensuring staff identify with the corporate goals.

Finally, at the service level, carriers are concerned to differentiate their service from many other very similar services. The prospective mega-carriers will all have to operate trucks and planes and ships of broadly similar quality, all meeting the same safety, pollution and noise regulations. By treating each type of service as a separate brand, carriers are doing what product companies have been doing for years – the marketing advantages are clear.

In the road freight sector, there are as yet very few great brands. When Exel Logistics was created within the National Freight Corporation (NFC), a brand awareness exercise was undertaken among 100 buyers of distribution services in the UK. A total of 93 separate company brands were identified, and each buyer named an average of only five or six. Amazingly, some buyers did not even name the companies that they used.

This situation is bound to change as freight companies become larger and need to establish a presence across the whole of Europe. Furthermore, branding for Europe – with its many different languages – is of crucial importance. Yet, curiously, in test marketing initials used as a company brand name do not fare well. A company launched using only initials will often have difficulty in establishing an identity: companies that succeed in this respect are usually those whose brands are already part of the international vocabulary, such as IBM or Fiat.

If anything, there is a greater problem with the branding of services. While consumer product brands, such as Perrier mineral water and Marlboro cigarettes, are recognized instantly, this is not true of freight service brands, even among users. A number of companies have recognized this as a problem and have taken steps to create and establish service brands. Nedlloyd is trying to do something similar with the rather anonymous activity of warehousing, using the brand name Districenters.

However, there is a long way to go. For example, 'dedicated contract distribution' accurately describes a service much in demand in the UK, but it hardly trips off the tongue. Its equivalent in Germany is *Massgeschneiderte-distribution* (literally, tailor-made distribution). What a marketing challenge it is for someone to create a pan-European brand name for these identical services.

## Building geographical and service coverage: a mega-carrier in the making

The Netherlands-based company Nedlloyd provides an excellent example of a carrier which has sought to build a bigger service portfolio and to broaden its geographical coverage. By examining the steps Nedlloyd has taken we can illustrate the opportunities and possible pitfalls of the move towards mega-carrier status. Our assessment is based solely on published press data and the company's own annual reports. In moving beyond its roots in shipping operations it is apparent that Nedlloyd has areas of strength and perhaps weakness. The strengths include:

- its potential for global logistics from liner shipping and road freight interests
- the fact that it originates from a country with powerful trading base centred on Rotterdam
- it can capitalize on the strong reputation of Dutch hauliers
- Dutch business culture is perceived by potential customers to be fairly 'neutral'

However, there are a number of areas of potential weakness:

- it is underdeveloped in some key service sectors (such as express and dedicated work)
- its geographical coverage of the EC still far from complete
- the company's financial and managerial resources are stretched as a result of its rapid expansion

To move beyond its traditional activities Nedlloyd has recognized that acquisition is the fastest way to achieve wider geographical coverage and build a service portfolio. By acquiring companies with specialist operations – such as the Dutch parcels carrier Van Gend en Loos – the potential mega-carrier buys into a new market and obtains new management skills. Nedlloyd has also acquired a number of other companies such as Transflash (UK), Messageria Emiliana (Italy), Andreas Christ and Union Transport (both in Germany).

However, the difficulty of obtaining the potential synergy between recently acquired companies may mean that, in the medium term, Nedlloyd's best prospect may be as a distribution architect for land services in Europe and global container logistics. In the long term the company could well achieve true mega-carrier status through its global logistics capability.

# Who Will Win the Great Mega-carrier Race?

## Strengths and weaknesses of principal competitors

The strengths, weaknesses and challenges faced by each type of company as they move beyond their current activity and territory are discussed in greater detail below. By forming a profile of the competitors in this way we can then consider whether, say, airlines have a greater opportunity than ocean carriers to become tomorrow's freight mega-carriers.

### Distribution companies

Many of the major national distribution companies have created well-branded services. For example, France Distribution System, a subsidiary of Bolloré Technologies, specialize in the distribution of fast-moving consumer goods in the French market, while in the UK Fashionflow, operated by Exel Logistics for Marks and Spencer, is a dedicated service for the movement of clothes. Retailers are important customers for these well-defined and branded services. What is more, many retailers have reached saturation point in their own markets and are therefore eager for expansion in a new larger single market. In turn, this could enable national distribution companies to 'piggy-back' their way into new markets as they seek mega-carrier status. So there would seem to be some clear advantages here for the distribution companies.

However, retailing – especially food retailing – does not always travel well (see chapters 5 and 6); and this will significantly slow the rate of geographical expansion for those companies who are only exploring the option of joining with their key domestic retail customers in ventures into new territory.

A key strength has to be the way large distribution companies offer one-stop shopping opportunities to customers. They frequently have a wide range of services on offer; often through subsidiary companies, each of which has one particular service as its speciality. However, one-stop shopping typically only applies to national markets, and real cross-border capabilities are the exception for many distribution companies.

## Liner shipping companies

Many of these companies have seen their market presence restricted because of liner conference and consortia agreements, but there are signs of significant changes (such as the break-up of the TRIO consortium that has dominated Europe–Far East trade). However, clearly defined national loading rights and tonnage limits mean that a shipping line may be part of a service calling at all major European ports but may only have a marketing presence in one or two countries. Therefore it is possible for a line to have UK loading and marketing rights but not be able to sell the same service to, say, French shippers.

The traditional ship-operating skills of the ocean carriers and liner companies have had to change dramatically in line with the technological changes in the industry (most notably containerization). To these skills have had to be added those required for complex terminal operations, as well as the developments brought about by the introduction of double-stack train systems in the USA. Some of the major lines are in a strong position to offer intra-European services to their customers (for example, German department stores importing goods from the Far East could be offered local delivery for other goods by, say, Hapag Lloyd). But as yet this large customer base has not really been exploited and shipping lines have, typically, been content to offer a relatively small portfolio of services. Many have concentrated primarily on door-to-door or port-to-port operations, with only the most limited added-value services.

## Freight forwarders

In the 1980s freight forwarders saw their traditional activities threatened from a variety of directions. The high-margin small-consignment end of their business has been attacked by the integrated parcels carriers offering guaranteed time-definite deliveries, while their lower-margin, high-volume cargo has been eroded by the decision of some air and ocean carriers to move into the retail end of the market and deal directly with shippers.

Big freight forwarding companies have a wide geographical presence both for sales and operational reasons (for example, customs clearance at borders, ports and airports). This presence, combined with a large customer base from a wide spectrum of industries, are strong plus points in the mega-carrier race.

However, they are undoubtedly handicapped by a perception of their services held by many shippers, who believe that freight forwarders have failed to develop a sufficient range of clearly branded services. Some freight forwarders have rightly been accused of trying to be all things to all people, saying in effect to shippers 'we have any service you need – just tell us what you want'. This contrasts with the branding of services by the domestic distribution companies and the integrated parcels carriers. In addition, freight forwarders within Europe are faced with the prospect of reduced revenues for customs clearance work after 1993 as the Single European Market (SEM) becomes a reality. Therefore, if freight forwarders are to feature in the mega-carrier race they need to focus their services with increasing accuracy. The Eurapid service introduced by Danzas is one sign of a changing approach.

## Integrated parcels carriers

The integrated parcels carriers are a relatively new freight transport phenomenon. Some of the key players, notably Federal Express and

TNT, have completely outgrown their domestic origins and are now set on a course of global expansion. Wide coverage is a prerequisite for parcels business due to the competitive nature of the industry and the very wide range of customers. But in Europe the parcels market has grown at different rates in each country, reflecting among other things regulatory and business interaction (such as postal monopolies). Thus the parcels networks are more developed in, say, the UK than in Spain.

However, in all the European countries the integrated parcels carriers are still expanding and are building denser networks (for example, TNT expanded their operations in Italy during 1990, opening 17 new depots). This expansion is largely driven by the economies of scale open to integrated parcels carriers. The mechanized systems developed to handle high volumes of traffic quickly make it advantageous to increase the flow, even if the yield per parcel falls somewhat.

Growth seems likely to come from two areas:

- increasing the package size handled, so that instead of having a cut-off point of perhaps 50 kg this is increased to 100 kg (a number of operators have been handling these higher weights for some time)
- encouraging shippers to switch from traditional groupage services to newer time-definite deliveries

However, importantly, growth could be lower than that achieved to date for two main reasons. First, when the integrated parcels carriers take on the larger consignments they are eating into a market in which freight forwarders and international road groupage operators are extremely strong, and in which there is only a limited advantage to be gained from central hubs and mechanized sorting. Second, universal improvements in IT could make it more difficult for the integrated carriers to sustain their competitive advantage (much of which has been built on superior IT capability).

## Airlines

Despite the similarity between some air freight carriers and integrated express operators, there is no doubt that many shippers still believe that airlines offer a fundamentally inferior service. The door-to-door or even floor-to-floor service offered by the integrated carriers with their closed loop systems gives them some important marketing advantages. However, many airlines are still happy to act as wholesalers and are not attempting to deal directly with any but the largest shippers. Some airlines, though, seem keen to take on the integrated carriers: 1990 saw the creation of an important multinational alliance between two airlines and an integrated small package operator, when in May, DHL, a leading courier and small-packages operator, sold minority stakes to the Japanese trading company Nissho Iwai, Lufthansa and Japan Airlines. Adding the airport-to-airport capability of the airlines to DHL's courier and parcels expertise is an important step towards the goal of a full-service global air cargo product.

On the cargo side of airline operations we can now see the rise of strategic alliances, most notably that concerning Lufthansa, Air France, Cathay Pacific and Japan Airlines. They have jointly formed a new umbrella company to develop an automated cargo information system, with the aim of providing faster and more efficient distribution throughout the world (Browne, 1991). The system will eventually link and coordinate regional distribution systems at a global level, and it will provide shippers and forwarders with direct access to the airlines' in-house computer systems, to give schedule and tracking information and to enable them to make cargo reservations. Shippers should be able to see the full range of services available and select the most appropriate one.

## An analytical approach to potential winners and losers

Throughout this chapter we have examined the nature of development in European logistics services, and in particular the rise of the mega-carrier. The task remains to make an assessment of whether it is possible to identify potential winners in the mega-carrier race – either by sector or by company. We have developed a straightforward framework for analysis by dividing potential mega-carriers into two main behavioural groups, which may be described as the 'traditionalists' and the 'adventurers' (table 10.6).

Among the traditionalists are numbered many freight forwarders and international hauliers. Freight forwarders are mostly concerned with facilitating the international movement of goods by buying in appropriate transport services and arranging the correct documentation. International hauliers will work either for the freight forwarders or directly for the shippers of goods, in what will often be long-established partnerships. It would be wrong to suggest that changes in the European marketplace will mean a collapse in demand for

**Table 10.6**  Classification of players in the European freight market

---

(a)  'Traditionalists'
This category includes many small to medium-sized freight agents and forwarders and international hauliers, as well as larger companies.


(b)  'Adventurers'
Here there are four subgroups, namely:

| | |
|---|---|
| Acquirers | Such as Federal Express, Nedlloyd, P&O, Lep, UPS and Inter Forward |
| Partners | Such as Sea-Land and Frans Maas, Dornbush Group Atlanta and Intersped, and Lufthansa and Air France |
| Co-operators | Such as Cavewood Transport (UK) and Marqueset SA (Spain) Stockeurop Logistics International (Association of small and medium-sized logistics companies in the UK, Ireland, France, Belgium and Germany) |
| Piggy-backers | Such as Exel Logistics–Fashionflow and Marks & Spencer, and TNT and News International |

---

either of these services. This will not happen, but there will inevitably be some modification of demand. For example, skills in handling documentation will become a less important feature of forwarding with the removal of cross-border formalities within Europe.

Moreover, these established freight companies in the traditionalist mould are likely to find that they will face increasing competition from the adventurers; which, we consider, fall into four groups.

First, there are the *acquirers*. This kind of freight company is actively expanding its geographical base and/or portfolio of services by buying companies in Europe. For example, Federal Express have bought Lex Systemline and Home Delivery Services (UK), SAIMEX (Italy), Elbe (Germany) and Transport Groep Alvracht (Netherlands). Some companies from outside the EC clearly see a need to develop their services in time for the launch of the SEM. The Swedish carrier Inter Forward acquired 18 companies within Europe, principally in the EC, in 1989 and 1990 (White, 1990).

Second, there are the *partners*. These are companies which have entered into a formal arrangement whereby not only are joint operations developed but there will also be joint marketing of services. Sometimes the partnership will extend as far as an exchange of shares. The essence of the arrangement is likely to be that the companies see mutual benefits from some shared strategic goal. The services of the partners will often be complementary, either in terms of service type and/or geographical coverage.

Third, there are the *co-operators*. The challenge for these companies is to find like-minded equivalents in other countries and to establish a working relationship with them. Tankfreight is a good example of a company adopting a co-operative strategy in Europe, having secured a working agreement with Rinnen, a German-based company with subsidiaries in France and the Netherlands.

Fourth, there are the *piggy-backers*; that is, freight companies which have strong associations with particular users of freight services within one country, and who extend that partnership to other countries. For example, the long association between Marks & Spencer and Exel Logistics (Fashionflow) in the UK has now been extended to France, to the mutual benefit of both companies.

Ambitious companies must follow one of the strategies within the adventurers' category. However, the specific way in which the strategy is pursued will depend to a considerable extent on the type of company involved. For example, distribution companies must look for acquisition or partnership, because organic growth or piggy-backing is sure to be too slow and it is doubtful whether they have the in-house ability to develop cross-border goods flow control (including customs management).

Given that distribution companies lack this key area of skills in both management and information systems, this may point to the opportunity for partnership, with or acquisition of, the experts in this field – the freight forwarders. It seems probable that we will see the emergence of some powerful combinations of major distribution companies and international freight forwarders in the next few years: this will be especially important in Europe with its strong freight forwarding sector.

Although the strengths of express operators and airlines may at first sight appear to be complementary, there are some deep-seated difficulties with partnerships, resulting from the essentially wholesale nature of airline freight operations. Therefore, when a partnership is struck up with one particular express operator, other users (express operators and freight forwarders) become suspicious about equality of treatment and seek alternative long-distance transport. For example, it remains to be seen whether, in the long term, Federal Express can overcome freight forwarders' initial hostility to their acquisition of Flying Tigers.

Perhaps a strategic alliance between an express operator and an ocean carrier would provide a launchpad for rapid global expansion. Moreover, there is really no service overlap, and the problem of wholesaler bias identified above would not be important. In addition, liner companies have a number of potential advantages:

- their global reach and the scope of their services
- financial muscle – buying ships requires considerable capital and shipping lines have well-developed skills at raising finance (essential for mega-carrier status)
- their wide spread of customers (international retailers and buying houses, manufacturers and basic processing industries)
- their market exposure in various geographical areas makes for less dependence on regional economic fortunes (for example in the event of a recession).

# Whither the Mega-carrier?

## Market dominance

A key question for the future of the mega-carrier concept concerns the size of these new companies. Is it indeed possible that some of them could contravene competition regulations within the EC by virtue of their dominant market position? In this context, it is revealing to consider what Max Grundhardt, managing director of the freight forwarding company Haniel, has been quoted as saying (CBI/TNT Express, 1990):

> Even if the largest freight forwarder teamed up with the biggest operator they would still have less than five per cent of the total market.

Clearly, definitions are important to this statement (such as what is meant by the total market). However, if we refer back to table 10.3, which showed the top 50 road-based transport companies in Europe, we can see the underlying truth of the comment. Using the companies and figures listed in table 10.3 it is clear that if the largest freight forwarder in Europe (generally agreed to be Danzas) teamed up with the largest distribution specialist (NFC) they would have between five and six per cent of the total European distribution market. A carrier of this size offering Danzas's geographical coverage together with NFC's range of services would have every right to be considered a mega-carrier, and yet there would be no question of it having a truly dominant market position. Moreover, that figure of six per cent is certainly something of an exaggeration, and the actual market share held by the companies listed in table 10.3 will be rather less than that shown, since:

• the revenue figure used by the survey compilers was based on the total worldwide revenue for the companies listed, whereas we are comparing this to the total west European distribution market
• the revenue figure for some companies includes non-transport and non-logistics activities such as property and travel

Given these points it is clear that, although mega-carriers will have a very different market role from that presently occupied by large carriers, they are unlikely to be dominant in the market as a whole. Naturally, their dominance may be somewhat greater in certain specific market sectors.

## Possible pitfalls?

If there is one factor above all others encouraging large freight companies to become mega-carriers it is the desire of logistics users for one-stop shopping. But is it possible that it will be too great a challenge to provide the tremendous service range and geographical coverage required by a multinational company wanting one-stop shopping? Are freight companies biting off more than they can chew?

There do seem to be some inherent difficulties in satisfying shippers' demands for true one-stop shopping. It should be noted that several of the largest freight companies within North America essentially provide a narrow range of services (mainly LTL), albeit across a wide geographical area. The more imaginative US companies such as Federal Express have sought to develop in a much broader way – but this has led to a number of problems. Until 1990 most of the top management of Federal Express in the UK had been in British hands, but this now has changed and managers from the USA have been brought in instead.

The enormous financial resources required to develop these far-flung networks also brings difficulties, and we have already noted the pressure placed on Nedlloyd as they finance rapid growth in the European market. In short, it has to be recognized that there are a variety of difficulties and pitfalls which face carriers as they expand the area that they cover and the service portfolio that they provide. Among the most significant are the following:

- it can be difficult to successfully develop strategic alliances across different business and management cultures
- apparent synergies may in reality be more difficult to exploit than anticipated (for example, the acquisition of Flying Tigers by Federal Express has failed to deliver the expected returns)
- it can be difficult to integrate information systems following mergers, joint ventures and strategic alliances
- there may be problems of control with rapid growth (such as Rockwoods' difficulties, which led ultimately to the company going into receivership)
- retreat is difficult – once a carrier starts to offer one-stop shopping then to step back from this strategy and try to select only higher revenue earning activities can result in the loss of key customers

The clear implication is that the concept of mega-carriers in the freight business makes good sense and that many shippers would welcome its development. However, the practical problems of becoming a mega-carrier are considerable. Could it be that some companies currently trying to achieve mega-carrier status will find that they are chasing a concept which is ahead of its time?

# Case Study    Nippon Yusen Kaisha (NYK): a global strategy

The traditional activity of NYK has been ocean transport, and the company have operated port-to-port services between Europe and the Far East since 1896. Shipping remains the company's principal business, and NYK control a fleet of 322 ships carrying some 70 million tonnes annually.

Low economic growth and uncertainty over the prospects for shipping led NYK to restructure and devise a strategy based on increasing their activities to encompass more door-to-door rather than merely port-to-port operation services. One result of this decision was the formation of NYK Line Europe in 1990, specifically to promote NYK's logistics activities in association with the Group's ocean transport and to further coordinate NYK's European operations.

Significantly, the NYK Group has devised a corporate strategy for the twenty-first century, known in-house as 'NYK 21'. The objective of 'NYK 21' is to move the company beyond sea transport to become a fully integrated logistics service; in short, to become a mega-carrier with a wide portfolio of services. NYK plan to achieve this primarily through the coordination of its large number of affiliated companies in air cargo, forwarding, warehousing and road transport. However, strategic acquisition is also an option, and may well be the preferred route in order to achieve rapid growth.

The corporate goal is to strengthen NYK's forwarding services, logistics activities, air cargo business and land transport, so that they provide 30 per cent of NYK's revenue (they currently account for 10 per cent). To do this NYK must build an integrated network to encompass sea, land and air services. A major part of this strategy rests on the continuing development of NYK Logistics Centres at key locations around the world.

## NYK's Logistics Centres

Logistics Centres are in operation worldwide, and additional centres are planned (see table 10.7). These centres provide more than warehousing: importantly, NYK see them as being focused on

**Table 10.7**  NYK Logistics Centres

| Location | Floor space (m²) | Started operation (to be opened) |
|---|---|---|
| Tokyo | 22 500 | 1987 |
| Kobe | 22 000 | 1989 |
| Taipei | 3 200 | 1989 |
| | 10 800 | 1975 |
| Hong Kong | 7 200 | 1988 |
| | 5 850 | 1990 |
| Bangkok | 10 000 | 1988 |
| Singapore | 20 000 | 1990 |
| Malaysia | 10 000 | (1991) |
| Sydney | 13 000 | 1989 |
| Los Angeles | 35 000 | 1989 |
| Toronto | 3 900 | 1986 |
| Copenhagen | 1 500 | 1985 |
| Dusseldorf | 7 700 | 1988 |
| Rotterdam | 5 000 | 1990 |
| Antwerp | 20 000 | (1991) |
| Milan | 20 000 | (1991) |
| London | 20 000 | (1991) |

*Source*: NYK, 1990

supplying a range of logistics services, such as inventory management and order picking, to their customers. NYK's Logistics Centre concept aims to give clients the benefits of centralized inventory control, in order to facilitate reduced inventory levels and transport utilization. Each centre will have expertise in land, sea and air transportation, with its own collection and delivery network. Information technology (IT) has been identified by NYK as the essential key to modern logistics, and each centre is networked with the others to provide global consignment tracking and tracing.

Some NYK Logistics Centres go even further in providing a range of services to customers. In Singapore, for instance, the Logistics Centre provides a Materials Requirements Planning (MRP) service for a Japanese electrical goods manufacturer: NYK consider this to be a largely untapped area for involvement by logistics suppliers.

MRP involves matching master production schedules with parts lists, vendors, dates and lead times, to ensure a least-cost and orderly arrival of materials for the production process. That arrival can, if appropriate, be on a JIT basis. Clearly, as the number of parts and vendors increases so does the complexity of the MRP system.

NYK contend that manufacturers can gain an advantage by contracting out MRP to experienced logistics specialists. The master production schedule can be transferred to NYK's computer, MRP can be carried out simultaneously and purchase orders may be issued to the vendors with or without NYK taking title to the goods. The merits to the client of such a system are stated to be:

- freedom from procurement arrangement and documentation
- freedom from monetary settlement with vendors
- human resources released for other productive tasks

The case study highlights the way in which a company with wide geographical coverage but a limited range of services has to add complex skills in areas such as inventory management and final distribution in the race to become a global mega-carrier. The NYK 21 corporate strategy is clearly ambitious. However, NYK's global capability, together with their strong links with many powerful manufacturers, suggests that they are well on their way to becoming one of tomorrow's mega-carriers.

Source: Paper given by Mr Akira Sugawara (Chairman, NYK Line Europe Ltd) entitled 'A European logistics strategy for a global Japanese company', 7th European Conference on Logistics (Eurolog), Madrid, April 1990

## Case Study   NFC

NFC is one of the largest freight companies in Europe, with an annual turnover of more than £1.4 billion. How it attained this high ranking is an extraordinary story, which has been told by its Chairman, Sir Peter Thompson, in a recent book (Thompson, 1990). This case study is drawn both from the book and from interviews with senior executives within NFC.

The origins of NFC go back to the immediate postwar period in the UK, when an extensive programme was launched to bring selected companies into state ownership. Many of these companies were large, and were considered to be pivotal in industries of key economic importance, such as steel, coal mining and shipbuilding. But, simultaneously, a large number of small hauliers were also 'nationalized'; this event effectively marked the beginning of NFC.

During the 1950s and 1960s there was an alternating sequence of nationalization and denationalization of various companies, depending on the political persuasion of the government in power. Yet, during all this time, the status of the nationalized companies in the haulage industry remained untouched; partly because no government thought that potential private-sector buyers would find them an attractive proposition.

NFC came into being as the holding company for nationalized haulage following the 1968 Transport Act. This Act also had the effect of bringing economic deregulation to the haulage sector; so NFC became, during the late 1960s and 1970s, increasingly exposed to competition from privately owned haulage companies. Parcels businesses were hit hard by new competition. National Carriers Limited (NCL), one of the two parcels companies owned by NFC, lost a pound sterling for every pound it earned in 1969. By 1975, NFC had operating losses of £16 million, which rose to £31 million after extraordinary items and interest were taken into account. Loan interest was a particularly onerous burden, since nationalized industries were financed entirely by debt, with fixed interest payments to be made each year. Therefore, if a nationalized business lost money it was forced to borrow to pay the losses – and so its interest burden would be much higher in the following year.

By 1980, it became clear to senior management within NFC that it would never be successful as a nationalized company. Under the leadership of Peter Thompson, the company proposed to government that there should be an employee buy-out. Under the plan, NFC would be owned by employees who had chosen to buy shares. As a result, they would participate in policy-making, but the managers would retain the authority to manage. The wealth created would be shared by all employees.

For the purposes of the buy-out NFC was valued at £53.5 million, and sold to its employees in February 1982. The result has been a transformation of the company, in no small part due to the commitment of employees who, as shareholders in the company, effectively worked for themselves. In 1982 there were 23 000 people on the payroll and the numbers were falling. NFC currently employs 33 000 around the world, and the total continues to rise. Financial results too have been impressive. For six consecutive years after the employee buy-out, NFC achieved annual compound growth in profits before tax in excess of 40 per cent. Growth in earnings per share was above 30 per cent.

In the late 1980s, NFC took two important decisions affecting the ownership and organization of the company. First, it became apparent that the 'internal market' operated by NFC for share trading could not be sustained for long. As a result, a decision was taken to obtain Stock Exchange listing, a complicated undertaking since it involved giving double voting rights to employee shareholders to retain employee control of the company. On 6 February 1989, this goal was realized, with NFC shares being traded on the London Stock Exchange for the first time.

The second key decision of the late 1980s changed the way NFC was organized. As NFC companies had expanded during the 1980s they had explored new market opportunities, with the result that overlap had developed in some of their activities. One unwanted consequence was that, in bidding for contracts, some NFC companies found that they were bidding against each other. A decision was taken to rationalize NFC's organization to eliminate this problem, which also provided an opportunity to re-brand some of the companies. The reorganization led to the creation of four separate divisions, each with its own specialization; namely, logistics, transport, home services (predominantly Pickfords Removals, a worldwide company), and travel and property. The major branding initiative was in the launch of Exel Logistics, which specializes in part or total supply chain management; from the transport of raw materials into the manufacturer, to work-in-progress, inventory management and distribution to the retailer, or even direct to the customer's home. The range of services is expanding all the time to cater for new demands in the contract logistics market.

The 1980s also saw a major shift in strategy regarding NFC's geographical area of operation. At the 1982 employee buy-out, virtually all earnings were from the UK. Since then there has been substantial diversification overseas, first in the USA and then in

Europe. Major US acquisitions have been Dauphin, Minuteman and DCI. Business has also been won in France and Spain, where Sadema has recently been purchased. Other acquisitions are expected soon in Germany.

In some respects, NFC has been late in its European expansion, compared with some of its competitors. However, given its unimpressive performance as a nationalized company up until 1982, and the demands on management time brought about by the buy-out, Stock Exchange launch and then reorganization, the achievements in less than a decade have been impressive by any standards. NFC is now a streamlined company with well-defined products, spanning the spectrum of logistics activities. While the company clearly has some way to go before it can be described as a European mega-carrier, the essential first steps have been taken towards this aim. In combination with its entry into the US market, NFC clearly has the potential to develop as a global player in logistics, mainly through the Exel Logistics Division, in line with its declared mission statement.

## Case Study    Lep Group: European Service Portfolio Builders

Lep is one the world's largest freight forwarders and already has transport operations on the continent, such as Lassen in Germany, to support its freight forwarding activities. However, as the national barriers come down the role for freight forwarders in the EC will change dramatically. There will be an increasing role for logistics and distribution companies – a fact which is recognized by Lep.

In 1985 Lep purchased Swift Transport Service with the intention of using Swift as a model for developing European operations. Swift specializes in time-definite services, such as just-in-time deliveries of components, for the automotive and consumer goods industries, operating both dedicated and common user services. In the UK, for example, Swift have a contract with Ford to collect, consolidate and deliver production components from suppliers to Ford's production plants nationwide. This same model of operations is in the process of being transferred to Lep's more recent acquisitions.

Continental acquisitions came in 1988; first Maro Trans and Jean Vincent in Belgium, followed by Steenbergen in the Netherlands. In 1989 the re-branded Lep Swift made a major move into the German market with its £8.7 million purchase of Wohlfarth. While the majority of Wohlfarths's business is domestic, it does have railheads in Paris, Milan and Madrid, offering Lep Swift access to the intermodal market in Europe, which is becoming increasingly important. In total Lep

**Table 10.8**   Lep Swift European network

| Country | Number of depots | Number of vehicles |
| --- | --- | --- |
| UK | 19 | 750 |
| Germany | 51 | 1250 |
| Belgium | 4 | 100 |
| Netherlands | 2 | 60 |
| Italy | 17 | 400 |
| Spain | 1 | 20 |
| Austria | 4 | 200 |
| Denmark | 5 | 500 |
| Total | 103 | 4280 |

*Source*: *Distribution*, 1990

Swift operate over 2100 vehicles in Europe from 76 depots spread throughout the countries shown in table 10.8.

Lep Swift recognize the importance of domestic freight flows, and although the company is well known for its international trunking services these have been grafted onto the existing and profitable domestic networks of the companies that they have acquired. Indeed, all Lep Swift's acquisitions earn between 60 and 80 per cent of their revenue from domestic activities, and it is intended that this balance will continue.

Lep Swift's strategy has been to concentrate on industrial customers who demand high service levels, with the goal of establishing long-term relationships with a few select clients (for example, Swift UK has worked with Ford for 30 years). At first sight this niche market approach may seem to preclude mega-carrier status. But Swift is only a part of Lep's total service portfolio, and the size of Lep's present operations together with their recent acquisitions means that the group has the potential to be considered as a European mega-carrier at some time in the 1990s. Significantly, closer links are already being forged between the freight forwarding activities of Lep International and the physical distribution activities of Lep Swift. The combination of extensive geographical coverage and skills in all areas of supply chain management will, in many cases, provide Lep with a competitive edge.

The thinking underlying the strategy to build a service portfolio that can satisfy sophisticated national logistics demands as well as provide international cross-border services is summarized by John Brotherton, Chief Executive of Lep Swift:

Freight forwarders are comfortable with the international environment; distribution companies in the main are not. So within the
Lep group we have a massive advantage. Lep Swift considers
that it has the advantage in having the facility to use the
contents and organization of the freight forwarding companies
within the Group. The Lep Group is in a very good position
because of its integration of distribution and freight forwarding
interests. This is a significant acknowledgement of the transformation of the freight forwarding market in Europe into one of
logistics and distribution.

In the meantime Lep has a profitable freight forwarding
business to run. . . But without a distribution culture in the
Group it would obviously leave us exposed in however many
years it took for the demise of freight forwarding in Europe.

Source: From an interview in *Distribution*, September–October 1990
Note: Since this interview, LEP Group has sold two Belgian companies
back to their original owner and Swift Transport Services has been
purchased from the parent company through a management buyout.

# 11

# Information Technology: Competitive Advantage or Necessity?

## Introduction

Information technology (IT) is an ill-defined term covering a wide area of technological applications including micro-electronics, data processing, robotics, communications, sensor applications and software packages. The common element linking these applications is the opportunity to improve information flows resulting from data capture and data analysis. It is this opportunity that makes IT important to logistics.

There is no doubt that the information component of logistics is growing in importance. Acceptable logistics services packages are no longer concerned only with the physical aspects of the service, but are becoming ever more concerned with the administrative, or information, aspects of managing that service. Increasingly, manufacturers and retailers demand that business be conducted electronically. Information systems have become a key ingredient of the logistics services package. Moreover, many companies see information systems as being a route to achieving sustainable competitive advantage; part of this chapter will, indeed, focus on whether IT implementation can actually produce sustainable advantage in logistics performance.

The field of IT is very wide, complex and rapidly changing. As a result, it is most useful to focus on a number of key issues rather than try to produce an all-embracing but superficial survey of developments which would be out of date even before publication. First, it is essential to examine the way in which IT fits into the framework of logistics activities. Second, we will highlight some of the difficulties caused by inadequate information systems and the lack of integrated IT applications, and evaluate the potential benefits that will flow from overcoming these. The third area of concern is to classify IT applications and assess their potential impact. It is then vital to identify examples of the ways in which logistics services providers have sought to use IT for competitive advantage. Finally, we consider whether the competitive advantage from IT is sustainable, and whether there are any lessons from implementation strategies that are important to prospective mega-carriers (see also chapter 10).

# IT Applications and Their Role in Logistics

The value chain concept (Porter, 1985) simply disaggregates the firm into its strategically relevant activities and provides a framework within which cost and the potential for differentiation may be examined (figure 11.1). As such it provides a useful starting point to consider the contribution that can be made by IT. To remain competitive a firm must control the major costs in its own value chain and in the upstream and downstream value chains of suppliers, distributors and end customers. Applications of IT have the potential to play a vital part in controlling costs and enhancing service quality.

Information technology is part of the value chain at every point. Every value activity has a physical and an information dimension,

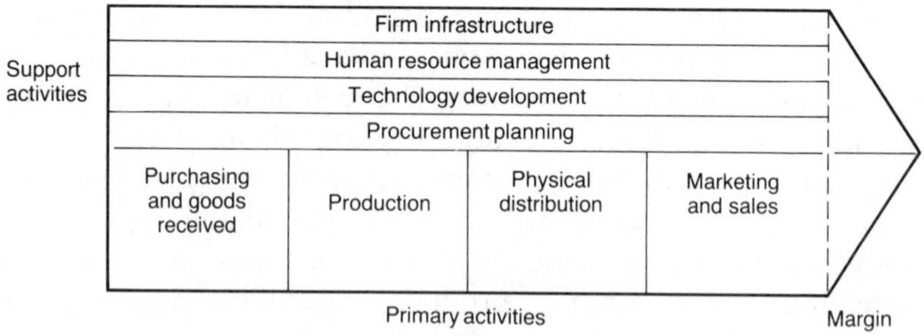

**Figure 11.1**  The value chain concept.
*Source*: Adapted with permission of The Free Press, a Division of Macmillan, Inc. from *Competitive Advantage: Creating and Sustaining Superior Performance* by Michael E. Porter. Copyright © 1985 by Michael E. Porter

because each value activity creates information and at the same time uses information. Consequently, IT in one value activity can have a direct impact on another activity, not least in the structure of costs. This applies not only to the value chain of a firm in isolation, but also to the value chains of their customers and suppliers. So, for example, a company can make a valuable contribution to the procurement and in-bound logistics activities of its clients by giving them access to its inventory and production scheduling database; their customers will know in advance what to expect, and the information will be up to date. Similarly, the firm could make manufacturing scheduling much more effective for its suppliers if it allowed them to have access to its forward orders database. And these could be suppliers of raw materials, or of services – say, logistics services providers.

Clearly, automating and using IT on your own is not enough. In order to really achieve a high level of benefits it is essential that suppliers also take part. This is demonstrated by an example from the automotive industry (*The Economist*, 1990b). At Nissan's UK factory in Sunderland the plant computer calls up the computer of its seat supplier, Akeda–Hoover, every day to schedule Hoover's daily production. Seats of each colour and style are scheduled in such a way that they can roll straight out of Hoover's door and into a car waiting on Nissan's assembly line.

Similarly, Ford estimates that it now carries out daily production scheduling with about half of the 1000 European suppliers with which they have electronic links. The importance for logistics services providers to be part of this electronic network is abundantly clear; gaps in the network will dramatically reduce the total potential benefits. Looking again at the above example from Nissan, if the carrier is unaware of the schedule for seats then they cannot play a full part in ensuring just-in-time delivery.

Changes are also evident in the way in which companies pay for goods. Instead of trading several slips of paper, each of which must be matched with physical parts, large manufacturers want to be able to send an order electronically to their suppliers and then transfer funds electronically when the goods are received. The 'goods received' element of the transaction can be done using bar-code technology and light pens or scanners.

However, a major difficulty at present is the essentially 'closed' nature of many of the IT systems used to support the firm's value chain. These systems can be considered as closed systems in several ways. For example, some information systems may only be applied to certain narrow tasks within a firm, such as computerized payroll systems. Other information systems may be closed because they are only applied in specific industry sectors (vertical systems such as ODETTE in the motor industry or CEFIC in the chemical industry). This is a major problem for logistics services providers, because logistics is essentially a horizontal activity, linking together as it does not only a company and its suppliers and customers but also external partners such as banks and customs.

In addition, many systems may be closed in the sense that their high cost excludes small and medium enterprises from access. This problem of disjointed information systems leads on to the overall consideration of problems caused by inadequate information transfer; something that correctly applied IT solutions could consign to past history.

# Inadequacies in Information Transfer: the Implications for Logistics

Organizations and enterprises concerned with goods movement need to have access to the same updated information at the right time in many locations. A number of weaknesses in the present systems for information transfer are evident among European trade and industry. First, it is expensive to handle documents connected with trade, and the cost is magnified when trade becomes international. Paperwork-related costs in international trade are estimated to be between 3.5 per cent and 15 per cent of the value of the goods (Frybourg, 1989). The costs arise because most information is entered manually and transferred by post or voice. It is estimated that some 80 per cent of computer output is subsequently 'input' again manually, due to poor integration between information systems and the limited use of IT applications such as Electronic Data Interchange (EDI).

Although growth in the application of EDI has been rapid, its use has to be regarded as being in its infancy. Greater use of EDI would ensure reduced data entry costs, reduced clerical errors, and reduced copying and transmission costs. In the UK alone, errors in document sets presented under letters of credit are estimated to cost exporters almost 80 million ecu a year (Dawson, 1989). This situation must change if competition in world markets in the 1990s is to be successful.

In addition, because information transfer is incomplete and

unreliable, resource planning is done using inadequate information. For example, many shippers plan despatch well before booking freight space; but if freight forwarders (by means of, say, an automated booking system) were aware of shippers' plans, there would be much more opportunity for consolidation and optimal routing.

Goods often arrive before documents. This causes difficulties because information from the documents will typically be needed downstream to allow the shipment to flow along the logistics chain. For example, there are potential delays at major transport interfaces such as rail terminals or ports where goods are transferred from one mode to another. In turn, delays lead to extra costs, both in terms of additional space requirements and storage management costs.

Customs arrangements made by industry highlight a further area in which information inadequacies present a problem and a cost. Overall customs-related administrative costs borne by the EC business community amount to 7.5 billion ecu (Cecchini, 1988). The Single European Market (SEM) will do much to reduce this burden, but developments in IT can contribute significantly, and will be of special importance for the large volume of external trade between EC member states and the rest of the world. IT developments include both data transfer activities, such as Direct Trader Input in the UK, where shippers and freight forwarders are able to make on-line clearances of imports and exports, and also expert systems to help with tariff number selection.

By 1992 it is anticipated that each EC member state should have its own customs mainframe computers, providing interfaces for all exporters and importers. One plan has these mainframes linked to the EC's mainframe in Brussels, which will control payment of duties, VAT and the collection of statistical information, no matter where a shipment is imported or exported within the EC. A potential problem for shippers, forwarders and carriers is that they will all have to be able to interface with the mainframes of existing member states if they wish to take advantage of streamlined customs systems.

Specific transport-related problems caused by inadequate information transfer occur in a number of areas. Among them are the underutilization of vehicle capacity and the relatively limited use of multimodal road–rail systems.

The Cecchini Report (1988) has commented on the existence of much underutilized capacity in the form of part-loaded and empty lorries. The causes of poor utilization are three-fold:

- freight market regulation restricting loading opportunities
- imbalances of freight traffic flows
- insufficiently good information on the whereabouts of loads and vehicles to carry them

Better information through the use of IT will therefore go some way to reduce empty running and improve vehicle productivity. If capacity utilization were improved by only 5 per cent, as a result of initiatives in the IT area, then operating cost savings of 390 million ecu a year could be made (figure based on 1986 EC freight traffic volumes and costs). At the social and environmental level, improved utilization of transport capacity confers safety benefits, and reduces congestion and pollution.

Multimodal road–rail transport using swap bodies and semi-trailers suffers from problems relating to information flow which have restricted its development. At multimodal terminals there can be delays caused entirely by information problems. IT can help to resolve these problems for multimodal transport, thereby ensuring greater economic, social and environmental benefits from improved road–rail co-operation.

Having examined some of the broader problems facing IT in logistics, the following section considers IT applications according to their classification, and assesses the benefits which can be expected from particular applications.

## Classification of Systems and Their Probable Benefits in a European Context

Given the wide-ranging definition of IT, it is helpful to categorize both actual and potential IT applications for logistics services. We broadly agree with Tarkowski and Irestahl (1988), who suggest that the many possible applications can be resolved into one of the following four categories:

- *transaction systems*, which process the daily transactions in the company (such as order processing and invoicing)
- *operative planning systems*, which coordinate resource utilization, such as capacity planning and the routing and scheduling of vehicles
- *controlling systems*, which measure and control costs and incomes, productivity and performance
- *directive information systems*, which support overall planning and

strategic decision-making (including simulation models such as Exel Logistics' AWARD system for warehouse layout)

The following assessment of IT systems according to their classification represents a distillation of the results from a 1989 survey carried out jointly by the FLEET and EUROFRET[7] consortia as part of the DRIVE programme of research into IT and road freight transport. This survey had the major aim of determining the scale of benefit that road freight operators across Europe are expecting from IT: hence the larger the expected benefit, the more likely it will be that operators will want to adopt a particular IT system. Although the survey was confined to road freight operators, many of the companies which took part have other interests such as combined transport and shipping. As such, the results provide a unique insight into the expected benefits from the various kinds of IT applications used in transaction systems, operative planning systems and controlling systems.

## Transaction systems

Transaction systems represent a key issue in IT development. Transport operators in many European countries (especially in the north) have long had computerized accounting and routine transaction systems. As discussed earlier in this chapter, the challenge for these operators is to link these systems with trading partners (such as shippers and forwarders) and governmental authorities (such as customs) to speed transactions, ease the burden of paperwork and gain competitive advantage. The expected scale of benefits from different transaction systems, as assessed by respondents to the survey, are shown in table 11.1.

A number of additional comments from the respondents highlight the divergent views taken about transaction systems by operators from different countries:

- Freight exchange has had a better record of success in some countries than others. In the UK, Datafreight and Cargofax both failed, whereas in the Netherlands, a closed system for freight exchange (Tradicom) has been reasonably successful among small and medium-sized companies, although larger ones are not keen to participate.
- Open systems for freight exchange (such as Teleroute and Transpotel) are not as popular as closed ones. Interestingly, in France, the Minitel system is used by small and medium-sized companies to search for freight; large companies are only occasional users.

**Table 11.1** Transaction systems: the expected benefits

| IT applications | Expected scale of benefit |
| --- | --- |
| Freight exchange (especially for backloading) | High |
| Paperless invoicing | High |
| Shipper/forwarder transactions | High |
| Forwarder/carrier transactions | High |
| Shipper/carrier transactions | High |
| Carrier/carrier transactions | Medium |
| Automatic debiting on toll roads | Medium |

Source: EUROFRET (1990)

- Greek and Spanish operators, with their low level of operating costs, are keen to see a pan-European freight exchange, as they believe that there is considerable business to be won.
- In the area of order processing, UK companies are significant IT users. A 1986 survey of 30 UK companies showed that 26 were already using IT (Peters, 1990). The position appears to be similar in the Netherlands and other north European countries. However, in southern Europe, there is much more manual processing of orders. As a consequence, the realization of the benefits from IT in inter-company transactions (see table 11.1) will occur at a varying pace. In northern Europe, where IT in order processing is well established, the benefits can be relatively quickly realized. This is not true in southern Europe.
- In Germany there is very heavy emphasis on shipper/forwarder transactions, no doubt reflecting the importance of 'spedition' companies in the operation of the German freight market.

## Operative planning systems

The views of the survey respondents on the expected scale of benefits from operative planning systems are shown in table 11.2.

Other points which emerge from the survey are as follows:

- Vehicle routing and scheduling is usually regarded as a manual task, even in many large companies. There appears to be more enthusiasm for IT systems in this area in the UK than elsewhere (see also chapter 6); most non-UK respondents were unfamiliar with existing software, and many were even unaware of its existence.
- Mobile telephones for driver communication are used more in Sweden than in any other country in Europe. This is partly explained by

**Table 11.2** Operative planning systems: the expected benefits

| IT applications | Expected scale of benefit |
| --- | --- |
| Voice communication between driver and base | High |
| Route planning based on real route network | Medium |
| Route guidance to driver | Medium |
| Information display for off-duty driver recreation (such as restaurants and cinemas) | Low |

*Source*: EUROFRET (1990)

Sweden's relatively sparse population and its harsh climate. The least use of mobile telephones is in Greece, Spain, Portugal and Ireland.

● In Greece there are a few dedicated radio channels by which companies may communicate with their trucks in and around Athens and Thessaloniki.

● In Germany there is little in the way of mobile communications between driver and base. This, without doubt, is because of the slow and restrictive approach taken by the Bundespost, which has a telecommunications monopoly in Germany.

## Controlling systems

The thoughts of respondents about the probable benefits from controlling systems are summarized in table 11.3.

**Table 11.3** Controlling systems: the expected benefits

| IT applications | Expected scale of benefit |
| --- | --- |
| On-line tracing of shipments | High |
| Automatic fleet position monitoring | High |
| Automatic cargo status updates | Medium |
| Consignment identification at loading and unloading | Medium |
| Electronic tachographs | Medium |
| Automatic scheduling of vehicle maintenance | Medium |
| Automatic reporting of accidents to base | Low |

*Source*: EUROFRET (1990)

A number of further points that emerged from the survey illustrate the way in which operators view these controlling systems:

- Despite the apparent enthusiasm for on-line tracking of shipments, there is little evidence of IT implementation. Companies specializing in express services are most advanced in this area. Otherwise, the usual routine is for drivers to telephone to report progress.
- In the area of general freight, the IDS (International Distribution System) tracking system is of some note. It was established by 12 Dutch hauliers, together with partners in a number of other countries.
- German operators appear to be especially enthusiastic about the monitoring of vehicle performance and the automatic scheduling of vehicle maintenance.

It must be pointed out that the FLEET and EUROFRET consortia did not include questions about directive information systems in their survey. As a consequence there are no results to quote. However, it should be noted that some of the operative planning systems (such as computerized vehicle routing and scheduling) can be used for strategic decision-making. The preference for operators for this kind of IT in one capacity therefore reflects on its potential as a directive information system.

It is clear from the above discussion that there is a spread of opinion about the perceived benefits of IT applications, not least by country. Given the varying importance of different countries with respect to economic strength and trading capacity, equal weight cannot be given to the results from each country. However, in our opinion, it is well worth taking special note of the views from the Netherlands, since its hauliers are often regarded as the best in Europe, and the country has enormous importance as a trading gateway. The views of Dutch operators regarding the importance of IT are summarized in table 11.4.

Having established the potential importance of IT, at least from the Dutch viewpoint, the following section considers the way in which IT can be, and has been, used by logistics services providers in their search for competitive advantage.

# Uses of Information Systems by Logistics Services Providers

Logistics services providers are already using information systems to gain competitive advantages (Browne, 1989). A wide variety of uses

**Table 11.4** Overall ranking of IT importance according to Dutch hauliers

| IT application | Rank |
|---|---|
| Electronic Data Interchange | |
|   with consigner/consignee | 18 ⎫ |
|   with customs | 4 ⎬ 22 |
| Tracking and tracing | 10 |
| Driver communication | 9 |
| Mobile document facility | 5 |
| Pan-European freight exchange system | 3 |

Note: the higher the number the greater the importance attached to the application by hauliers.
*Source*: Netherlands Economic Institute, internal report, 1989

and implementations have taken place, and in order to clarify the implications of these it is possible to consider the strategies under two broad headings, based on the industry competitive analysis developed by Porter: first those which are essentially aimed at achieving a competitive advantage through lower costs; and second those where a strategy of service differentiation is most important (Porter and Millar, 1985).

## *Strategies based on lower costs or better resource utilization*

A good example of a strategy based on better resource utilization through linking information systems can be found in the brewing industry. A UK subsidiary of Grand Metropolitan makes extensive use of a computerized vehicle routing and scheduling (CVRS) package to control their delivery operations. At one of their sites the CVRS system is linked to the company's sales order processing system. Coordinating the sales processing and CVRS means not only better vehicle productivity, but faster delivery and, ultimately, lower inventory levels and consequent savings.

In many road transport sectors, further enhancements of computerized freight systems include the introduction of direct data transmission between depots and vehicles (replacing radio communications) and computer-controlled collections. These allow a customer's telephoned order to be keyed straight into the computer, to be electronically transmitted direct to the collection vehicle, with no need for a hard-copy collection note. The consequences are savings in both documentation and the reduced risk of error due to information being re-keyed incorrectly.

Multimodal transport is an area in which there is significant scope for the development of competitive advantage based on reduced costs or better resource utilization. This type of road–rail transport (see above) can blend the differing efficiencies of road and rail, but problems relating to information flow have so far hampered developments (particularly in Europe). For example, if a freight forwarder cannot access the rail operator's information system they will be unable to offer high-quality transport using a multimodal service, and so they will use road transport alone. The development of double-stack trains in the USA could well provide an information systems model for change in Europe. This would help to ensure greater economic, social and environmental benefits from improved road–rail co-operation, together with competitive advantages through lower costs for long-distance movements.

## Strategies based on service differentiation

Firms providing logistics services can use information systems to gain competitive advantages in a number of ways based on service differentiation strategies. For example, they can use IT to:

- add value to a basic service by means of stock and inventory management
- develop new freight market sectors which are less contestable than established ones
- differentiate their service from that of competitors by means of tracking and tracing systems
- introduce switching costs by, say, offering customers terminals for freight reservation

There are strong links between adding value and developing new market sectors which are less contestable. As freight markets have tended to become more competitive through deregulation, these twin aims have spearheaded the strategies of many freight companies. This has been especially true for larger companies, whose traditional areas of business have been eroded by strong competition from small low-cost entrants. IT offers an opportunity for the larger companies, which have the capacity for major IT development, to differentiate their services on offer from those of the new entrants. The key point, of course, is whether customers can be found for these new added-value services with a strong IT dimension. Dedicated contract distribution is a prime example of a service which is implicitly underpinned by IT capabilities and which cannot be performed by small operators.

A number of major European freight companies are also exploring the use of IT as a strategic weapon to promote the idea of single operator control. By integrating all the stages of the processing for a shipment on a Europe-wide basis, and linking major shippers into their information systems, carriers can develop a strategy based on 'one-stop shopping' for their customers.

Tracking and tracing systems using EDI technology and bar codes for packages are most advanced in the parcels and express freight sector (for example, the Federal Express 'Cosmos' and Securicor 'Tracka' systems). In part, this is a response to the high service levels that these transport companies are trying to achieve, but it is also a reflection of their own internal requirements, influenced by the very high volume of consignments that they handle. After the package is picked up its details are collected, typically via a bar code and hand-held scanner, and sent electronically to a central computer. At various points on its journey the package is scanned again, allowing the company to identify its location. Apart from better customer service three additional advantages follow from the use of tracking and tracing:

- The application of automatic identification and EDI allows customs authorities to be notified about consignments before the arrival of the goods, thus speeding clearance.
- Tracking and tracing allows companies to carry out internal audits. By adding extra scanning points companies can monitor how long a package takes at each stage of its journey and so identify bottlenecks.
- Providing shippers with more and better quality information brings carriers closer to their customers.

The parcels carrier UPS has also announced plans to upgrade its service to customers, with the development of its UPS Net (a worldwide information system). Significantly, the catalyst for this development came from the desire to integrate several newly acquired companies (11 companies acquired in Europe over a 12-month period), as well as the competitive pressure to provide higher service levels. UPS have acquired a number of companies with skills in this area – notably Roadnet Technologies, which specializes in the production of digitized maps.

The use of IT as the 'glue' to hold a geographically diverse operation together in this way is very exciting. Rapid expansion across a wide area and the development of new service types and standards are prerequisites for competitors in the race to become the freight mega-carriers of the 1990s. The role of technology in enabling geographically dispersed groups to coordinate their activities better has been noted if not universally accepted (Rockart and Short, 1989). In particular, the scope for different place–same time, different time–different place or different time–same place communication has important implications for global carriers, to promote efficient operations and to weld diverse management teams (Manheim, 1990).

Ultimately, tracking systems may become more important for slower transport systems, where the scope for delay in absolute terms is greater and where there is time to use the information for production scheduling. For example, radio cartridges have been attached to containers carrying car parts from the Far East to the USA. The cartridges contain data on the parts in the container, together with information on the whereabouts of the consignment. The consignee can then use this information to schedule their assembly line production in the most appropriate way.

There are a number of examples of transport firms seeking to moderate the influence of strong buyers by introducing a switching cost (an expense which a company incurs when it buys from a new supplier) to 'lock in' customers. A typical way of doing this is for a company to supply their clients with hardware, such as a terminal which allows the client to have access to simple order placing facilities or order progress monitoring. Some space reservation systems operated by airlines suggest a strategy based partly on switching costs. British Airways (BA) have installed a computerized system for cargo reservation called CARAT, for use by a number of their larger customers. Not only does this allow BA to differentiate their product, but it also means that the costs of making the information input are transferred to their customers.

Many of the examples of the use made of IT in logistics services come from companies which are prospective mega-carriers (see also chapter 10). This is no surprise, because IT is one of the key weapons being used by these companies in their race to achieve mega-carrier status. The airlines are thought by some to have a significant lead in their ability to apply information systems for competitive advantage. This belief stems from the tremendous impact of computerized reservation systems (CRS) and, in particular, the SABRE system developed by American Airlines, which has fundamentally altered the way in which airlines compete. We conclude this chapter by considering, first, whether the examples given above really do represent an opportunity for sustainable competitive advantage and, second, if there are any lessons for IT implementation that prospective mega-carriers should observe.

## Conclusion: Competitive Advantage or Necessity?

The model of achieving competitive advantage through IT, propounded by a number of management gurus, is very attractive. However, there are significant doubts as to whether many of the advantages are sustainable. Companies have already built many of the obvious ideas for systems that can rapidly change their product's position in the market. In addition, competitors have learnt to blunt the impact of information systems designed for competitive advantage. The key way to do this has been to copy the system – often by banding together with other companies who are also worried about the innovator's competitive edge. For example, New York retail banks joined together to build a network of cash dispensers to compete with the lead that Citicorp had gained. By being second in the field companies may find they can achieve the same advantage at lower cost, because some of the technology has been prototyped and tested by their go-ahead and innovative rival.

Manheim (1990) argues strongly that implementing, say, EDI alone will not be sufficient by itself to produce a competitive advantage. He cites the following reasons for this view.

First, for EDI to be effective there have to be partners – it is not a game that is really worth playing on your own. Many of the partners will themselves be supplying or buying from competitors of the firm that wants to implement EDI. For this reason EDI tends to be adopted at about the same time by groups of companies in an industry sector.

Second, leading companies typically find it in their own interests to help others to implement EDI, because it is in better trading links that the maximum benefits can be realized. As Manheim says:

> Thus the very dynamic of EDI works against it being a source of unique competitive advantage for any single company. Rather when

an industry segment does begin to move toward adopting EDI, it becomes a competitive necessity for all firms in that industry; if a firm does not keep up with its competitors and business partners, it will face a competitive disadvantage.

There is little doubt that this view holds true not only for EDI but for IT applications in general.

But even if IT does not provide an instant 'technological fix', producing immediate and sustainable competitive advantage, it does provide a platform on which firms can build competitive advantage. However, they can only do this by creatively exploiting the changes in trading relationships and corporate behaviour which result from the growing importance of IT.

Importantly, the way in which a company approaches the implementation of IT can influence the likelihood of success in obtaining a sustainable competitive advantage. For example, IT strategies that are dependent on outside consultants, or on well-known models such as SABRE and American Hospital Supplies, may be easily copied – a competitor merely needs to employ a similarly capable consultant. By contrast, IT strategies that encourage grass-roots involvement and tinkering (analogous to the Japanese *kaizen* concept) mean that the subsequent IT applications will be much harder for competitors to copy; because they are in fact part of the corporate culture in which they were developed.

Further important aspects of IT implementation were identified by Copeland and McKenney (1988), on the basis of their in-depth analysis of the use of computerized reservation systems by the US airline industry. Three of the issues that they identify have a special significance for prospective mega-carriers:

- IT can be a source of economies of scale and scope
- technological experience is vital
- 'learning by doing' is very important

The potential use of IT to achieve economies of scale and scope contains an important message for prospective freight mega-carriers. While it has long been recognized that there are economies of scale in freight transport, many of these have stemmed from technological vehicle developments (for example, larger trucks and ships), and their impact has been less marked than in, say, the manufacturing sector. Information systems will provide mega-carriers with an opportunity to make their scale of operation count in terms of market share. The new technology required to operate sophisticated tracking and tracing systems at a global level is extremely expensive. Indeed, the cost is so high that only the largest companies can afford to acquire it. As a result, the requirement for IT is driving certain sectors towards rationalization. This is most notable in the express parcels sector; but can also be seen in distribution, where IT for inventory management, vehicle routing and scheduling, and delivery order processing through EDI all play an important role.

Understanding the technology, learning how to use it and applying it operationally are inextricably linked. Yet even some of the larger freight carriers (especially outside the express and airline sector) have relatively poorly developed information systems and lack management skills in this area. Furthermore, and as we argued in chapter 10, to become mega-carriers they must develop a wider geographical range and increase their service portfolio. Both of these imperatives put tremendous pressure on management resources and existing information systems. One potential route to building skills and gaining experience in this area is through co-operative pre-competitive projects (such as the EC-funded ESPRIT programme). In a number of recent European initiatives (such as DRIVE and COST 306) freight carriers have played an important role – gaining experience at a relatively low cost. The ability to implement workable information systems solutions at the right time and within budget will be of vital necessity in the mega-carrier race.

## Case Study   IT for the New Railway Age

The majority of the examples of IT implementation used so far in this chapter have come from road-based operations. It is therefore perhaps appropriate to consider the activities of the railways in this field. The following case study looks first at two Europe-wide developments in IT for rail freight services, Hermes and Docimel. The second part of the study focuses on two French developments; first 'Customer Liaisons' and then the wittily named 'SESAME'.

### International IT projects

#### HERMES

At present a number of European railways use computerized tracking and tracing systems and telecommunications to enable them to be certain of the whereabouts of their wagon fleets. However, when the wagons cross a European border and come under the control of another railway authority the national systems are of little use. Anecdotal evidence refers to wagons being 'lost' on other rail systems for months at a time. Clearly, this was not good enough as European traffic flows became increasingly international. Consequently, the principal European rail authorities have acted in a concerted way to develop 'HERMES' – a Europe-wide system for wagon location. With the implementation of Hermes no longer will a wagon, and therefore the consignment it is carrying, disappear into a 'black hole' on moving from one rail system to another.

The original basic function of wagon location envisaged for HERMES is being enhanced to provide:

- advice of despatch and arrival
- frontier transit notification
- wagon damage reports
- notice of incidents in transit

## DOCIMEL

DOCIMEL goes beyond HERMES, and has the objective of replacing the consignment note relating to the goods by an EDI-based system designed to eliminate the transfer of all information using paper. In the short term, pilot projects will be developed with rail customers in the automobile, chemical and home appliance sectors, the first stages becoming operational in 1991.

## *SNCF's IT projects*

In terms of rail technology and development, the French railways (SNCF) are often held up as a model or vision of the future for European railways. It is therefore especially interesting to note the views of their freight sector on developments involving information systems. Commenting on French railway's commitment to the development of IT (or 'telematics'), J. P. Bernadet, the Vice-Director of Freight SNCF, stated in 1988 that:

> Computer based monitoring of consignment movements will indeed be one of the most innovative dimensions in renovating the SNCF's freight product and one of its major assets.

He went on to give details of SNCF developments in this field:

> To meet changing requirements on the market and the needs of companies and to develop customer loyalty by being at the forefront of their logistics organization and their management

system, we (SNCF Freight) are currently developing a telematics project for freight business management which . . . will be based on two systems . . .'customer liaisons' and 'SESAME'.

The two IT projects are discussed in more detail below.

### Customer Liaisons

The aim of the 'Customer Liaisons' project is to provide carrier–customer partners with a completely open added-value service, which takes into account the constraints of the two parties and their requirements in terms of information, software and additional services *independent* of the equipment. In order to improve the quality of the rail freight service, consignment note data and current shipment status have been given priority. As Bernadet noted in 1988:

> The project seems to be particularly appreciated by customers who are still too often worried about the obscurity surrounding our (SNCF) traffic. . . .

### SESAME (Système d'Exploitation et du Suivi des Activités Marchandise)

This second project, which will be developed in parallel with the above, reflects the need to develop an information system which will fundamentally improve the link between the railways and their customers. Fierce competition for traffic from road-based operators, who already have information systems to link them to shippers for many routine transactions, has stimulated SNCF to develop a system that will cover the entire transport cycle. The resulting system, 'SESAME', will encompass information transfer from receipt of the rail customer's orders right through to provision of information on charging, administration of tariff documents, invoicing and accounting.

Two important points emerge from SNCF's IT developments:

- *Open systems.* SNCF seem to have decided on the right strategy in seeking to build information systems that are 'open', rather than being reliant on any one hardware supplier. This open-systems approach will be aided by the development of standards such as Edifact.
- *Consignment visibility.* SNCF have rightly recognized that if rail is to compete with road-based operations then the rail companies have to act in the area of information services. In seeking to become more integrated with their customers, the railways must develop more accessible information systems that give shippers the confidence to use their services in the knowledge that details of the consignment can be accessed at any time.

Supply-side Logistics

The final word rests with Bernadet:

SNCF (Freight) is preparing for a cultural revolution in the years to come: there will be new working methods, real time information processing, step-by-step elimination of paper, new types of communication with customers, integration with other companies, all of these . . . will contribute . . . to increasing our resources as an operator providing a comprehensive service.

Source: J. P. Bernadet (Vice-Director, Freight SNCF), 6th Eurolog Conference, 1988

# Part III
# The Future

# 12
# Will Transport Prices Fall?

## Rationale for Transport Price Falls

The most striking aspect of deregulation in trucking markets in the USA was the fall in rates for both FTL and LTL services. A key question is whether the same pattern can be expected in Europe. During 1989 and 1990 the information technology company GE Information Services (GEIS) commissioned a survey to evaluate expected changes in European logistics. An intriguing finding to emerge from the survey (Byrne, 1990) was the divergence between shippers and carriers in their expectations about transport price changes. No less than 83 per cent of shippers (manufacturers and retailers) believed that transport prices would fall by the mid-1990s. By contrast, 62 per cent of carriers felt that transport prices would remain stable or even increase. The principal aim of this chapter is to investigate whether, on the basis of the objective evidence available, it is the shippers or the carriers who are correct.

In chapter 8 we described the principal supply-side developments in logistics, and considered the extent to which national models of deregulation provide a useful insight into EC changes and responses. What is important in this chapter is to try to quantify the possible scope for price reductions in transport. The focus is on road haulage for two reasons. First, road is currently, and seems certain to remain, the dominant mode for goods transport in Europe. Second, the thrust of deregulation and many changes resulting from the Single European Market (SEM) will critically affect the road haulage sector (for example, cabotage freedoms and reducing border delays).

The proponents of future transport price reductions point to two key developments to support their assertion:

- continuing deregulation of road haulage will lead to more competition, fewer empty hauls and lower prices
- the implementation of the SEM will mean reduced border delays and therefore greater vehicle and driver productivity

Looking at the first of these developments in more detail, we can see that the following reasons underpin the view that there will be more competition and fewer empty hauls:

- at the international level there will be easier access to markets as permit limitations cease to matter
- at the national level further softening of price and capacity regulation can be expected in several markets (Germany, for example)
- importantly, there will ultimately be access to new markets through cabotage operations
- easier access to markets combined with improved information flows will lead to a reduction in the number of goods vehicles running empty

The SEM will not only increase trade between member states but will also lead to reduced delays at borders. Instead of treating movements between, say, France and Germany as an export from France, the movement will become little different from a domestic sale, with no need to clear customs at the border and little likelihood of any vehicle check either. Fewer controls and reduced delays at borders will reduce direct operating costs and administrative overheads for international truckers, and rates could well fall as a consequence. Estimates vary, but significant reductions in journey time for international trips are to be expected by the mid-1990s if and when border delays are reduced. The scope for time savings is considerable, and we return to this later in the chapter.

However, the picture is complicated and there is little doubt that any decreases in transport prices will vary in different markets and will be driven by different underlying factors. The complicated interplay between the different factors is shown in figure 12.1, illustrating how there will be important differences between the causes of price reductions in national and international markets. The first half of this chapter will focus on the scope for price changes in national markets, with the second part devoted to developments in international haulage. The chapter ends by exploring the combined impact of these changes.

Proposition ——▶ Where ——▶ Mechanism

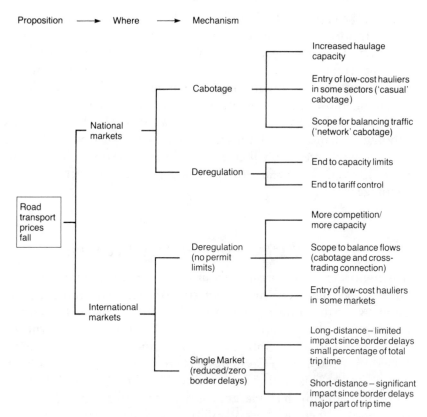

**Figure 12.1**   Road haulage prices will fall.

## National Markets

National freight markets are affected by their own governments' decisions about regulatory change and by the cabotage freedoms introduced in July 1990 throughout the EC. Cabotage affects national markets by giving non-resident international hauliers the opportunity to work in national markets. There is no reason to suppose that gains in economic efficiency resulting from the removal of cabotage restrictions will be the same in each sector of the road freight market; each has different scope for achieving efficiencies. To assess the potential impact of the removal of cabotage restrictions, both the macro- and micro-levels of road haulage operation must be considered.

At the macro-level the key issue is the amount of domestic traffic that will be captured by international hauliers from other countries. This proportion of the total domestic traffic, say $X$ per cent, is important to identify because it is related to the maximum reduction in empty running which can be achieved by the removal of cabotage restrictions. Reduction in empty running is an important key to obtaining improvements in operating efficiency and will, it is argued, drive down domestic prices. We can call this the 'direct' effect of cabotage. At the micro-level we are more concerned with the scope that cabotage freedom will give for changes in the operating practices of individual European road hauliers; the 'indirect' effect of cabotage.

## Direct effects of cabotage freedoms

It is important to be precise about exactly what cabotage freedoms allow. The right to carry domestic or national traffic depends critically on the country of registration of the vehicle. Thus, before cabotage freedoms were introduced in 1990 a German firm, say, could have had an operating centre in France but would have been forbidden from using a German-registered truck to perform a French national trip. This restriction has now been lifted, provided that the German company has the appropriate cabotage permit, and as a consequence there is the possibility of reducing empty running. A hypothetical example is used in figure 12.2 to illustrate a cabotage operation and to show how empty running may be reduced.

In figure 12.2a there are 10 international truckloads going from C to A and 10 domestic truckloads from A to B. There are no backloads in either case. With cabotage restrictions in force foreign hauliers perform the international movements from C to A, but are not allowed to backload from A to B. This domestic traffic is, in effect, reserved for national hauliers, who must themselves return empty from B to A because there is no suitable traffic for backloading.

Cabotage restrictions as in figure 12.2a therefore result in 20 empty truck movements between A and B alongside 20 full ones, which is not a sensible use of available capacity. As figure 12.2b shows, the removal of cabotage restrictions enables international hauliers to take goods from A to B as backloads, reducing empty running to zero. The contentious point is, of course, that national hauliers lose work to those from another country because the foreign

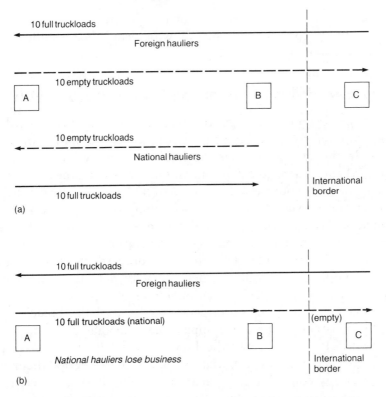

**Figure 12.2** Cabotage restrictions and empty running: truck movements (a) with and (b) without cabotage restrictions.

haulier is able to offer a low price, having already secured their international loads at C bound for A.

There is clearly a major gain in operational efficiency; at best 10 international movements can be used to eliminate 20 empty domestic movements (including the domestic legs of international movements) following the removal of cabotage restrictions.

More generally, and by extension, if $X$ per cent of domestic traffic is captured by international hauliers, then up to $2X$ per cent of domestic empty running could be eliminated. From a transport users' (and green) point of view this does make the removal of cabotage restrictions attractive. But there are important operating and business constraints to be considered. Prominent among these are the directional balance of freight traffic, the prices charged for work and the quality of service offered by international hauliers in comparison with local hauliers. In practice, reductions in empty running will be nowhere near the theoretical potential. The reasons for this assessment are considered in the following detailed case study of the impact of cabotage in France.

## Direct effects of cabotage: a French case study

The introduction of cabotage freedom has been fiercely opposed by many national road hauliers; this is true for almost all EC member states. In the case of the German haulage industry with its highly regulated and protected environment, this was to be expected. But in the case of other countries the strength of the reaction has surprised a number of observers. Particular concern has been expressed by road hauliers in France, which is a major transit country in the EC and which underwent national haulage deregulation in the late 1980s. The hauliers' chief fear has been that since domestic markets are now highly competitive introducing new capacity onto the market will have a disastrous effect on national hauliers' profitability. It is revealing to examine in some depth the case of the French road freight industry and the direct impact that cabotage may have.

Between 1987 and 1990 the French road haulage market was progressively deregulated, so that by the end of this period there was no longer any control over capacity or price – although a reference tariff does remain in existence. Access to the market has now been granted to any haulier who can meet certain qualitative conditions, while the reference tariff merely provides a starting point for negotiation between carrier and shipper.

French deregulation (see also chapter 8) has been managed carefully by the government in an attempt to moderate the effects of increased national competition. Yet, despite this management, and the growth in French national traffic (8 per cent a year from 1987 to 1990), average transport prices per tonne–kilometre fell by 5.3 per cent, 7.4 per cent and 3.5 per cent for 1987, 1988 and 1989 respectively. Indeed, these price reductions are all the more significant since, during the same period, transport costs such as wages, fuel, depreciation and insurance have risen (figure 12.3).

There is no doubt that in theory, given France's central position, cabotage freedom will exacerbate the decrease in transport prices, with many foreign international hauliers already either carrying loads to and from various French regions or transiting the country. To evaluate the expected level of increased competition it is necessary to assess the extent to which foreign vehicles are travelling empty in

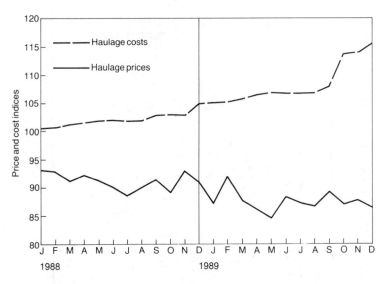

**Figure 12.3**   French haulage costs and prices, 1988 and 1989.
Source: *Camions Magazine*, May 1990, 2 bis Rue Mercoeur,
75011 Paris, France

France. A report published by the Observatoire Economique et Social de Transport (OEST) contained an analysis of the difference between imports and exports by French region for foreign EC hauliers, thus revealing the potential 'caboteur' capacity (Selosse and Salini, 1989). For example, it is shown in table 12.1 that Belgian hauliers deliver to the Paris region just over one million tonnes more than they take out, and therefore can be said to have one million tonnes of potential caboteur capacity available for a French domestic movement before they return to Belgium (details for all regions are presented in table 12.1).

From table 12.1 it is clear that there are many opportunities for foreign hauliers to undertake cabotage as part of their total international trip. But the figures are misleading, since a large proportion of the available capacity cannot be utilized. For example, in the northern region of France, Belgian hauliers deliver 3.521 million tonnes more than they carry back to Belgium. Yet it is doubtful whether the Belgian hauliers will be able to find French customers for the short-distance domestic routes that they could exploit on their way back from northern France to Belgium.

A further constraint on the effective use of the available capacity concerns internal freight flows. For cabotage to be attractive, the

**Table 12.1** Empty running by region in France for foreign hauliers based on imports minus exports for 1987 (thousand tonnes)

| French zone | Country of origin of haulier | | | | | | Total |
|---|---|---|---|---|---|---|---|
| | Belgium | Holland | Germany | Italy | UK | Spain | |
| Frontier Nord | 3521 | 221 | −64 | −39 | −19 | −98 | 3521 |
| Frontier Est | −229 | 87 | −644 | −32 | −23 | −62 | −903 |
| Frontier Italie | 25 | 16 | 55 | −33 | 0 | 8 | 71 |
| Frontier Espagne | −17 | −14 | −48 | −20 | 1 | 635 | 535 |
| Ouest | 246 | 69 | 63 | −48 | 0 | 57 | 387 |
| Paris | 1021 | 800 | 945 | 164 | 20 | 130 | 3081 |
| Est | −159 | 26 | −170 | −105 | 1 | −36 | −444 |
| Lyonnais | 222 | 111 | 171 | −90 | 6 | 37 | 457 |
| Provence | −5 | −22 | −81 | −43 | −2 | −12 | −165 |
| Sud Ouest | 13 | −18 | −30 | −72 | 1 | 58 | −49 |
| Centre | 34 | 7 | 28 | 3 | −1 | 0 | 71 |
| Total | 4672 | 1283 | 224 | −316 | −16 | 717 | 6563 |

Note that a positive figure indicates empty vehicle capacity available for cabotage.
*Source:* Selosse and Salini (1989)

direction in which foreign haulier spare capacity is available has to coincide with the direction of a significant domestic traffic flow. It is clear that the only way spare foreign haulier capacity available in, say, Paris can be used is if there is demand for space outwards from the Paris region. The regional interaction of international and domestic goods flows for France is shown in table 12.2. What emerges is that many of the internal flows are not in the same direction as foreign hauliers' spare capacity. So, although German hauliers bring into the Paris region 945 000 tonnes more than they take out (table 12.1), they cannot easily utilize this capacity because French domestic flows are not balanced; domestic traffic arriving in the Paris area exceeds departing traffic by over 3.2 million tonnes (table 12.2).

## Indirect effects of cabotage

A further disappointment arises when assessments are made of the probable proportion of domestic traffic which could be captured by international hauliers; it is likely to be somewhat limited. In the UK for example, one study established that a maximum of only about 1 per cent of domestic traffic would be captured by non-UK international

**Table 12.2** The interaction of international flows by region with French national flows in 1987 (thousand tonnes)

| French zone | International French hauliers | International Foreign hauliers | National |
|---|---|---|---|
| Frontier Nord | 1127 | 3521 | −506 |
| Frontier Est | −79 | −903 | −605 |
| Frontier Italie | −158 | 71 | 2207 |
| Frontier Espagne | −411 | 535 | 832 |
| Ouest | −29 | 387 | −814 |
| Paris | 1091 | 3081 | 3210 |
| Est | −68 | −444 | −3737 |
| Lyonnais | 95 | 457 | 322 |
| Provence | −384 | −165 | −1074 |
| Sud Ouest | −495 | −49 | 320 |
| Centre | 1 | 72 | −156 |

Note that a positive figure indicates empty vehicle capacity available for cabotage.
*Source*: Selosse and Salini (1989)

hauliers (Cooper, Browne and Gretton, 1987). This was calculated using the very simple method of establishing the extra capacity that would be available from foreign international hauliers if cabotage restrictions were relaxed.

Surprisingly, the position does not appear to be so very different in France, despite the greater importance of transit traffic and the greater size of the country; both factors which encourage many international hauliers to believe that it will be a good prospect for cabotage. Estimates of the likely impact of cabotage in France vary: the French Ministry of Transport consider that 1 per cent of French domestic freight could be captured by caboteurs, while the FNTR (the principal trade association for road transport operators) believe that up to 3.5 per cent of freight could be at risk (Artous, 1990).

These findings should to some extent allay the fears of domestic operators who believe that foreign international operators will take a large part of their domestic business. Moreover, they should consider just how readily their client companies will switch business allegiances to foreign-based international operators. Many of these potential competitors for domestic business will be unsuitable. For example, many hauliers from southern Europe carry agricultural products with seasonal distribution patterns. Few users of haulage services with an all-year requirement will be interested in using these hauliers unless their seasonal arrival coincides with business peaks. Furthermore, and especially in northern Europe, the purchasing of transport services is no longer made on an *ad hoc* basis. Users have increasingly moved towards purchasing tailor-made transport and distribution services, often with sophisticated IT links between carrier and shipper. It is hard to see how 'casual' cabotage will make any kind of major impact on established relationships of this type.

Nevertheless, despite these inhibitors to cabotage, the French road haulage industry is very worried. Typical of articles discussing cabotage and French haulage was one which appeared in the French *Camions Magazine* in April 1990: 'Les transporteurs français craignent le pire [French transport operators fear the worst]'. This likened the prospect of foreign caboteurs to a military invasion: 'Ils se sont lancés dans une nouvelle bataille de la Marne face à l'envahissement à armes inégales [They have been thrown into a new battle of the Marne against the invasion of unequal forces]' (Chardin, 1990b).

The reaction of French road hauliers seems at first sight to be unnecessarily pessimistic. But while there are doubts over the direct effects of cabotage, it may well be that cabotage is the key to important changes in operating patterns for the larger carriers (the future European mega-carriers, see chapter 10). At the micro-level of road haulage operation one cannot doubt the real value of removing cabotage restrictions. The larger freight operators who are currently establishing Europe-wide freight networks for client companies anticipate substantial benefits from cabotage freedom. Consider, for example, the hypothetical situation in figure 12.4, where a carrier establishes a small network based on three locations for a client company.

In figure 12.4a are shown the daily directional requirement for truck movements which results from the activities of the user company. With cabotage restrictions there would be 80 truck movements, of which 30 are empty.

However, with cabotage freedoms, trucks can be efficiently redeployed after moving from the base (where they are registered) to location C, since they are now allowed to complete an onward national movement from C to A, enabling them to undertake further work between location A and the base. With cabotage freedom only 50 truck movements are required, not one of them empty (figure 12.4b). The benefit of removing cabotage restrictions is therefore the elimination of 30 empty truck movements which, using the network illustrated, could translate into a 37.5 per cent reduction in total transport price for the client company. Although, once again, actual balances of flows may not bring quite such substantial gains in practice, there could nevertheless be significant savings since 'network' cabotage will be planned to meet the known needs of transport users, which is far less true of the casual cabotage assessed earlier (Cooper, 1990b).

From discussions with larger European transport providers in the road freight sector it is clear that they are anticipating large business benefits from network cabotage. Savings of 37.5 per cent may not be readily realized, but even 5–10 per cent would represent a significant increase in operating efficiency; with the consequent price advantage being sought by shippers. It is the larger operators who will be best able to exploit the possibilities of network cabotage, because they possess the scope in terms of marketing and IT systems to derive economies of scale.

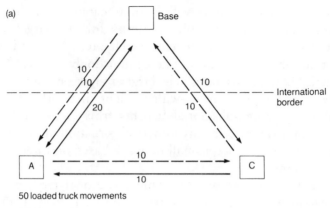

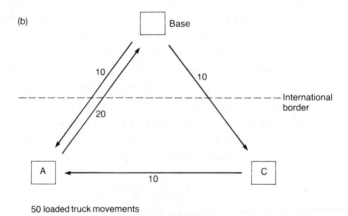

**Figure 12.4** Transport networks (a) with and (b) without cabotage restrictions. _ _ _ _ _, empty running; _____, loaded running; points A, C and Base are equidistant.

# International Markets

## *Deregulation effects*

For many years, international movements between European countries (including EC member states) have been governed by a complex system of permit authorizations affecting the rights of hauliers to undertake particular journeys. As discussed in chapter 8, this permit system is changing to one in which control will be concerned only with quality and not with capacity. As an interim measure in the period between 1988 and 1993, multilateral permits are being increased at a rate of 40 per cent a year. These permits allow an operator considerable freedom to carry goods on an *international* movement anywhere in the EC, regardless of the operator's country of registration.

At present most international traffic between EC member states is carried by a haulier from the country of origin or destination, rather than by a 'cross-trader' from a third country (for example, a French haulier taking goods between Denmark and Germany). Only hauliers from the Netherlands have really exploited the cross-trading opportunities available within the EC. However, the existence of a much greater supply of multilateral permits, which are ideal for cross-traders, could well encourage this type of activity by hauliers from all member states.

The main question is what effect complete capacity deregulation (that is, no permit limits to capacity) will have on international freight rates for goods moving between member states. In short, the answer is not very much – and there are several reasons underlying this.

First, it is important to remember that for several years international road freight movements between many member states have in practice been free of any capacity control. For example, permits are not required for movements between the UK and the Netherlands, and there are no limits on the number available for Dutch hauliers wishing to go to Italy. Even on routes where there are limits to the number of permits there was little evidence of permit shortages during the latter half of the 1980s. Because of the relative freedom of access to most international markets there is already considerable overcapacity on many routes, and it has to be doubted whether the extra capacity attracted to a route as a consequence of further deregulation will really impact severely on prices.

The second point is that although international transport prices have been subject to reference tariffs which set an upper and lower band for rates, these have been largely ignored in practice. Shippers have been free to negotiate the best rates they can with carriers, and for many routes international rates have typically been low.

Third, imbalances of traffic have an almost overwhelmingly important influence on international freight rates (Browne, Doganis and Bergstrand, 1989). To illustrate this point consider the prices charged for a sample of loads into and out of the UK during 1990

**Table 12.3**  Impact of cargo flow imbalances on haulage prices

| Route | Full load price *outwards* from UK (£) | Full load price *inwards* to UK (£) |
| --- | --- | --- |
| London–Milan | 800 | 1400 |
| London–Paris | 350 | 700 |
| London–Frankfurt | 500 | 800 |
| London–Amsterdam | 400 | 700 |
| London–Antwerp | 250 | 400 |

*Source*: Information from international hauliers, 1989–90

(table 12.3). As the table shows, in each case, the imbalance of traffic means that the price charged for a load leaving the UK is dramatically lower than for in-bound traffic – often only half the price.

## Single Market effects

Delays at borders for European road hauliers have been estimated to cost up to 830 million ecu a year (Cecchini, 1988). However, this macro-economic analysis does not reveal the extent to which border delays may influence prices for particular international journeys, nor the micro-economic opportunities for price reduction if delays were to be reduced or were to cease altogether.

In simple terms, a major impetus for reduced prices comes from the greater productivity that will result from fewer border delays. At present, average end-to-end speeds for international journeys within the EC are often as low as 25 km/h. Estimating average border delays is at best an inexact science. The consultants Ernst and Whinney undertook a study for the European Commission which attempted this evaluation: the border delays that they noted are shown in table 12.4 and, indeed, these figures were used in the calculation of the macro-economic cost of delays referred to in the Cecchini Report (1988).

An analysis of table 12.4 suggests that if the delays were removed then average speeds for international journeys would rise to 31 km/h. The resulting increased productivity means that fixed costs can be spread over far more revenue-earning kilometres. As a consequence, an increase in average speeds of as little as 6 km/h could result in a

**Table 12.4**   Border delays, 1988 (in hours)

|        |         |        | To      |       |         |      |
| ------ | ------- | ------ | ------- | ----- | ------- | ---- |
| From   | Belgium | France | Germany | Italy | Holland | UK   |
| Belgium | —      | 4.03   | 2.91    | 11.66 | 1.44    | 4.50 |
| France  | 3.76   | —      | 2.61    | 7.58  | 1.81    | 4.64 |
| Germany | 3.35   | 2.98   | —       | 7.74  | 1.43    | 4.85 |
| Italy   | 6.63   | 5.87   | 4.90    | —     | 5.70    | 7.72 |
| Holland | 1.54   | 2.30   | 1.72    | 8.27  | —       | 3.96 |
| UK      | 4.16   | 5.01   | 4.36    | 9.75  | 4.21    | —    |

*Source*: Ernst and Whinney, 1988

fall in rates of 17 per cent, on the assumption that the load factor remains at 70 per cent (typical for international long-distance haulage). The increased productivity means, of course, a considerable increase in the available truck capacity, and it is possible that load factors will fall. However, the greater freedom of market access, combined with the growth in international goods movements, should help to offset this.

But the analysis suggested above is still rather general; border delays clearly have very different impacts for short- and long-distance trips. Using running and standing costs from published cost tables, together with revenue and operating information from road haulage companies, it is possible to calculate costs and revenues for international road journeys of 1200, 500 and 200 km (table 12.5a).

When the calculation is repeated with the assumption of no delays at borders (table 12.5b), it becomes clear that hauliers may be able to make a greater profit per tonne–kilometre, since fixed costs are spread over more revenue-earning tonne–kilometres. But there will be increased competition from further deregulation, while the removal of border delays themselves increases the available truck capacity. As a result, hauliers will almost certainly be forced to pass on the windfall profit in the form of lower prices to shippers; at best making the same profit per tonne–kilometre.

The scope for reduced prices on the three journeys of different distances is illustrated in table 12.5c, assuming that hauliers seek only to maintain profit levels and that savings are passed to shippers in the form of lower prices. What emerges most clearly is that the scope for reduced prices is much greater on the short-distance

**Table 12.5**  Impact of border delays on transport prices for trips of different distances

|  | Trip A | Trip B | Trip C |
|---|---|---|---|
| (a)  Costs and revenues assuming 1990 level of border delays | | | |
| Distance (km) | 1200 | 500 | 200 |
| Journey time (hours) | 48 | 8 | 4.5 |
| Border delays (hours) | 6 | 2 | 1.5 |
| Total time (hours) | 54 | 10 | 6.0 |
| Percentage due to delays | 11% | 20% | 25% |
| Cost per trip (£) | 1740 | 531 | 243 |
| Revenue per trip (£) | 2000 | 600 | 300 |
| Cost per TKM (pence) | 10.4 | 7.6 | 8.7 |
| Revenue per TKM (pence) | 11.9 | 8.6 | 10.7 |
| Profit per TKM (pence) (with border delays) | 1.5 | 1.0 | 2.0 |
| | | | |
| (b)  Costs and revenues assuming zero border delays | | | |
| Distance (km) | 1200 | 500 | 200 |
| Journey time (hours) | 48 | 8 | 4.5 |
| Border delays (hours) | 0 | 0 | 0 |
| Total time (hours) | 48 | 8 | 4.5 |
| Percentage due to delays | 0% | 0% | 0% |
| Cost per trip (£) | 1646 | 499 | 220 |
| Revenue per trip (£) | 2000 | 600 | 300 |
| Cost per TKM (pence) | 9.8 | 7.1 | 7.9 |
| Revenue per TKM (pence) | 11.9 | 8.6 | 10.7 |
| Profit per TKM (pence) (with no border delay) | 2.1 | 1.4 | 2.9 |

(c) Potential rate reductions if hauliers seek only to maintain trip profitability at 1990 levels and pass on the savings to shippers

|  | Trip A | Trip B | Trip C |
|---|---|---|---|
| Trip profit (1990 level) | 1.5 | 1 | 1.5 |
| Cost per TKM (pence) (with no border delay) | 9.8 | 7.1 | 7.9 |
| New price (pence/TKM) | 11.3 | 8.1 | 9.4 |
| Reduction in rates | 5.08% | 5.10% | 12.67% |

Assumptions: Load of 14 tonnes per vehicle; running costs of 75 pence per kilometre; standing costs of £15.55 per hour.
*Source*: cost data from *Motor Transport* cost tables (1990) and therefore based on UK costs

international journeys, since even though border delays are reduced in absolute terms they are much more significant as a proportion of total transit time. For long-distance journeys the key constraint on productivity is the need for drivers' rest periods and the limits on the maximum driving period within the EC (nine hours at present). Referring to table 12.5c, we see that a shipper using road haulage for a journey of 1200 km may expect savings of 5 per cent if border delays cease. However, the shipper who is using road haulage for short-distance cross-border movements can anticipate some dramatic savings – a reduction of 13 per cent in real terms on current rates.

Data are available from a somewhat more complex model used to investigate the effects of border delays on prices for three specific routes (Hurn, 1990). The routes investigated were London to Milan, Eindhoven to Lille, and Brussels to Arnhem.

The model took as its starting point the border delays already noted in table 12.4. Two scenarios were developed: a first, 'optimistic' scenario in which it was assumed that border delays would cease by 1993; and a second, 'pessimistic' scenario that assumed some continuing delays despite the move towards the SEM (table 12.6).

Both scenarios suggest there is scope for significant rate reduction on shorter-distance cross-border movements. Transport deregulation

**Table 12.6**  Scope for transport price reductions in 1993 on certain specific international routes within the EC

|  |  | Possible transport price reduction if border delays cease (%) | |
| --- | --- | --- | --- |
| Routes | Distance (km) | Optimistic scenario | Pessimistic scenario |
| London to Milan | 1015 | 8 | 3 |
| Eindhoven to Lille | 220 | 15 | 10 |
| Brussels to Arnhem | 180 | 13 | 10 |

The optimistic scenario assumes that current border delays (1990) cease completely in 1993.
The pessimistic scenario assumes that some border checks remain in force in 1993, but that delays are significantly reduced compared with 1990.
*Source*: based on an analysis in an unpublished dissertation by M. Hurn at the Polytechnic of Central London, 1990

and the abolition of border controls will allow inventory to be held according to real patterns of supply and demand. This implies a greater concentration of inventory in fewer locations, with potentially significant savings for European industry, and the scope for future mega-carriers to exploit network cabotage opportunities.

# Which Markets and Which Sectors will be Most Affected?

The combined impact on road transport prices of the changes described in the preceding sections is illustrated in table 12.7. International prices are more affected than national prices, because the main thrust of the Community's policy has been towards international rather than national transport.

**Table 12.7** Summary of the reductions to be expected in road transport prices, 1990–2000

|  | National (%)[a] | | International (%) | |
|---|---|---|---|---|
|  | Long distance | Short distance | Long distance | Short distance |
| Specialized transport | 0 | 0 | 1–5 | 1–5 |
| General haulage | 1–5 | 0 | 5–10 | 10–15 |

[a] Cabotage freedoms will act as a catalyst to drive prices down in the highly regulated German market

Within international transport, easier access to the market combined with reductions in border formalities will increase competition and drive down unit costs. Two categories of savings will be especially noticeable:

- where border delays are lengthy in absolute terms (such as at the Italian and Spanish borders at present)
- for short-distance cross-border trips, where any delay at the frontier has a significant impact on total trip time

Competitive influences will be more important in general haulage and will have less effect on specialized work (such as hanging garments) or where added-value services such as inventory management are provided by the transporter. There are several reasons for the greater impact on general haulage:

- there are few barriers to entry (for example, capital required is low and skills are not in short supply)
- there are limits to the economies of scale in some key sectors of general haulage, such as the FTL business
- the buyer–seller link between the shipper and the carrier is typically weaker in general haulage than in specialized transport, and is not based on long-term contracts

Nevertheless, it is important to remember that international road haulage has been market-driven for many years, and so the competition effect of the measures will be evolutionary rather than revolutionary. A number of other factors join together to moderate the scope for downward pressure on prices:

- Many international truckers already schedule their journeys so that the driver's rest period coincides with foreseeable border delays, thus limiting the real scope for improvements in all journey times.
- Continuing parochialism on the part of many shippers (especially the small and medium-sized companies) will reduce the opportunity for international hauliers to cross-trade.
- EC provision already exists to introduce new quantitative restrictions 'when a serious disturbance to the market is likely to persist'. A serious disturbance includes one of the following circumstances:
  - if the average profits of carriers are insufficient to secure the profitability of a properly managed undertaking
  - if the capacity of international road haulage is substantially in excess of demand
  - if there has been a significant increase in the number of carriers going bankrupt
  - if there has been a significant increase in unemployment
  - if the environment is seriously threatened by congestion

Transport prices for national haulage will also come under attack, albeit less fiercely than in the international arena. We have already noted the decline in road haulage prices in France following national deregulation. The freedom to perform cabotage can only exert further downward pressure on prices; the key question being how powerful that pressure will be.

Our analysis strongly suggests that casual cabotage will have only the most limited impact – both in terms of tonnes lifted and on prices charged to shippers. In the short term, some hauliers from low-cost countries will certainly try to exploit opportunities in what are perceived to be easier, wealthier markets. But this approach becomes self-defeating over time; because the longer the low-cost haulier spends in the high-price, high-cost market, the more nearly their costs will approximate to those of the national hauliers. Moreover, the trends towards a logistics approach by shippers and greater service specialization by carriers, and the move to a contractual rather than transaction-based relationship between the two parties further reduce the opportunities for casual cabotage.

However, if casual cabotage can be dismissed as a short-term irrelevance, the same cannot be said for network cabotage. There is undoubtedly scope for organized cabotage by large transnational transport and logistics services providers. By balancing flows and improving resource utilization, these companies will be able to remain profitable in the more competitive markets of the 1990s. In the long run, this greater efficiency will become an important competitive advantage, and will be one of the forces that changes the shape of the market and favours the growth of mega-carriers.

The less specialized the transport service, the more important the immediate impact of cabotage will be. This has implications for the relevance of cabotage across different sectors of the haulage industry. For example, national long-distance, FTL movements will be most under attack, whereas foreign vehicles and drivers will not really be in the market for specialized high street deliveries.

# Conclusions

The consequences of transport price reductions and the greater ease of moving products across borders can be summarized as follows:

- to make European industry more competitive at a global level (logistics costs are a major factor cost in some sectors, and transport costs are a significant proportion of logistics costs)
- to allow industry to locate stockholding according to more rational supply and demand factors (since borders will no longer dictate distribution patterns)
- to encourage more road freight, leading to more road congestion, and possibly to make it more difficult to persuade shippers to use rail or road–rail combined transport for marginal shipments

- to change the optimum gateway ports for European world trade (for example, with reduced inland transport prices, it could be argued that Marseilles or Genoa could replace Rotterdam as the best gateway port for Europe–Far East liner services)
- to lead users of transport services to select regional hauliers, bringing together the functions of domestic and international operators in an integrated way
- further to encourage manufacturers and retailers to source supplies from peripheral regions of Europe, where costs such as wages may be low

However, we began this chapter by noting the conflicting views of shippers and carriers in relation to future transport prices, and it is important to return to this fundamental question. The analysis that we have presented leads us to conclude that prices are unlikely to rise, but that the extent of any fall is highly dependent upon which sector of the market is being considered. We have concentrated here on the dramatic institutional changes facing European logistics, such as deregulation and the abolition of border formalities, all of which will tend to push prices down. But other, less predictable, changes could occur in the longer term. For example, road haulage prices would rise if fuel taxes were sharply increased as part of a Europe-wide package of environmental measures, and productivity gains could be offset by growing road congestion on urban and inter-urban routes. It is these longer-term issues, centred on the environment, which are addressed in the next chapter.

# 13
# Green Logistics

## Introduction

Concern for the environment has long ceased to be a preoccupation of fringe lobby groups; it has moved into the mainstream of governmental and business interests. Neither governments nor companies can now afford to be negligent towards the environment, especially in the advanced economies of Europe, the USA and Japan. Regulation is increasingly designed to limit the adverse environmental impacts of various economic activities. This has resulted in initiatives as diverse as restricting the emissions of sulphur dioxide from the chimneys of coal-fired power stations, to making grants available to farmers so that they conserve parts of their property that are rich in wildlife (for example, wetlands and woodlands) rather than cultivating them.

Similarly, companies have been very careful to present a green image to the public. Advertising, in particular, is often aimed at proving the green credentials of a company. For example, Enron Corp promotes its natural gas as 'the energy choice' for a cleaner, safer world. The Audi car company, in its European advertising, emphasizes that all models within its range are already equipped with catalytic converters as standard, even before it becomes a mandatory requirement across the European Community (EC).

Both the users and providers of logistics services have good reason to be concerned about their environmental credentials. The transport and storage of goods is at the centre of logistics activities for many companies, and can be problematic. Companies producing or carrying hazardous goods have special cause to be worried; the environmental consequences of accidents are potentially very serious. BASF, the German chemicals combine, now has a policy of consigning its goods by rail and inland waterways whenever possible, because it is thought that there is a greater risk of accidents on the roads.

However, the environmental impact of logistics activities must be considered in wider terms than simply the *kinds* of goods that are stored and transported. In particular, all kinds of freight transport activity have consequences for the environment, and the acceptability of these consequences is increasingly being called into question. Without doubt, it is the lorry which is most frequently characterized as the environmental 'villain of the piece'.

Many studies (see, for example, Wardroper, 1981; Whitelegg, 1988) have already catalogued the environmental complaints against lorries, which include pollution from exhaust gases, noise from engines and tyres, vibration and visual intrusion. There are also safety concerns, as lorries involved in serious accidents often cause fatalities, because of their size and momentum. Taking a broader view, many environmental pressure groups consider road freight transport to be wasteful of energy, which in turn contributes to a more rapid depletion of the world reserves of fossil fuels and to global warming; according to one study lorries produce 16 per cent of the $CO_2$ emissions that can be attributed to road transport (IVECO Ford, 1990a).

With increasing frequency, we now hear calls to restrict the use of lorries, with the aim of bringing about environmental improvement. As a result, many cities now impose night and weekend restrictions on lorry operation. But some 'solutions to the lorry problem' are unlikely to be successful until we understand *why* business wants to use lorries in the way that it does. In particular, we must recognize that lorry operation is a consequence of logistics planning, and that until the objectives of logistics planning are understood, attempts to control the growth of lorry traffic in the interests of the environment are unlikely to succeed.

Earlier chapters have already referred to 'supply chain management', and this phrase is the key to understanding the role of lorries in the movement of goods. Increasingly, companies are concerned with looking at their flow of goods and materials in an integral way, rather than in separate stages. Logistics therefore represents a holistic approach, in which component supply, production of finished goods and their distribution to, say, retail outlets must be considered as a continuous stream of activity. Crucially, this leads to the recognition that each element of the activity impacts on some or all of the others. Successful logistics planning means making sure that advantage is gained from exploiting trade-offs between these different elements; for example, storage and transport.

The evidence of successful logistics planning can be seen all around us. Two industries which have had an especially deep involvement with logistics are car manufacturing and consumer electronics. This has resulted in a number of important consequences for transport. Ford's engine plant in South Wales, for example, sends engines to car assembly locations all over Europe; engines are no longer made locally alongside each car production plant. Similarly, in electronics, many computers are now made to order, rather than being available off the shelf. Shortening product life-cycles, improved manufacturing techniques and innovations such as the just-in-time delivery of components have all meant that electronics has become a demand-led rather than a supply-led industry.

It is beyond the scope of this chapter to consider all possible logistics innovations, and their impact on transport and the environment. However, by examining in the following section just three of the more important ones, namely centralization of inventory, 24-hour lorry operations, and just-in-time delivery, we will be able to understand more about companies' motivations in relation to logistics and the consequences for transport. It is then possible to see what initiatives are needed to reduce the environmental impact of road freight transport in particular, and this is the focus of the concluding sections of the chapter.

# Innovation in Logistics: the Impact on Transport and the Environment

## Centralization of inventory

One of the classic relationships in logistics is the trade-off between warehousing and transport: as the number of warehouses is increased, the cost of operating them also increases, but transport operating cost falls, for a constant throughput of goods through the warehouse. This rule is usually presented as a diagram, to illustrate the implications for combined warehouse and transport operating costs and the choice of an optimum number of warehouses in a distribution system (see figure 13.1).

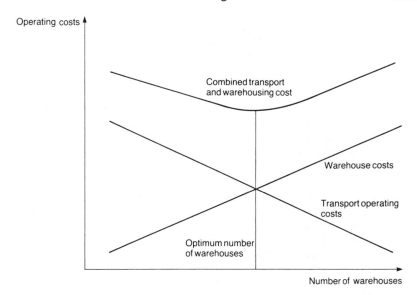

**Figure 13.1**   Trade-off in transport and warehouse operating costs.

Over the years, there has been a modification of the rule, which now takes into account the cost of holding inventory in warehouses. Variations in this cost have been formulated into the 'square root law' (Maister, 1976), which states that safety and cycle inventory requirements are related to the square root of the number of warehouses in a distribution system. Thus, moving from a system of ten depots to a completely centralized system using one depot would, in theory, reduce the inventory requirement by 68 per cent (McKinnon, 1989).

Although there are some important objections to an unbounded application of the square root (see, for example, Das, 1978), practice has shown that it performs reasonably well (Sussams, 1986). For this reason many companies, and especially those carrying high-value inventory, have been keen to convert to a system of distribution based on a central, national warehouse, rather than maintain a network of, say, ten regional warehouses.

The powerful attraction of inventory cost reduction can be illustrated well using a hypothetical example. A system of decentralized warehousing which is typical of many European operations is shown in figure 13.2a; it is designated here as Scenario 1. Under Scenario 1 there are three production locations and four warehouses,

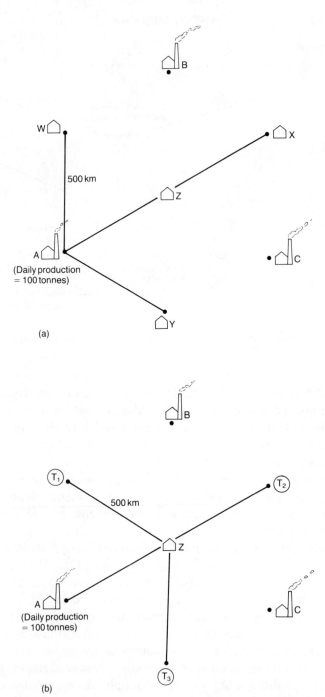

**Figure 13.2** Primary transport for alternative systems of warehousing. (a) Scenario 1: decentralized warehousing. (b) Scenario 2: centralized warehousing.

as illustrated. The distribution system has both primary and secondary transport components. Primary transport is concerned with the transport of goods from factories to warehouses, while secondary transport entails the final delivery of goods from warehouses to the customer.

In many cases, the centralization of warehousing, in itself, has little impact on secondary transport, since breaking-bulk for final delivery has to take place with or without centralization. We have assumed in figure 13.2 that both the warehouses and their replacements, the transit points, are carefully located to minimize secondary distribution. No change in secondary distribution is therefore implied in the switch from warehouses to transit points. Consequently, figure 13.2a concentrates on the primary transport and the location of facilities within the distribution system. Furthermore, for analytical simplicity, suppose that we are dealing with a 'balanced' distribution system, with each production location generating the same output and each warehouse processing the same throughput of goods.

Assume that production location A sends a daily vehicle load of 25 tonnes to each warehouse. Given the geometry of the distribution system in figure 13.2a, production location A thus generates 5000 vehicle–kilometres each day (including return trips by vehicles) in primary transport movements to warehouses.

Next, suppose that the production company decides to centralize its inventory holdings at warehouse Z (see Scenario 2, figure 13.2b). As a consequence, warehouses W, X and Y simply become transit points for goods, still marking the interface between primary and secondary transport, but without any inventory holding. This may readily be achieved by using the network facilities of a distribution contractor to re-channel goods in transit, or by using demountable systems (swap bodies) at secure lorry parks (Cooper and Doganis, 1982).

The purpose of retaining the interface between primary and secondary transport is, of course, to ensure that goods being delivered to customers are carried on the right size of vehicle; secondary transport vehicles are often small–medium in size to meet the conditions for urban delivery, while primary transport vehicles are often as large as possible to secure technical economies of scale (and thus low unit costs) on long-distance hauls along major highways. Inventory centralization therefore has little impact on secondary transport, but dramatic consequences for primary transport, as illustrated in figure 13.2b for Scenario 2. First, the entire daily production of 100 tonnes from production location A is channelled to the central warehouse Z, from where redistribution to transit points T takes place. Second, the number of daily vehicle–kilometres rises from 5000 under Scenario 1 to 7000 under Scenario 2, an increase of 40 per cent.

For the production company, a major benefit to compensate for the increasing cost of primary transport must come from savings in inventory. In table 13.1 it is shown how these savings weigh against increased costs for primary transport, using two different values for

**Table 13.1** Costs and benefits[a] arising from the centralization of inventory (that is, a change from Scenario 1 to Scenario 2)

|                                                                        | (ecu per day)            |
| ---------------------------------------------------------------------- | ------------------------ |
| (a) Costs                                                              |                          |
| Increase in primary transport                                          | 2000 × 1.2<br>= 2400     |
| (b) Benefits                                                           |                          |
| Reduction in inventory cost<br>(for low-value goods at 500 ecu per tonne) | 250                   |
| Reduction in inventory cost<br>(for high-value goods at 10 000 per tonne) | 5000                  |

[a] The calculations in table 13.1 are carried out as follows:
The increase in primary transport:

(a)  Scenario 1 return distances comprise three trips of 1000 km (from A to W, Y and Z) and one of 2000 km (from A to X). The total is therefore 5000 vehicle-kilometres.
(b)  Scenario 2 return distances comprise four trips of 1000 km (from A to Z) and then a further three trips of 1000 km (from X to T1, T2 and T3). The total is therefore 7000 vehicle-kilometres.

Scenario 2 therefore generates 2000 more vehicle–kilometres each day than Scenario 1.
Primary transport costs are 1.2 ecu per kilometre. For inventory costs it is assumed that there are ten stock turns each year and that the interest rate is 10 per cent. In using the square root law to calculate inventory reduction arising from centralization, the move from four warehouses to one gives a 50 per cent reduction in inventory.
Note that it may also be possible to achieve savings in warehouse operating costs as a result of centralization if economies of scale come into play (see Williams, 1974). These costs have not been assessed because no assumptions have been made about warehouse size.

inventory. The figures relate to the entire distribution system illustrated in figure 13.2.

From table 13.1 it is clear why savings in inventory costs have been an important focus of logistics policy for many companies which are producers of high-value goods; the savings more than outweigh increased costs in primary transport (by a ratio of more than 2 to 1 in our example). It is only for products with a relatively low value that centralization does not work. As table 13.1 shows, for low-value products the increased cost of primary transport can outweigh the savings in inventory.

The worry for environmentalists is that advanced economies, in the course of becoming wealthier – as has been the trend in the EC – tend to transport larger volumes of high-value goods. Consequently, the attraction of centralized inventory becomes stronger and more primary transport is generated. In the case of our hypothetical example the increase in primary transport is 40 per cent, which has major implications for pollution, visual intrusion and fuel consumption, together with increased demand for road space.

Back in the 1970s, Lichfield developed the idea of a 'planning balance sheet' to assess the merits and demerits of different planning schemes, and to make a judgement of the relative worth of different schemes (Lichfield et al., 1975). This idea may readily be extended to logistics with respect to environmental impact. But if we construct an 'environmental balance sheet' for centralized inventory, it is easy enough to find many negatives (such as increased pollution) but much harder to find positives; only a smaller aggregate land-take for warehousing would appear to qualify. In logistics, this is the crux of a potentially serious problem, which is only just becoming more widely recognized. A commercial decision, such as inventory centralization, represents a sensible outcome for a company when it only has to consider its own internal costs. Yet this decision has extensive social implications which are the cause of growing public sensitivity. If companies should be made, in any way, to internalize more of the social and environmental costs they generate through their activities, the consequences for logistics planning will be severe.

## 24-hour lorry operation

The decision to operate lorries round the clock is often linked to warehouse centralization. As supply lines between customer locations and warehouses become longer – as a result of centralization – there is the danger that levels of customer service will deteriorate. The multiple-shifting of vehicles is one way of ensuring that, for example, inventory is replenished more promptly and that out-of-stock situations are avoided.

However, some companies have introduced round-the-clock working of lorry fleets for the benefits that this practice can bring in its own right. The initiative has often come from manufacturing, where many companies run factories on both day and night shifts. By spreading their fixed costs, notably the capital costs of machinery, these companies reduce their unit production costs, and this helps them to remain competitive.

Some freight companies also see a potential benefit in the more intensive use of their expensive capital equipment, especially vehicles. This represents doing more with less. Why not use vehicles on two or even three shifts in each 24-hour period, rather than only during the daytime?

At present, the benefits of round-the-clock operation are not alone sufficiently great to induce many companies to switch from day-only operations. This is partly due to labour costs being a high proportion of total operating costs. Paying drivers extra money for working unsocial hours means that many of the gains from spreading fixed costs (such as vehicle licences and insurance) and reduced investment (such as a smaller vehicle fleet) are undermined by higher labour costs. In one study of round-the-clock operation, it was calculated that the overall saving, compared with day-only working, is of the order of 4–6 per cent; the exact figure for any one company will depend mainly upon the length of vehicle replacement cycles (Cooper and Tweddle, 1990). For many companies, savings of this order may not be considered sufficiently high to justify a switch to round-the-clock working of lorry fleets.

However, from an environmental point of view there are some benefits from round-the-clock scheduling of vehicles, although these must be carefully assessed against certain disbenefits. One of the main benefits is reduced fuel consumption. One company carried out a test programme of fuel consumption, the results of which were reported in Cooper and Tweddle (1990), and are shown here as table 13.2.

It is shown in table 13.2 that improvements in fuel consumption of between 4 and 6 per cent could be obtained by running vehicles at night rather than by day. The company conducting the test also found that these savings could be further enhanced by fitting aerodynamic aids.

**Table 13.2** Results of company fuel consumption tests (litres per 100 kilometres)

|                     | Aerodynamic aids | |
|---------------------|:----:|:-------:|
|                     | With | Without |
| Daytime operation   | 42.19 | 45.04 |
| Night-time operation | 40.65 | 42.21 |

*Source*: Cooper and Tweddle, 1990, *Logistics and Distribution Planning*, Kogan Page, London

Furthermore, it is important to realize that the future potential for saving fuel by operating at night is likely to increase as growing daytime congestion on roads adversely affects fuel consumption figures. It is not inconceivable that, by the end of the century, it will be possible to save around 10 per cent on fuel consumption by running at night.

Not all freight companies, of course, will readily be able to introduce night-time operation for their vehicle fleets, because customers restrict the times for delivery, often for safety or security reasons or to avoid noise disturbance to nearby residents. The best opportunities will be for operators supplying retailers that use distribution centres that are open at all times, or manufacturers in continuous process industries.

## Just-in-time deliveries

Just-in-time (JIT) delivery is widely regarded as one of the most successful innovations in logistics in recent times. A great number of manufacturers, and even retailers, have changed their delivery practices to JIT, and there are specialist freight companies which offer JIT as a service to clients. Indeed, the importance of JIT has been so widely recognized that many people outside the logistics sector, including the media and the general public, are aware of it.

Many applaud JIT as a major advance in supply chain management. But what of the environmental implications of JIT? Is JIT to be welcomed or should it treated with rather more circumspection than has hitherto been the case?

In chapter 4 we discussed the principles of JIT and its importance as an inventory-free production method, particularly in electronics and motor manufacturing. Since Taiichi Ohno, widely regarded as the father of JIT, transformed manufacturing at Toyota, many others have quickly followed. The pioneers of JIT brought about important changes, not only to the manufacturing process but also to transport.

The implications of JIT delivery for transport are indeed dramatic. Instead of a large vehicle delivering, say, weekly, the requirement is for much smaller vehicles to deliver daily or, in some cases, several times each day.[8] For many large Japanese manufacturers, this has not caused a problem, since component suppliers are often located near the factory gate; the giant Toyoda works is a case in point. However, in Europe, where planning controls are often tight and component suppliers long-established at distant locations, JIT means an extensive use of the public road network. This inevitably means environmental deterioration, with several, smaller vehicles being used to carry the same amount of goods as a single large vehicle that was used before the introduction of JIT. The result is more fuel consumed and more pollution.

Assuming that vehicles are run fully loaded, five vehicles each of 5 tonnes capacity could be used in a JIT operation in place of a single vehicle with a capacity of 25 tonnes. It is shown in figure 13.3 that using the five smaller vehicles results in the consumption of 165 litres

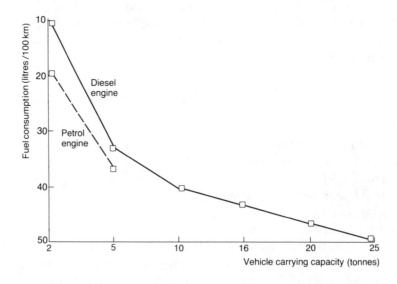

**Figure 13.3** Fuel consumption figures for vehicles of different carrying capacities.
*Source*: Based on data from *Commercial Motor* tables of operating costs

of fuel per 100 km, whereas the larger vehicle would use only 49 litres. This represents more than a two-fold increase in fuel consumption.

In addition to increased air pollution and greater energy use, there will also be the likelihood of greater noise disturbance and visual intrusion, as more small vehicles are used in place of large ones. Vibration might be reduced, but this is the only aspect of JIT deliveries that could lead to a favourable outcome. Otherwise, taking the 'environmental balance sheet' approach, it is evident that JIT can lead to road transport practices which are hostile to the environment.

Moreover, another consequence of JIT may be the transfer of goods from rail to road, a development which is generally considered to have negative environmental consequences. In a comparative study of France and the USA, Garreau, Lieb and Millen (1991) noted that the users of logistics services used road to a greater extent following the introduction of JIT. Rail was the loser, although there are circumstances in which rail can successfully adapt to JIT practices. SNCF, for example, delivers to one of France's largest chemical groups at Noyan from one of its distribution centres or *plateforms* (meaning a terminal the activities of which include not only transfer and handling, but also warehousing, sorting, conditioning, distribution in consignments according to shipper instructions and even product assembly; see *Cargo Systems*, 1990).

Finally, it must be recognized that some manufacturers are requesting JIT deliveries from suppliers in the mistaken belief that it saves them money. Unthinkingly applied, JIT can be inappropriate to a company's needs and, as a result, more expensive in the wrong context.

The problem arises because JIT is widely perceived as a mark of logistics excellence. No manufacturer wants to display ignorance, and many hasten to introduce JIT deliveries within their manufacturing schedules. But JIT must form part of an integrated manufacturing plan designed to eliminate excessive holdings of inventory (see the McDonnell Douglas case study in chapter 4). In isolation, the frequent delivery of small consignments of, say, components will not be enough to bring benefits to companies. Worse still, some companies would find they are incurring disbenefits if they looked more closely at all their costs, this being especially true of those which are not sufficiently in touch with the pricing practices used by their suppliers. Some of these suppliers will readily agree to supply on a JIT basis, but will invoice the client company on a higher tariff to recoup the additional costs of delivery. This action can readily wipe out gains sought elsewhere by the manufacturer when introducing JIT.

Such an outcome is rather an uncomfortable one to contemplate: the supplier is happy because he is keeping his client happy; the client is happy because his manufacturing is now served according to the latest fashion for JIT delivery; but environmental groups are entitled to feel aggrieved because there is no tangible gain to the economy resulting from the switch to JIT; and the environment suffers because more, smaller vehicles are on the roads, carrying the same amount of freight as the fewer, larger vehicles that they displaced. Clearly, in logistics as in any other area of business, following fashion can be no substitute for careful planning.

# A Regulatory Framework for Green Logistics

This book is essentially about the business of providing logistics services; it does not set out to provide a detailed examination of all aspects of government policy that might affect logistics, as well as other kinds of business activity. For this reason we do not consider, say, differences in employment legislation between EC member states (except for a brief mention of drivers' working hours), or varying taxation policy. However, given the growing role of regulation to protect the environment, it would be unwise to neglect the consequences of government policy that is specifically designed to make logistics greener. Three possible regulatory initiatives, each with the purpose of minimizing the environmental impact to some degree, are examined in this section; namely, improving the design of lorries, making road transport comparatively more expensive, and encouraging the use of combined transport systems.

## Improvements in lorry design

Given that lorries are the main target of environmental pressure groups, there is some merit in using policy instruments to bring about improvements in lorry design that would make the operation of lorries less harmful to the environment. Yet such an approach would bring about only relatively limited benefits. For example, improvements in engine design can reduce fuel requirements, noise and pollution; and better suspension design can lead to less vibration. But it is difficult for design changes to make much difference to a lorry's visual intrusion, or its demand for space on congested roads.

Furthermore, in the context of some logistics innovations, improvements in the design of lorries will do little more than slightly ameliorate the effects of environmental deterioration. Take, for example, the centralization of inventory, considered above. In moving from Scenario 1 (decentralized warehousing) to Scenario 2 (centralized warehousing), there is a net environmental loss which cannot be fully reversed by the simple expedient of improving lorry design.

Consequently, it is unlikely that the improvement of lorry design, as a sole policy measure contemplated by government, will be sufficient to satisfy the green lobby. Further measures will certainly be sought. Technological fixes will not on their own be sufficient to reduce the environmental impact of lorries significantly; changes in operating practices are also essential.

## Making road transport comparatively more expensive

A number of logistics innovations appear to have occurred partly because transport is regarded by companies as a relatively cheap input, compared with other logistics activities. Again, consider the example of the centralization of inventory. Because companies, in analysing their costs, have come to the conclusion that transport is cheap, they are happy to spend more on it, because the extra cost is so readily recouped in savings on inventory. But if transport is suddenly made more expensive, then the trend towards centralization could be reversed.

However, the scope for making road freight transport in particular more expensive may not be great, given the wider political implications for governments. It is shown in table 13.1 that primary transport costs under Scenario 2 would have to be raised by 2600 ecu per day to balance the cost savings in inventory for high-value goods. This means more than doubling transport operating costs.

Government could seek to achieve this increase by raising taxation on fuel. But since fuel costs are often only about 30 per cent of total operating costs in transport, this would mean the introduction of a swingeing fuel tax. There must be serious doubts about the preparedness of governments to introduce policies aimed at raising fuel duty to very high levels. A hostile reaction could be expected, not just from the business community, but from others such as private motorists, whose fuel costs may also need to rise as part of a general policy of making transport more expensive. In addition, the global competitiveness of European companies must be considered. The policy aim must be to retain the business advantages of logistics innovation while minimizing any adverse environmental impact.

## Combined transport

Combined transport represents the great hope of the environmental pressure groups and the railways alike, promising relief from congestion and pollution caused by lorries, and at the same time restoring the commercial fortunes of the railway companies. The key feature of combined transport is its intermodalism: goods are switched between road and rail (and sometimes sea) in the course of a single journey from, say, producer to customer. Central to the idea of combined transport is the ability of each transport mode to make the contribution that is best suited to its operating characteristics. Therefore, in many cases, the role of road transport will be to perform collection and delivery services around towns and cities, while rail will be used for long-haul work between major centres of production and consumption.

Combined transport comprises no fewer than three separate technological systems. The first of these is based upon maritime and continental containers. Most railway companies in Europe have well-established subsidiaries which are responsible for moving containers (for example, Transfracht in Germany, CNC in France, and Freightliner in the UK). These subsidiaries are particularly geared to the movement of containers from ports, so serving shipping lines operating to and from the Far East, North America, Australasia and elsewhere.

However, containers have a restricted application in inland transport. Containers on ships must be stacked, so they must be sturdy in construction. In turn, this makes them heavy – too heavy for road hauliers since they unduly restrict payloads. Consequently, the preferred technologies for combined transport restricted to inland movements are 'unaccompanied' road–rail transport (trailers, semi-trailers and demountable bodies) and accompanied road–rail transport (complete vehicles comprising tractor units and semi-trailers and so on, together with drivers). These two technologies for inland work complete the trio of technologies in European combined transport, but it is important to point out that road–rail transport services are unevenly spread. France and Germany (with Novatrans and Kombiverkehr respectively) have the most extensive road–rail services – both have been extremely successful.

Kombiverkehr is jointly owned by a consortium of hauliers using the road–rail services and Deutsche Bundesbahn, which is the minority shareholder. As shown in figure 13.4, growth in the number of units (semi-trailers and demountable bodies) has been impressive, from around 20 000 in 1969 to nearly 650 000 in 1989, representing an annual growth rate of about 5 per cent.

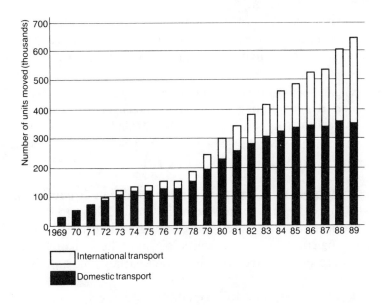

**Figure 13.4**   Carryings by Kombiverkehr, 1969–89.
*Source*: Kombiverkehr annual report, 1990

In recent years, the major source of growth has been international work, which now comprises 45 per cent of units moved. This trend seems likely to continue as economic integration develops within the EC.

The success of both Kombiverkehr and Novatrans in developing a new market for international combined transport (ICT) has not gone unnoticed. In its final report on ICT for the Commission of the

European Communities and a number of railway-related organizations, the A. T. Kearney Consulting Group reached the following key conclusion:

> As a substitute for road transport, international combined transport possesses intrinsically, in terms of performance and economic competitiveness, the features sought for by users, and can contribute to reducing the obstacles to international road transport caused by infrastructure saturation and environmental and social pressures.
>
> (A. T. Kearney, 1990)

The critical word in the above conclusion is the word 'intrinsically'. Essentially what the A. T. Kearney report is saying is that the technical characteristics of ICT make a transfer of goods from road to rail a good prospect. Yet there are serious barriers to realizing this goal, as the second conclusion in the report recognizes:

> Realising the optimal development potential of international combined transport requires setting up an international network, improving overall performance, reducing costs and making full use of productivity reserves, as well as an aggressive marketing policy.
>
> (A. T. Kearney, 1990)

The report goes on to say that, if these conditions are fulfilled, then ICT volume could triple between 1990 and 2005, to reach 43.2 million tonnes. In the interests of creating an improved framework for green logistics, such an achievement must be welcomed. But, in one crucial respect, we feel that the A. T. Kearney report on ICT does not go far enough.

The key point is that ICT operators are the customers of the railway companies, and unless major steps are taken to reform the organization of the railway companies, then the promise of ICT is unlikely to be realized. We can already see the root of the problem in current Kombiverkehr operations. In Germany, Deutsche Bundesbahn (DB) not only provides train services for Kombiverkehr, but also provides train and wagonload services in its own right. But because DB, in effect, runs its business according to revenue-maximizing principles, it sees Kombiverkehr as a threat to achieving some of its business objectives. This point is explained in figure 13.5. In a wagonload rail service, DB collects wagons from the private sidings of a customer, marshals them into trainloads at location A and sends

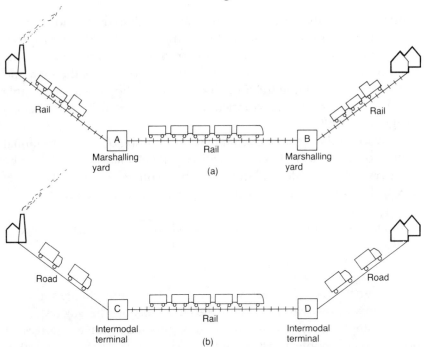

**Figure 13.5** Rail and combined transport operations: the modal contributions (a) railways (wagon-load); (b) combined transport.

them to location B. Here wagons are once again marshalled and sent to their final destinations. If Kombiverkehr were to take over this work it would mean that the collection and delivery operations would be completed by road rather than rail. Since this means a loss of revenue by rail (which still performs the line-haul work in either case) DB is not always supportive of Kombiverkehr.

Clearly, conflicts of interests of this kind cannot promote the development of ICT in Europe; and the problem becomes much worse when a number of railway companies have to co-operate, especially when they have different business priorities. The construction of the Channel Tunnel has highlighted this last aspect, with revenue-maximizing DB finding it difficult to agree a joint freight strategy with profit-maximizing British Rail.

In our view, both ICT and the conventional services of the railways are unlikely to reach their full potential without dramatic change in the organization of the railways in the EC, which is currently a serious burden to progress. This problem is fully recognized by the European Commission, which sent a paper on transport policy (COM(89)566 final) to the Council of the European Communities in

January 1990. In the paper, it was argued that there should be a separation of infrastructure and operations in the EC, a proposal which has provoked fierce opposition from some quarters. Rogissart from SNCB (Belgian railways), for example, condemns the plan and attributes the declining freight market share of the railways (see table 13.3) to distortions in competition which favour road hauliers (Rogissart, 1990).

However, others take a different view; Amatore, of the International Union of Railways (UIC) recognizes the challenge faced by the railways, notably deregulation of the haulage sector (Amatore, 1990). He acknowledges current deficiencies, saying that:

> In some countries staff numbers go up and down according to the type of government which is in power. It is obvious that such practices cannot lead to rational planning.

But, further, Amatore foresees the need for major changes in both operations and organization. In the first category he suggests that marshalling operations, terminal runs and locomotive changes at borders will become a feature of the past; and, not before time, that

**Table 13.3**  Market shares of freight transport in Europe

| | Total intra-EC billion tonne–kilometres performed | | | |
| | Road | Rail | Inland waterway | Total of the three modes |
|---|---|---|---|---|
| 1986 | 651 | 147.6 | 92.1 | 891 |
| 1987 | 696 | 146.1 | 89.2 | 931 |
| 1988 | 756 | 147.3 | 94.7 | 998 |
| *Annual growth rates* | | | | |
| 1986–7 | 6.9% | −1.0% | −3.1% | 4.5% |
| 1987–8 | 8.6% | 0.8% | 6.2% | 7.2% |
| *Modal split* | | | | |
| 1986 | 73.1% | 16.6% | 10.3% | 100% |
| 1987 | 74.7% | 15.7% | 9.6% | 100% |
| 1988 | 75.7% | 14.8% | 9.5% | 100% |

*Source*: Europa Transport Annual Report, 1988

efficient trainload work is the forte of the railway, and one it needs to concentrate upon. But the key to progress must be in the organization of railways in Europe. At the very least, as Amatore says:

> . . . relations between railways and governments will have to be clarified, since the limited managerial autonomy of railway prevents them from achieving their commercial and financial objectives.

To many observers, the railways represent an example of 'Eurosclerosis' at its worst, with excessive government interference making it difficult for them to operate efficiently. If the railways were to be invented now, to best serve the EC, no-one would organize them according to their present structure. Reform of railways institutions is urgently required, and not only for them to serve a green role.

Many freight companies, sometimes those with extensive road transport interests, are keen to see a good rail alternative to road. They see the need to transfer more freight from road to rail as congestion worsens on roads, simply to satisfy the needs of client companies in retailing and manufacturing.

Ideally, there should be a three-fold approach to reform:

1  There should be a separation of responsibility for track and operations, as there is now in Sweden. This would make the railway operating companies more responsive to the needs of users of logistics services (such as freight forwarders and shippers).
2  Rail operating companies from the private sector should be allowed to compete with their public-sector counterparts. This means giving private operators track access throughout the EC, to allow them to develop successful pan-European services for client companies.
3  There should be one track authority for rail throughout Europe. This is necessary to ensure that network bottlenecks (such as the one between Germany and the Netherlands) are overcome and that technical differences (such as the loading gauge) are minimized.

We do, of course, recognize the formidable problems of implementing these proposals, which many would say are too radical. But are they any more radical than other, greater proposals which have wide support within the EC, notably economic and political union of the members states? It is difficult to see why the monopoly of a railway company should be seen as immutable.

The railways need radical institutional reform; otherwise they cannot live up to the role that is increasingly expected of them by both environmental groups and industry. Without reform, innovation by the railways will remain stifled. (As Bernd Metzinger, the president of Hupac and Danzas International, reminded everyone at the Euromodal 1990 conference, combined transport was initiated by the hauliers and the freight forwarders, not the railways.) Furthermore, if rail is not stimulated to innovate and compete, rather than to complain about the terms of competition, there is concern that rapid environmental deterioration and increased congestion will lead to calls to restrict the activities of the haulage sector. If this means re-regulation, then it will certainly result in rail winning business back from the hauliers – but it will not be the way in which to re-invigorate the European economy.

## Environmental Planning by Companies

While waiting for reform of railway organization in Europe to provide a gateway to green logistics, many road-based freight companies would do well to see how their operations could be made greener. There is considerable merit in taking a three-stage approach, the first being an *environmental audit* of a company's logistics activities. Some companies will even want to make this publicly available; for example, Norsk Hydro sees environmental interests as being synonymous with the public interest (Thomas, 1990). Second, there must be a *listing of actions* required to achieve reduced environmental impact, and then a *priority ranking* of the actions.

Many freight companies have considerable scope for reducing the environmental impact of their activities. An understanding of that scope can be readily achieved through an environmental audit which is designed to highlight those activities which have adverse consequences for the environment. Many of these activities and their consequences will be obvious, such as the pollution effects of operating vehicles. However, others such as the use of CFCs in cold storage, wasted heat from refrigerator plants, or the use of packaging materials which are difficult to recycle, may be less obvious.

By careful consideration of all aspects of a company's logistics activities, a comprehensive assessment of the environmental impact can be made. The list can often be a long one. For example, a working group within NFC, the UK-based freight conglomerate, listed no fewer than 70 kinds of environmental impact resulting from its activities. However, it is important to note that many of these impacts were not related to logistics, including as they did such activities as switching off lights in empty rooms.

Once these different kinds of environmental impact have been identified, it is then necessary to go on to consider what actions might be taken to reduce their scale. In each instance a choice of options is available, and it is important to find the preferred option in terms of both the cost of the action and the environmental benefit that will result. This can be quite a sophisticated exercise, perhaps necessitating the conversion of all benefits into money terms, and using shadow pricing as appropriate.

Finally, actions designed to reduce environmental impact can be given a priority ranking, according to their costs and benefits. In a number of cases there will be the bonus of identifying actions which can be worthwhile in their own right, without counting the external benefits to the environment. Cold storage may be a case in point, where waste heat from refrigeration units is often simply ducted into the open air. It may be worth following the example of countries which lead in the conservation of energy, such as Sweden, where waste heat is routinely used to heat buildings adjacent to the cold store. But this is not without its problems, since most heat from cold storage is produced during the summer months when it is not needed to heat, say, offices.

However, a crucial point needs to be made about the environmental audit and action designed to make a company's logistics activities greener. It will be very unusual for a 'quick fix' of one of two actions to have a significant effect. More often, effective environmental planning will require a coordinated plan of action, covering a number of related logistics activities. Only by a deep diffusion of actions throughout the logistics function will any significant gains for the environment result. In turn, companies might then be able to enjoy a marketing dividend from their actions.

We began this chapter by noting how various producers and manufacturers had been able to promote themselves as green; there is no reason why logistics services companies should not follow their example.

# 14

# Into the Twenty-first Century

## Introduction

Logistics has made a considerable contribution to business in the second half of the twentieth century. For many companies, improved management of the supply chain has been the key to achieving competitive advantage. This has happened in a variety of ways. At its simplest level, by making supply chain costs more transparent it has been possible for managers to become more cost-competitive through trade-offs in the supply chain between different logistics functions. Increased spending on transport, for example, has often been more than compensated for by savings in warehouse and inventory costs. At a more sophisticated level, some manufacturers have redesigned products and production methods to take special account of logistics. This is especially true of the electronics and automotive industries, where greater 'commonality' between products has simplified the procurement of components, improved quality and brought more flexibility to manufacturing: specifications for finished products can now be switched at a much later stage of the production process, to take account of changes in demand.

In this way, logistics can provide a key input even to product planning. Improvements in manufacturing practice, underpinned by logistics concepts, mean that the product lead time from drawing board (or computer screen) to market can be substantially reduced. As a result, manufacturers can respond more quickly to new demands in the marketplace, or gain a lead over competitors by being the first to create new market niches with the introduction of innovative products. Japanese companies in the automotive sector have been particularly adept at 'fast-tuning' products to markets. A case in point is in the market for inexpensive four-wheel-drive vehicles. Makers such as Suzuki, Isuzu and Daihatsu first created the niche, then had it all to themselves as other manufacturers raced to catch up. With European manufacturers typically having a seven-year or more product development cycle, compared with the four-year Japanese one, closing the gap has been difficult.

The 1990s will therefore see many manufacturers trying to match the pacesetters in logistics, not only in the electronics and automotive industries, but also in other market sectors. This process is bound to continue into the twenty-first century, since the laggards are a long way behind and it will take longer than a decade to catch up. It is more than just a question of copying techniques; company cultures will often need substantial redirection to instil the right kind of competitive values in the context of a rapidly changing business environment.

For Europe, there are some special considerations to be taken into account. Importantly, there is the changing face of Europe itself. The 'Iron Curtain' between East and West has all but disappeared, and this has important implications for patterns of trade within Europe, and so for logistics. Europe is a small, crowded continent and there is justifiable concern about environmental deterioration as Europe's economy continues to grow. Together, these two *external* factors will have a crucial impact on logistics in the twenty-first century. But there will also be *internal* factors at work. First, we need to consider user strategies in logistics, which are changing fast in Europe. Second, what about the strategies of providers of logistics services? How might these change or, more pertinently, how *should* they change as we move into the twenty-first century? We discuss both external and internal factors in the following sections.

# The Changing Face of Europe

As we pointed out in chapter 2, the character and structure of the three main trading blocs in Europe, namely the European Community (EC), EFTA and Comecon, have changed substantially over recent years. In particular, the strongest of the trading blocs, the EC, has turned into a powerful magnet for countries in the other two. Thus the composition of the trading blocs themselves seems certain to be different in the next century, and Comecon is likely to have disappeared as a formal association of countries in eastern Europe. There is the strong possibility that the EC will comprise around 15 countries, rather than the current 12. But perhaps more important than this potential enlargement is the growth of trade between East and West.

At present, trade volumes are relatively small, but there is massive potential for growth. This may arise in a number of ways. In the first place there is agriculture. Much of eastern Europe contains very fertile land which is currently not very productive: state control of agriculture failed to produce yields in line with potential. However, in future, there is every prospect that eastern Europe agriculture will revive, and that farmers will seek new markets in the West. The main obstacle that they now face is the EC's Common Agricultural Policy (CAP).

One of the original aims of the CAP was laudable enough, namely to make the EC self-sufficient in food. In the immediate postwar period this aim had its merits, but critics now see the CAP rather more as a protectionist measure. By providing guaranteed agricultural prices the CAP has encouraged farmers to overproduce. Much of this overproduction is then sold on world markets at subsidized prices, since European farming is, on average, high cost. At the same time high import tariffs lock out agricultural products from countries outside the EC.

Farmers in eastern Europe have a ready potential market on their doorsteps, but a high tariff wall will keep their products out unless there is major reform of the CAP. However, with reform, farmers in eastern Europe stand to become more prosperous by selling in the EC. In turn, this prosperity would create new markets for consumer goods, from which EC manufacturers can benefit. This, at least, is the prospect. Realization will involve the negotiation of many difficult economic and political hurdles.

However, it would be an oversimplification to suggest that trade between eastern and western Europe would mainly comprise agricultural products heading West, with manufactured goods returning in the opposite direction. A number of countries in eastern Europe used to have a very strong manufacturing base. Czechoslovakia, for example, once contained some of Europe's leading industries, notably in the armaments and automotive sectors.

There is considerable scope for reviving manufacturing capabilities in eastern Europe. Often the preferred path will be through joint ventures with companies in western Europe, or in the USA and

Japan. So far, most of the prime movers for joint ventures have been in the automotive sector. Fiat is probably ahead of the field, having developed manufacturing links with eastern Europe since as long ago as 1912. Importantly, Fiat maintained and developed these links in the 1950s and 1960s when few western European companies were prepared to commit themselves to a long-term involvement with eastern European countries (an example is their joint venture in 1954 with Zastava, the Yugoslavian motor manufacturer). More recently, Fiat has pursued a number of other agreements, ranging from product licensing to technology transfer, in Poland and the Soviet Union (see table 14.1).

The reasons for Fiat's strong association with eastern Europe are complex. The three most important ones are:

- The desire to reduce its heavy reliance on the Italian market. Fiat had 57 per cent in 1989, down from 61 per cent in 1986 (Done, 1990).
- The threat of increased competition, particularly from Japanese manufacturers. Fiat's strong position in Italy is partly due to import restrictions, which have limited Japanese cars to under 1 per cent of the market. (These restrictions are due to end as part of the 1992 completion of the SEM, but only a partial relaxation of the restrictions is likely.)
- The mature and saturated car market in western Europe. All the rival manufacturers are attempting to reduce product cycle times and improve quality control, but this will not be a guarantee of selling more new cars.

Signor Gallo, Fiat's Executive Vice President for International Activities, has summed up both the problem, and Fiat's reaction to it, in the following quotation:

In Western Europe there is already strong competition in a fairly saturated market. With growing Japanese presence it will become more and more crowded with not so much growth in the market. You make a great effort to gain just a decimal point of market penetration. The big market of the future is eastern Europe. (Done, 1990)

Yet seeing eastern Europe as an untapped new market is only part of the strategy; there is also the attraction of low-cost production. Essential to Fiat's plans will be the ability to feed cars produced in eastern Europe into its western European sales network. Fiat is already selling Zastava's Yugo 45/55 range under the Innocenti brand name in Italy, and plans are well advanced for single sourcing involving Zastava in Yugoslavia and FSM in Poland.

Joint ventures are not, of course, the only route open to bring

**Table 14.1** Fiat's commitments in eastern Europe

| Company/location | Car produced | Output per annum | Type of deal |
|---|---|---|---|
| *Poland*[a] | | | |
| FSM, Bielsko Biala | 126 (1974) | | Under licence |
| | Micro (from 1991) | 160 000–250 000 | |
| FSO, Warsaw | FSO 1300 | | Under licence |
| | Tipo (from 1995–6?) | 120 000 | |
| *Yugoslavia* | | | |
| ZCZ, Kragujevac | Yugo 513 | | 1968 acquired 18.5% |
| | Yugo 45/55 (Fiat 127 derivative) | | equity stake in ZCZ |
| | Yugo 311/511 (Fiat 128 derivative) | | (negotiating an increase) |
| | Uno Sting/Formula | | |
| *USSR* | | | |
| VAZ, Togliattigrad | Fiat 124 derivative – Lada (from 1970) | 660 000 | Production/technology contract |
| Yelaz, Yelabuga | Panda (from 1992) | 300 000 | Production/technology contract |
| | A93 (Uno derivative from 1993–4) | 300 000 | 30% equity stake in A93 |
| | Tipo/Tempra (from 1995–6) | 300 000 | Production/technology contract |

[a] There are plans for an engine and gearbox plant to supply both FSO and FSM.

*Source:* Adapted from K. Done's 'Fiat's Grand European Design', *Financial Times* 9 July 1990 and updated by Fiat UK Ltd, London

about the revitalization of manufacturing in eastern Europe. In a number of cases, state-run companies have been privatized outright. Hunslet Holdings, for example, has taken a 51 per cent shareholding stake in Ganz, the former state-run railway engineering company in Hungary. Similarly, Lafarge Coppée, a leading French cement company has taken control of East Germany's largest cement producer (Karsdorf) and its main sanitary-ware company (VEB Keramische Werk).

However, for many businesses, the key point is not so much *how* change will be achieved, but *whether* it will be achieved. Eastern Europe does, of course, have good potential for economic growth. At best, the growth rate could be dramatic, given sufficient co-operation from the West. Industry could thrive and so generate the necessary wealth for people in eastern Europe to buy the consumer goods that they appear to want so desperately, given the long years of denial.

Yet there is nothing certain about this outcome. Above all, the politics of eastern Europe remain very fluid as attempts are made to revive democratic traditions such as multi-party voting in elections. Yugoslavia is threatening to fragment and suffers from hyper-inflation. Bulgaria, at its recent elections, put the Communist party back in power. There is nothing uniform about eastern Europe, despite appearances to the contrary during the postwar period.

While there remains political uncertainty, there will be corresponding uncertainty for businesses contemplating investment in eastern Europe. Investment is likely to be a risky proposition perhaps well into the next century. Yet, in many cases, companies also know that it will be a risk not to invest.

If we assume the best-case scenario, and suppose that there is a revitalization of eastern European economies and a resulting boost to trade, then the challenge for logistics will be considerable. In particular, communications remain a major problem in eastern Europe.

Transport infrastructure is generally poor, with few motorways or high-grade railway lines. As a result, transit times are slow, an important consideration when moving perishables, such as many agricultural products. Similarly, telephone systems are often outdated and inadequate. An acute shortage of lines means that even simple telephone calls from one part of a country to another can take time to arrange. Much longer waiting times are often necessary for inter-national calls. With severe problems affecting even such a basic tool of business as the telephone, the prospect of EDI seems a long way off.

Clearly, the scale of investment needed to bring the standards of both the transport infrastructure and the communications infrastructure up to the best of west European standards will be considerable, running into many billions of ecus. For some countries, there is hope of aid from the EC, but this could be limited by the need to show some direct benefit to the EC itself. Thus Yugoslavia, which provides land transit between Greece and Italy, may be well placed compared with, say, Romania, which is not on any intra-EC trade route.

Some countries in eastern Europe have gone as far as to express an interest in joining the EC directly. There are many reasons for them to pursue this aim, mostly economic ones. If successful, it would enable them to draw directly upon EC regional funds, with the aim of promoting rapid economic development. An important element of regional aid would be infrastructure improvement. However, sharing in the success of the EC means rather more than building new roads; there are important economic adjustments to make. Switching from a command to a market economy raises the prospect of unemployment for a workforce which has hitherto enjoyed guaranteed jobs. The transition will be traumatic, as workers in the former East Germany have discovered following unification.

It would be wrong to underestimate the length of time it might take for a workforce to ditch the values of a command economy in favour of those belonging to a market economy. After all, there are few people from eastern Europe who have had any experience of market economies. Even the oldest workers would have started their careers in the 1940s. Furthermore, restrictions in travel in the postwar period meant that few people from east European countries were able to go to live, work and learn in the West, even if they wished. Indeed, the possible introduction of Western ideas into eastern Europe, including those concerning management practices, would have been deeply frowned upon (or worse) during the postwar era.

The lack of appropriate managerial skills in eastern Europe is likely to prove to be one of the largest problems facing future business developers in the region. It will affect not only the users of logistics services, such as the manufacturers, but also the providers of logistics services, such as hauliers and shipping lines. The fear, quite commonly expressed, that hauliers from eastern Europe will make fast inroads into the European market for logistics services, seems very overstated. Soviet shipping was, for many years, represented as a bogeyman to Western interests, because of its predatory pricing policies, based upon a desire to earn hard currency. But even when the Soviet Union was firmly wedded to the ideas of the command economy, the fear was much greater than the reality (Bergstrand and Doganis, 1987). To suppose now that eastern European hauliers pose a threat to companies such as Frans Maas seems little short of absurd.

# The Environment

Throughout this book, the theme of deregulation has been a recurring one, not least because of its importance in transforming markets for logistics services. Deregulation of communications industries, and the ending of the monopoly of the national PTTs, will help to stimulate the better use of information technology (IT) in European logistics. In transport, the deregulation of haulage markets has already begun to transform the ability of freight companies to respond to the rapidly changing needs of their customers.

However, the future is not one of unbounded development, especially for the road-based freight companies. Although many of them may have been liberated from the more stifling effects of economic regulation, it is more than possible that some form of re-regulation will come into force in the twenty-first century. Here the motive will have less to do with protecting railway traffic (as in former times) and more to do with protection of the environment.

We have already discussed the probable expansion of road haulage at the expense of rail, unless there is a radical change in the way railway business is conducted (chapter 13). However, as concern for the environment grows, adding more lorries to already congested roads will not be helpful. Lorries are already subject to extensive bans on their use in some countries (see table 14.2), and the likelihood is that more restrictions will be called for.

The irony is, of course, that car traffic vastly exceeds lorry traffic; the relative proportions are typically in the order of 5:1. And even significant growth in lorry traffic is unlikely to change this relationship, given the growing demand for car use. Yet most governments in EC countries are reluctant to restrict the use of cars, for fear of the political fallout – lorries are a much easier target.

Increasing congestion and the need for better environmental protection seem very likely to lead to a more concerted approach towards curbing lorry traffic than the current *ad hoc* approach. One

**Table 14.2** Restrictions on the movement of goods vehicles in selected European countries

| Country | Nature of ban | Hours of ban |
| --- | --- | --- |
| Austria | Vehicles over 7.5 tonnes and when drawing a trailer | 15:00 Saturday–22:00 Sunday plus public holidays |
| France | Vehicles over 6 tonnes laden weight<br>Vehicles carrying dangerous goods | 22:00 Saturday–22:00 Sunday and bank holidays<br>12:00 Saturday–24:00 Sunday and evenings preceding bank holidays |
| | (British vehicles returning to Channel ports are exempt, but must not use autoroutes; refrigerated vehicles not restricted if at least three-quarters full of perishable goods) | |
| Germany | Vehicles over 7.5 tonnes laden weight | 00:00–22:00 hours Sundays and public holidays (with certain exceptions); Saturdays from 07:00, June–September |
| Greece | Goods vehicles, except those carrying perishables | 18:00 Saturday–24:00 Sunday |
| Eire | Customs crossings, except by special request and fee payment | Restricted to between 09:00 and 17:00 hours daily |
| Italy | Goods vehicles with loads in excess of 5 tonnes<br>Mont Blanc Tunnel | 09:00–20:00 Sundays and public holidays<br>Sundays and French and Italian public holidays |
| Spain | Goods vehicles, except those carrying perishables<br>Vehicles carrying dangerous goods | Sundays and public holidays<br>12:00 Saturday–24:00 Sunday, public holidays, 1 and 31 July, and 1 and 31 August |

**Table 14.2** (*cont.*):

| Country | Nature of ban | Hours of ban |
|---|---|---|
| Switzerland | Goods vehicles over 35 tonnes | 00:00–12:00 Sundays and public holidays; 22:00–04:00 daily 1 April–31 October; 21:00–05:00 daily 1 November–31 March |

*Source*: adapted from IVECO Ford (1990b), Watford

possibility is for there to be restrictions on lorries using particularly congested corridors; permits may be required for lorries to use certain roads at designated times of day. The interesting question is that of who should administer any such permit system, especially when some routes cross international borders.

There is an argument in favour of involvement by the EC Commission, not least to ensure that national interests do not predominate over Community ones. Yet here we are on sensitive political territory. Many politicians would resent further authority being transferred towards the centre in EC affairs.

However, for most businesses, the issue is not so much about who does the controlling but the consequences of control itself. Crucially, both users and providers of logistics services should act to ensure that government, either at the national or EC level, does not re-regulate road freight transport by default.

For example, users should more carefully consider the environmental consequences of their logistics plans, such as the centralization of inventory. It may be better for them to develop new logistics strategies, notably more local production, if it helps to minimize the use of transport. The nightmare scenario for some companies will be for them to have developed single plant production and centralized inventory, only to face severe restrictions on the movement of goods between factory and warehouse and from warehouse to customer. The resulting loss of customer service will be hard for them to reverse with any speed, given the investment already made in existing facilities such as warehouses.

For their part, the providers of logistics services need to adapt their operational practices to take more account of the environment. Reduced empty running of lorries, for example, not only helps to improve competitiveness, but is environmentally friendly. Clearly, many freight operators already see advantages in, say, network cabotage (see chapter 12), which helps to reduce empty running and so reduce prices to customers. As some lead, others will have to follow in order to remain competitive.

Green practices in logistics need to be noticed. There is nothing wrong in promoting the fact that strategic changes in logistics can make an environmental contribution. Both users and providers will need to consider more carefully environmental aspects of their activities, ranging from strategic planning right down to the use of appropriate packaging materials and waste disposal. The concerns of the twenty-first century, which will be dominated by quality-of-life issues, make it essential for companies to be proactively green, rather than waiting for someone to brand them as unnecessary polluters, deserving drastic control of their activities.

Hauliers, and other providers of logistics services, therefore need to mature as businesses, to ensure that they create an image for themselves in line with their environmental achievements. They need to become more adept at public relations and advertising. All this is consistent with the changing shape of businesses as providers of logistics services. In chapter 8, we marked out the progression of freight companies from proprietorial beginnings to the development of a more corporate approach to business. The environment will be a severe test of the corporate credentials of many freight companies in the twenty-first century.

# User Strategies in Logistics

Dramatic improvements in the efficiency of European logistics are possible, according to our survey in chapter 7. What is more, they are necessary if European-based companies are to remain competitive in the twenty-first century.

The powerful economies of the USA and Japan, together with the newly industrialized economies of the Pacific Rim, will continue to provide a major challenge to the EC. Companies working within the Community not only have this challenge to contend with, but also the twin uncertainties of internal competition within the Community as the SEM takes shape and the changing face of eastern Europe. Every opportunity has to be taken for them to become better companies.

Logistics clearly has a key role to play in making companies more effective competitors. In manufacturing, production continues to become more 'footloose', with companies seeking out those locations which offer advantages in relation to wage rates, industrial relations records and government grants; the actual country of production is often a relatively unimportant consideration. Footloose manufacturing puts a new emphasis on excellence in logistics; sourcing and distribution requirements change dramatically with a change in production location. It follows that responsibilities for logistics must assume a new importance if companies are to compete successfully.

The approach of Japanese companies is instructive in this respect. A number of them, including Sony, Honda, Toshiba and Toyota, have set up manufacturing bases near to newly established export markets. Once local manufacturing comes on stream, the local products are often just as good as those exported from Japan. Many observers have put this down to innovative trade union agreements or excellence in quality control or, more generally, superior management techniques. What is often neglected is the crucial role of logistics, which needs to be highly adapative in support of manufacturing. In effect, logistics is the key ingredient of strategies which are based upon the idea of 'thinking globally, but acting locally'.

Excellence in logistics cannot be achieved without resources for planning, and the ability to influence the decision-making process within companies. Sony's 100-strong logistics department is at the centre of much of the decision-making within the company, because the importance of logistics in modern manufacture is so well appreciated. How many Europeans can claim a team which has even a tenth of that number?

Sony, and many other Japanese companies, clearly demonstrate the importance of systematic logistics planning within companies. Only by taking a comprehensive approach to logistics within a company can new ideas be fully exploited, from the sourcing of components, through to assembly and final distribution. The complexity of logistics, as a common thread to so many company activities, must not be underestimated; and under-resourcing of logistics planning is certain to lead to sub-optimal approaches which bring only limited advantages to companies.

In our survey of companies based in Europe (in chapter 7) we concluded that there were significant weaknesses in logistics planning, particularly within industrial logistics. Part of the problem appears to be that many of the older-established companies have a management hierarchy which is not responsive to new priorities such as logistics planning. All too often the most powerful directors will be those in production or sales; logistics will often not be represented in its own right, but will be the sub-responsibility of, say, the distribution director. Here we have a problem. Logistics must not be regarded as a function of the distribution of manufactured products – the reverse is true. It therefore follows that the distribution director is usually quite the wrong person to assume responsibilities for logistics planning which inevitably, as a horizontal activity, cuts across manufacturing and sales functions. Even worse, the title 'logistics director' is often given to the distribution director to make him appear more important, with absolutely no change in responsibility. Logistics planning has to be taken more seriously than this.

Clearly, there is a fundamental need both to establish the importance of logistics for companies and to devise a framework for effective logistics planning within European companies, which reflects their own special managerial styles and traditions. Simply copying the Japanese will not always work. Logistics has to become established as a key responsibility in companies, but part of the problem is that there are too few logistics professionals. Most are almost entirely self-taught and there are few education and training programmes available for logistics. Additionally, there seems to be a frequent failure to grasp the speed at which business is changing, and the rate at which new skills need to be acquired.

Another point to recognize is that the preferred style of logistics decision-making will need to vary between countries, according to the prevailing management style. In Germany, with many companies operating in a highly structured way, there is scope for creating logistics departments which have well-defined functional responsibilities to other major areas of company activity, such as production and marketing. The approach in France is likely to be different, since in many French companies there is a tendency to refer most decision-making to the highest level. Logistics planning therefore needs to work in close association with chief executives. There is, therefore, unlikely to be any one format for logistics planning that will have a universal application to European companies. The influence of different cultural styles of management, according to country, is likely to persist.

However, this is not to rule out convergences in Europe, which will increasingly have a growing influence on logistics planning. The trend towards concentrating on core business, for example, is not unique to any one European country; it is very much a pan-European trend. As a result, there are good opportunities for third parties in logistics, as more companies wish to divest themselves of, say, transport and warehousing responsibilities.

Growing concentration of ownership, together with a preoccupation with core business, is likely to lead to a changing demand for logistics services among users. Many will be looking towards the bulk purchase of logistics services from a reduced number of suppliers. Indeed, this trend can already be recognized in the USA, where a survey of executives by Lalonde and Masters (1990) indicated a fall of 33 per cent in the number of carriers likely to be used in 1995, compared with 1988. The implications of this change become even more dramatic when placed against the expected increase in the use of third parties for logistics services (see chapters 4 and 9). These impacts will tend to place each buying decision for logistics services at a higher level in the organizational structure of the user company. With this trend being mirrored in Europe, the profile of logistics within companies will be raised further as more senior managers become involved with purchase decisions.

Another development which seems certain to lead to better decision-making in the purchase of logistics services concerns pricing. At present, pricing practices for European transport, in particular, are often unnecessarily complex, with a whole variety of pricing options. Pricing practices for international transport in Europe are especially complex. For example, a product made in Essen and sold to a customer in Lyon will sometimes be priced 'free German border'. This means that the producer will pay for the transport from Essen to the German–French border, with the customer paying for transport between the border and Lyon. It is hard to imagine US producers selling on the basis of, say, 'free Texas border'; with transport costs being divided between producer and customer. More often the product will be sold either 'ex-works' or 'delivered' with, respectively, the customer or the producer paying for all transport costs.

The trend is for similar arrangements to be made in Europe. Using the UK as an example, less than 50 per cent of products sold internationally from the UK in 1985 were sold either ex-works or delivered (see figure 14.1); the picture was probably similar in other European countries.

Importantly, changing the basis of pricing changes the basis for control of the supply chain. With ex-works pricing, the customer

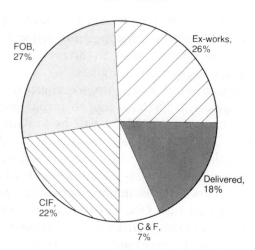

**Figure 14.1** What terms of sale do you use for your continental European customers?
*Source*: CPDM 1985 survey of current practices of UK exporters to Europe.

takes control of the supply chain. With delivered pricing, control responsibilities rest with the producer. In the coming years, improved control of the supply chain, as a result of decision-making responsibilities becoming more clear-cut, should bring significant benefits to European users of logistics services. It is not such good news for some suppliers of logistics services, notably freight agents and forwarders, who have made a living out of the complexities of arranging transport in Europe.

Lastly, it appears inevitable that there will be an increasing emphasis on quality in logistics services as we enter the twenty-first century. As logistics control is more tightly exercised by companies at either end of the supply chain, the monitoring of services will become significantly more important. At present, quality monitoring of logistics services is in its infancy. To improve quality, users must develop vendor rating systems for their transport suppliers, as they have done for their suppliers of more tangible products. This also requires a change from the adversarial approach and the selection of the cheapest option. Instead, what is needed is a commitment to longer-term relationships between supplier and provider, because this will ultimately prove most advantageous to users.

## Provider Strategies in Logistics

One of the dominant themes of the early years of the twenty-first century will be the role of the mega-carrier. Until a few years ago, few companies had any stated ambition to obtain mega-carrier status in Europe, as defined by a complete portfolio of freight services and representation in most countries, especially in the EC. A number of companies now aspire to the role.

Arguably, the 1990s will be the testing ground for the mega-carrier concept in Europe. There will probably be failures among those currently chasing mega-carrier status. Those remaining in the race, possibly joined by new entrants from the USA and Japan, may choose to redefine their role as some competitors go down. One probable outcome is that some may prefer to concentrate on specialist logistics tasks in Europe, such as LTL or express, rather than attempt a full portfolio of services ranging from FTL to dedicated contract distribution. Partnerships with other mega-carriers will give access to all the services that one-stop users of logistics services may require.

However, partnerships can be fragile, especially between large companies. So even if, in the 1990s, there is some slimming down of service portfolios by logistics companies, it is likely that the turn of the century will see attempts to expand them once again. These mega-carriers will have decided that it is, after all, possible to provide a comprehensive range of services in a manageable way. More sophisticated applications of IT will probably be at the heart of this belief.

A pan-European logistics capability is but a step away from a global logistics capability. The 1980s saw the arrival of the global express company. The beginning of the 1990s sees the rise of potential mega-carriers such as NYK and Nedlloyd, which are developing combined intercontinental and transcontinental services from origins in liner shipping. In Europe, there may, by the twenty-first century, be the opportunity for them to add rail to their modal portfolios, if the current monopoly of railway companies on railway operations is removed. As we have strongly argued in chapter 13, there are compelling reasons to allow competition in rail freight.

Whatever the precise form of the mega-carriers in the twenty-first century, the conduct of many of them will certainly be far removed from their origins. The proprietorial style which may have characterized their earlier history will have been fully replaced by a corporate attitude to business. This change has been slow in coming to the freight and logistics business for a variety of reasons, including ease of entry for small operators. But for those companies close to assuming a full corporatist strategy, with a sophisticated approach to key business activities such as planning, research and development and marketing, their new-found skills will be quickly exercised. Better branding, both of logistics companies and their services, will be an important weapon. Similarly, it will be necessary for them to defend market positions by promoting the value of their work. Nowhere will this be more important than with respect to environmental questions. A failure to communicate achievements in reducing environmental impact could lead, by default, to political initiatives towards transport re-regulation, a development that few providers and users of logistics services would welcome.

However, despite the growth of the mega-carriers, there will still be many small providers of logistics services: the economics of the sector will ensure that they will maintain the ability to compete. This is especially true of the owner–operator in haulage, the smallest business unit in the market for logistics services. Both as a subcontractor and as a local provider of services to small users, the small haulier is sure to survive.

The future of the medium-sized operator is less certain, and it is more difficult to identify their long-term advantages in the marketplace for logistics services. They are neither small enough to earn a living at the margin of the market nor large enough to develop many of the attributes (such as IT networks) that are now widely expected of companies with some kind of corporate structure. It will become more apparent throughout the 1990s and into the next century that medium-sized hauliers, especially those with around 20–80 vehicles, will prosper if they can promote their services in two ways. First, they can appear to be more 'user friendly' than the mega-carriers, especially to the smaller user. Second, they can gain strength by co-operation, through creating networks in association with similar companies. There are already signs of this happening, but mainly as a defensive measure in anticipation of increased competition from the mega-carriers. But co-operation needs to be promoted as a virtue, rather than being seen as sign of desperation. Co-operators will need to stress their ability to 'act local' wherever a delivery has to be made within the network.

We have already noted the increasing expectation of users of logistics services in relation to the quality of logistics provided by third parties. However, the goal of better quality could prove to be elusive. The main advances are likely to be made in the 'closed' logistics environments. These include warehousing and IT, where activities can be planned and executed more or less according to the specified requirements of logistics users. The major challenge will be in transport because it represents an 'open' environment for logistics. Lorries carrying goods for customers will have to compete for space along with other road users; there is no prospect of road capacity reservation by freight operators. In addition, road traffic is subject to severe disruption as a result of serious road accidents. This already plays havoc with delivery schedules. The prospect for the early part of the twenty-first century, with higher traffic volumes, is less than reassuring. Electronic solutions, such as automatic collision avoidance systems, currently seem a long way off, despite all the best efforts of the EC's research programmes.

It therefore appears that transport will increasingly become the weakest functional link in the supply chains of many companies. Some may want to make greater use of rail rather than road; its more disciplined operating structures make it less prone to accident and consequent delay. But it is also clear that the organization of rail as a business needs urgent reform if it is to fulfil the increasingly high expectations of potential users.

Lastly, it is important for providers of logistics services to have a clear idea of their own business objectives for the year 2000 and beyond. It is insufficient to wait for users to define their logistics services needs; being reactive will not be the way to win business in the future. This point again encapsulates one of the main themes of this book, that many large providers of logistics services have been transformed from proprietorial enterprises to corporate ones, often in a fairly short space of time.

The continued success of these large providers will depend on the continuing transformation of their business into corporate enterprises which contain high levels of skill, particularly in planning and marketing. The potential rewards for success will be substantial in the multi-billion ecu market for European logistics services. Of course it will be expensive to finance business development which involves a more substantial investment in new business skills – but this is beginning to weigh lightly against the likely consequences of non-investment as the business environment for logistics services becomes ever more demanding.

# Notes

1 The name Germany is used in the text in recognition of unification. However, a number of figures and tables, using data from the 1970s and 1980s, will refer just to West Germany.
2 Gross value-added represents the contribution of a given economic sector to the creation of a nation's wealth. It is calculated by subtracting from the final value of production the value of consumption of goods, services (the 'intermediate inputs') and fixed capital.
3 This section draws extensively on work carried out by the Oxford Institute of Retail Management (OXIRM) at Templeton College, Oxford into the internationalization of retailing. OXIRM researchers have done much original work to highlight the processes of retail internationalization and we are grateful to them for allowing us to draw so extensively on their studies.
4 The results differ in detail from the preliminary findings reported by the authors in the *International Journal of Logistics Management* (Cooper, Browne and Peters, 1990). This is because of a modification in the classification of companies and an increase in the survey sample for each performance indicator.
5 Part of this section is based upon an article published by James Cooper in *Transport Reviews* 11, 1, January 1991. For a fuller analysis of the consequences of deregulation in Australia, the UK and USA, see his article entitled 'Lessons for Europe from freight deregulation in Australia, the UK and the USA'.
6 Although West and East Germany are now united, there remain major differences in their freight sectors. This account of the German freight sector relates mainly to what was West Germany, up to October 1990. The former East Germany effectively adopted West German transport regulations from January 1991.
7 We are grateful to the members of EUROFRET for allowing us to quote from their survey.

8  Some JIT delivery systems have been designed on the basis of consolidation whereby a carrier collects consignments from suppliers and delivers to the assembly plant. This clearly entails the continued use of larger vehicles and falls outside the scope of the analysis in chapter 13.

# References

Amatore, P. 1990: The future of the railways in an integrated European system. *Rail International*, April.

Artous, A. 1990: La pression va d'abord venir de la recherche de fret de retour. *Camions Magazine*, April.

Austen, H. 1818: Biographical note. In Austen, J., *Persuasion*. London.

Baldwin, R. 1989: The growth effects of 1992. *Economic Policy*, 4 (Part II) No. 9, October.

Barret, S. 1988: Freedom for Irish road freight. *Transport*, 9(9), September.

Bergstrand, S. J. and Doganis, R. S. 1987: *The Impact of Soviet Shipping*. London: Allen and Unwin.

Bernadet, J. P. 1988: The French railway: case; telematics for logistics. 6th Eurolog European Logistics Conference, Milan, November.

Boatman, J. 1989: Quality in retail distribution. *Focus*, 8(2), March.

Bonnafous, A. 1988: The experience of trucking deregulation in France. OECD Seminar on Road Freight Deregulation, Experience, Evaluation, Research, Paris, 2–4 November.

Bowersox, D. 1988: Logistics – the route to quality. *Focus*, 7(7), September.

Browne, M. 1989: Using EDI for competitive advantage in logistics: implications for the transport industry. Paper presented to the ESTI Conference on Logistical Information Systems, Paris, December.

Browne, M. 1991: Prospective freight mega-carriers: the role of information technology in their global ambitions. Paper presented to the 24th Hawaii International Conference on System Sciences, Hawaii, January.

Browne, M. and Cooper, J. 1989: Developing effective strategies for cooperation in international freight transport. Paper presented to the 19th Biennial ICHCA Conference, Stockholm, May.

Browne, M., Doganis, R. and Bergstrand, S. 1989: *Transhipment of UK Trade*. London: British Ports Federation/Department of Transport.

Bulley, P. 1989: JIT: the impact on purchasing. *Purchasing and Supply Management*, April.

Byrne, S. 1990: *European Shippers Survey*. GE Information Services, London.

Canny, J. and Rastatter, E. 1988: US trucking deregulation since 1980. OECD Seminar T9 on Road Transport Regulation: Experience, Evaluation, Research, Paris, November.

*Cargo Systems* 1990: Towards 50 freight 'plateforms'. May.

CBI/PA Consulting Group 1990: *Information Technology: the Catalyst for Change*. London: Mercury Books.

CBI/TNT Express 1990: *Transport and Distribution*. London: Mercury Books.

Cecchini, P. 1988: *The European Challenge: 1992*. Aldershot: Wildwood House.

Chardin, D. 1990a: L'heure est au libéralisme plus tempéré. *Camions Magazine*, May.

Chardin, D. 1990b: Les transporteurs français craignent le pire. *Camions Magazine*, April.

Christensen, L. R. and Eastburn, M. P. 1985: Introduction of a computer system for delivery planning – Argyll Stores – case study. *Focus* 4 (6), November–December.

Christopher, M. 1986: *Effective Logistics Management*. Aldershot: Gower (first published in 1985 as *The Strategy of Distribution Management*).

Christopher, M. 1990: Profit through logistics. *Storage Handling Distribution*, 1990.

Cooper, J. C. 1990a: The UK distribution industry. In J. C. Cooper (ed.), *Logistics and Distribution Planning: Strategies for Management* (revised edition). London: Kogan Page.

Cooper, J. C. 1990b: The consequences of cabotage for transport users (freight). ESTI Seminar: Common Transport Policy, 29–30 May, Brussels.

Cooper, J. 1991: Lessons for Europe from freight deregulation in Australia, the UK and the USA. *Transport Reviews*, 11(1), January.

Cooper, J. and Browne, M. 1989: A great journey of change. *Eurobusiness*, 1(5), February.

Cooper, J. C. and Doganis, R. S. 1982: *The Economics of Demountables in Distribution*. Research Report No. 7, Transport Studies Group, Polytechnic of Central London.

Cooper, J. and Johnstone, M. 1990: Dedicated contract distribution: an assessment of the UK market place. *International Journal of Physical Distribution and Logistics Management*, 20(1).

Cooper, J. C. and Tweddle, G. 1990: Distribution round the clock. In J. C. Cooper (ed.), *Logistics and Distribution Planning: Strategies for Management* (revised edition). London: Kogan Page.

Cooper, J. C., Browne, M. and Gretton, D. 1987: *Freight Transport in the*

*European Community: Making the Most of UK Opportunities.* Research Report No. 14, Transport Studies Group, Polytechnic of Central London, March.

Cooper, J., Browne, M. and Peters, M. 1990: Logistics performance in Europe: the challenge of 1992. *International Journal of Logistics Management,* 1(1).

Cope, N. 1990: Walkmen's global stride. *Business,* March.

Copeland, D. G. and McKenney, J. L. 1988: Airline reservations systems: lessons from history. *MIS Quarterly,* September.

Corporate Intelligence Group 1990: *Retailing in Europe.* London.

Das, C. 1978: A re-appraisal of the square root law. *International Journal of Physical Distribution,* 8(6).

Davies, R. L. and Treadgold, A. D. 1988: Retail internationalisation: trends and directions. Paper presented at an OXIRM briefing at Coopers and Lybrand, London, 8 July.

Dawson, R. 1989: Time to meet the challenge. In *Institute of Export Handbook.*

Dicken, P. 1986: *Global Shift: Industrial Change in a Turbulent World.* London: Harper & Row.

*Distribution* 1990: Genuine focus. September–October.

Done, K. 1990: Fiat's grand European design. *Financial Times,* 9 July.

EC Commission (DG III) 1989: *Panorama of EC Industry.* Brussels: The Commission.

*Economist, The* 1988: Europe's internal market. 9 July.

*Economist, The* 1989: The lure of 1992. 18 November.

*Economist, The* 1990a: Not all sweeteners and light. 28 July.

*Economist, The* 1990b: A survey of information technology. 16 June.

EUROFRET 1990: Alternative RTI strategies for RFI scenaria (Volume I), 3rd Deliverable to EC DG XIII, April.

*Euromonitor* 1987: *Grocery Distribution in Western Europe.* London: Euromonitor Publications.

Eurostat 1989a: *Carriage of Goods (Railways) 1987.* Luxembourg.

Eurostat 1989b: *Europe in Figures: Deadline 1992.* Luxembourg.

Eurostat (continuing series): *Energy and Industry.* Luxembourg.

Fenton, N. 1985: Articled numbering and data communications. *The Institute of Physical Distribution Management Conference Proceedings.* March.

Ferguson, A. 1989: Britain's best factories. *Management Today,* November.

*Financial Times* 1991: The FT European Top 500. Week ending Friday 11 January.

Fisher, P. 1990: Standard required. *Truck,* November.

Flanagan, J. 1985: Multinational as we know it is obsolete (US markets falling to Japan). Interview with Peter Drucker, 26 August 1985. In Forbes (1990).

Forbes, M. 1990: Just-in-time distribution. In J. C. Cooper (ed.), *Logistics and Distribution Planning: Strategies for Management* (revised edition). London: Kogan Page.

Fraser, I. 1990: Now only the name's the same. *Eurobusiness*, April.

Freight Transport Association 1989: The free movement of goods. In *EC – Towards the Single Market 1992*. Freight Facts Series, August.

Friedman, A. 1988: *Agnelli and the Network of Italian Power*. London: Harrap.

Frybourg, M. 1989: Telematics in goods transport. ECMT Round Table 78.

Garnett, N. 1988: Ploughing a furrow to 1992. *The Financial Times*, 6 June.

Garreau, A., Lieb, R. and Millen, R. 1991: JIT and corporate transportation requirements: an international comparison. *International Journal of Physical Distribution and Logistics Management*, 21 (2) Bradford: MCB University Press.

Gibson, G. and Treadgold, A. 1990: Retailing in continental Europe: the opportunities and the costs. In N. Sanghavi and A. Treadgold (eds), *Developments in European Retailing*. Yeovil, Somerset: Dower House.

Handy, C. 1989: *The Age of Unreason*. London: Business Books.

Hambros Bank Ltd, February 1989, *European Road Transport and Distribution: Towards 1992*.

Hitchin, J. 1987: Untitled presentation to the Annual EPOS Conference, organized by the journal *Retail and Distribution Management*, Barbican, London (reported in *RDM*, 15(6), November–December 1987).

Hodd, M. 1987: Shipper control slashes cost. *Cargo Systems International*, February.

Hooper, J. 1989: Barcelona's old Spanish practices. *The Guardian*, 5 December.

Hudson, M. 1989: *Portugal to 1993*. Special Report No. 1157, Economist Intelligence Unit, London, January.

Hurn, M. 1990: The impact that the completion of the Single Market will have on European freight rates. Unpublished MSc dissertation, Polytechnic of Central London.

Institute of Grocery Distribution 1990: *Aldi*. Letchmore Heath, Hertfordshire: International Key Account Profiles.

IVECO Ford 1990a: *The Truck and the Greenhouse Effect*, Watford.

IVECO Ford 1990b: *1992 – The Long Haul Into Europe*. Watford.

*Journal of Law and Economics* 1978: The beneficiaries of trucking regulation (unattributed article). No. 21, October.

Joy, S. 1964: Unregulated road haulage: the Australian experience. *Oxford Economic Papers*, 16(2), July.

Kandler, J. 1989: Recent deregulation and proposed European harmonization in the Federal Republic of Germany: the attitudes of the parties concerned. Paper presented to the CERTES conference Transport Occupations and Regulation in the 1993 European Perspective, Paris, 9–11 May.

Kanter, Rosabeth Moss 1989: *When Giants Learn to Dance*. London: Simon & Schuster.

A. T. Kearney 1987a: *International Logistics: Battleground of the '90s*. Chicago: A. T. Kearney Inc.

A. T. Kearney 1987b: *Logistics Productivity: the Competitive Edge in Europe*. Chicago: A. T. Kearney Inc.

A. T. Kearney 1990: Preparatory study for a combined European transport network. Report of A. T. Kearney Consulting Group, Press File Abstract, 31 January.

Kellaway, L. 1990: EC given reassurance on chip industry's problems. *The Financial Times*, 6 September.

LaLonde, B. J. and Masters, J. M. 1990: Logistics: perspective for the 1990s. *International Journal of Logistics Management*, 1(1).

Levitt, T. 1983: The globalization of markets. *Harvard Business Review*, 61, May–June.

Lichfield, N., Kettle, P. and Whitbread, M. 1975: *Evaluation in the Planning Process*. Oxford: Pergamon.

*Lloyd's Shipping Economist* 1990: Opinion divided on tunnel's impact. February.

Lynn, M. 1990: The industrial ideals of IVECO. *Business*, April.

MacPherson, S. 1987: *Data Communications for Retailers*. NCC.

McKinnon, A. C. 1989: *Physical Distribution Systems*. London: Routledge.

Maister, D. H. 1976: Centralisation of inventories and the square root law. *International Journal of Physical Distribution*, 6(3).

Manheim, M. L. 1990: Global information technology: globalisation and opportunities for competitive advantage through information technology. Unpublished paper forming part of the Strategic Informatics Research Programme at Northwestern University; presented at IWGSI meeting, Paris, March 1990.

*Materials Handling* 1989: How information technology keeps Argos ahead. December.

Melly, P. 1990: Stepping up the M&A pace. *Freighting World*, 18 May.

Montgomery, D. and Hausman, W. 1985: Managing the marketing/manufacturing interface. *P A Journal of Management*, 2(2).

*Motor Transport* 1989: Logistics is the game. Bill Parsons of Federal Express interviewed by John Aldridge, 18 January.

Murrell, G. 1988: Management of the retail supply chain. *Logistics Today*, 7(2).

Mussannif, Y. and George, F. 1987: *Focus on European Retailers*. London: Banque Paribas Capital Markets Ltd.

NFC Contract Distribution Report 1989: *Managing the European Supply Chain*. Bedford.

NOB Wegtransport 1988: *Wegvervoer in Cijfers: Editie 1988*. Rijswijk.

Parkes, C. 1990: Unknown warrior. *Business*, March.

Peters, T. 1987: *Thriving on Chaos*. New York: Alfred Knopf.

Peters, M. J. 1990: Information technology and distribution. In J. C. Cooper (ed.), *Logistics and Distribution Planning: Strategies for Management* (revised edition). London: Kogan Page.

Porter, M. E. 1985: *Competitive Advantage*. New York: Free Press.

Porter, M. 1990: *The Competitive Advantage of Nations*. New York: Free Press.

Porter, M. E. and Millar, V. E. 1985: How information gives you competitive advantage. *Harvard Business Review*, July–August.

Quarmby, D. 1985: Distribution, the next ten years – the market-place. *Focus*, 4(6), November–December.

Quarmby, D. 1988: The importance of quality in retailing. *Focus*, 7(7), September.

Raghunathan, T. S., Bagchi, P. K. and Bardi, E. J. 1988: Motor carrier services: the US experience. *International Journal of Physical Distribution and Materials Management*, 18(5), MCB University Press, Bradford.

*Retail and Distribution Management* 1988: Europe 1992: the opportunities and the threats. November–December, comment column.

Rimmer, P. J. 1987: Contemporary freight transport issues. In P. J. Gilmour (ed.), *Logistics Management in Australia*. Melbourne: Longman Cheshire.

Rockart, J. F. and Short, J. E. 1989: IT in the 1990s: managing organizational interdependence. *Sloan Management Review*, Winter.

Rogissart, J. 1990: The common transport policy has lost its way – why? *Rail International*, April.

Rushton, A. and Oxley, J. 1989: *Handbook of Logistics and Distribution Management*. London: Kogan Page.

Schweitzer, R. P. 1988: The experience of private trucking in the United States since the Motor Carrier Act of 1980. OECD Seminar T9, Paris, November.

Selosse, P. and Salini, P. 1989: *Cabotage: quelles opportunités?* OEST Report.

Sharman, G. 1989: What 1992 means for logistics. *The McKinsey Quarterly*, Spring.

Sohal, A. and Howard, K. 1987: Trends in materials management. *International Journal of Physical Distribution and Materials Management*, 17(5).

Sparks, L. 1987: Electronic communications in wholesale distribution. *Focus*, 6(7), October.

Sparks, L. 1988: Change in UK retail distribution. *Focus*, 7(4), May.

Stanton, L. 1989: Asda's two year plan. *Motor Transport*, 29 November.

*Storage, Handling and Distribution* 1990: Order of magnitude. January.

Sugawara, A. 1990: A European logistics strategy for a global Japanese company. Paper presented to the 7th European Conference on Logistics, Madrid, April.

Sussams, J. E. 1986: Buffer stocks and the square root law. *Focus on Physical Distribution and Logistics Management*, 5(5).

Tarkowski, J. and Irestahl, B. 1988: *Transport Administration*. Lund: Studentlitteratur.

Thomas, D. 1990: Turning over a new green leaf. *Financial Times*. 24 October.

Thomas, T. 1988: Mayne Nickless gets bigger and leaner. *Business Review Weekly* (Australia), 25 March.

Thompson, P. 1990: *Sharing the Success: the Story of NFC*. London: Collins.

Translink 1990: France nationalises Europe. *Translink's European Deal Review*, 17 July.

Treadgold, A. 1988: Retailing without frontiers. *Retail and Distribution Management*, November–December.

Treadgold, A. 1989: Retail trends in continental Europe. In *Responding to 1992: Key Factors for Retailers*. London: Longman.

Tugendhat, C. 1971: *The Multinationals*. London: Eyre & Spottiswoode.

United States General Accounting Office 1987: *Trucking Regulations: Price Competition and Market Structure in the Trucking Industry*. Washington, DC, February.

Walman, B. 1989: Untitled presentation to the 10th EPOS Conference, London.

Wardroper, J. 1981: *Juggernaut*. London: Temple Smith.

Waters, C. D. J. 1990: How efficient is UK inventory management? In J. C. Cooper (ed.), *Logistics and Distribution Planning: Strategies for Management* (revised edition). London: Kogan Page.

Wheatley, M. 1989: Taking stock of the system. *Management Today*, December.

White, M. 1990: Swedes sweep in. *Motor Transport*, 1 November.

Whitelegg, J. 1988: *Transport Policy in the EEC*. London: Routledge.

Williams, J. 1974: *Food Distribution Costs – Results of an Interim Study of Wholesale Transportation and Warehousing Costs*. Monograph 3, National Materials Handling Centre.

Womack, J. P., Jones, D. T. and Roos, D. 1990: *The Machine That Changed the World*. Oxford: Maxwell MacMillan International.

Zinn, W. and Grosse, R. E. 1990: Barriers to globalization: is global distribution possible? *The International Journal of Logistics Management*, 1(1), 1990.

# Glossary

**bilateral permit** A type of permit which is negotiated between two governments to allow international haulage operations between their respective countries. Typically, a bilateral permit will be required for each international haulage movement that is undertaken (*see also* multilateral permit, permit quota).

**brown goods** Electrical consumer goods for domestic use such as televisions, radios, hi-fi equipment, VCRs, kettles, shavers and so on (*see also* white goods).

**buying group** A joint purchasing organization, set up by independent retailers or wholesalers. The buying group purchases in volume, thereby securing discounts from suppliers; it also often provides a corporate identity for the independent retailers to share.

**cabotage** In the road freight industry, cabotage means domestic work wholly carried out within one country by a foreign haulier.

**cash and carry** A wholesale outlet which sells to small traders, who generally collect the goods themselves.

**casual cabotage** Cabotage undertaken in an opportunistic fashion by an international haulier, and not as part of a planned, coordinated operating system (in contrast to network cabotage).

**centralization** Selection of a central inventory holding point, with the aim of minimizing inventory; often used to indicate a concentration of inventory into several large warehouses.

**CIF** (cost, insurance and freight) Terms of sale for an international consignment, in which the final price paid by the purchaser to the supplier includes the ex-works price of the product together with insurance and freight charges to the port of entry. The purchaser assumes all responsibility for subsequent land movements (*see also* FOB, ex-works pricing, delivered pricing, terms of sale).

**co-makership** Manufacturers and component suppliers may work so closely together that the relationship is referred to as co-makership even though the companies are separate legal entities (*see also* co-shippership).

**combined transport** the use of more than one mode of transport for the movement of goods, typically road and rail for inland movements or sea and rail/road for inter-continental movements.

**common user** A description of services such as storage and transport which are made available to a wide range of customers. The opposite of a dedicated service.

**co-shippership** When users of logistics services entrust their logistics needs to a single service supplier and establish a very close relationship this may be referred to as 'co-shippership', since it is analogous to co-makership.

**convenience store** A store which sells a wide range of products, including groceries. Opening hours are usually from early in the morning to late in the evening.

**co-operative** Similar to a buying group, but one which formally embraces the principles of the co-operative movement, established in Rochdale, UK in the nineteenth century.

**corner shop** A small, often family-run, business which sells mainly groceries in a very local catchment area.

**cross-trading** International haulage performed between two countries by an operator who is resident in neither country.

**customer service** Typically, this consists of a mix of product availability and consistency, delivery lead time, timing of deliveries and the condition of the goods on arrival.

**dedicated service** When a company providing logistics services dedicates all or part of their resources, such as vehicles and warehouses, to a single customer this is referred to as a dedicated service. It is the opposite of a common user service.

**delivered pricing** Terms of sale in which the final price paid by the purchaser to the supplier for a consignment includes all delivery costs to the purchaser's premises (*see also* CIF, ex-works pricing, terms of sale).

**deregulation** The removal or relaxation of governmental restrictions previously applying to market entry and the rules of operation.

**derogation** An exemption from the provisions of an EC Directive or Regulation. A derogation may be self-awarded by a member state or sought from the European Commission, depending on the circumstances (*see also* EC Directive, EC Regulation).

**EC Directive** A Directive is issued by the European Commission and must be complied with by the member states. A member state may, however, use domestic law to meet the provisions of the Directive (*see also* derogation, EC Regulation).

**EC Regulation** A Regulation is issued by the European Commission and it represents directly binding law upon the member states (*see also* EC Directive).

**EC Resolution**   A Resolution is passed by the European Commission and member states are expected to comply with its provisions (*see also* EC Directive, EC Regulation).

**ex-works pricing**   Terms of sale in which the final price paid by the purchaser to the supplier for a consignment is exclusive of all transport and insurance costs (*see also* CIF, FOB, pricing, delivered pricing, terms of sale).

**fast-moving consumer goods (FMCG)**   Products sold for everyday use in large quantities; applied to items such as processed foods, snacks, detergents, toothpaste, and so on. The products will typically be branded.

**FOB** (free on board)   Terms of sale in which the final price paid by the purchaser to the supplier for an international consignment comprises the ex-works price together with transport costs to the port of embarkation (*see also* CIF, ex-works pricing, delivered pricing, terms of sale).

**free border pricing**   Terms of sale similar to FOB, but applying to a land border rather than a port (*see* FOB).

**free frontier pricing**   A synonym for free border pricing.

**freight forwarder**   An agent who acts as a broker for transport serices, particularly for the carriage of international goods. A freight forwarder may also provide international transport services (*see also* shipper).

**general haulier**   A haulier who is able to carry a wide variety of products in all-purpose vehicles. The choice of vehicle may preclude involvement in some specialized operations (such as the transport of hanging garments or refrigerated goods).

**gross vehicle weight**   The maximum weight at which a vehicle, together with its load, is allowed to operate on public roads.

**harmonization**   The process initiated by the European Commission which aims to remove distortions to competition between EC member states.

**haulier**   A road freight operator who carries goods on behalf of other people (*see also* own-account operator, general haulier).

**hypermarket**   A large store selling food and non-food items. Precise definitions vary, but a commonly accepted one is based on a selling space in excess of 2500 square metres, with at least 35 per cent devoted to non-food items. Hypermarkets often occupy out-of-town sites and have extended shopping hours.

**independent**   A retail business with a limited number of outlets. They are often family-run and affiliated to buying groups or voluntary chains.

**intermodal transport**   A synonym for combined transport.

**lead time**   (1) The elapsed time between initial product design and production/availability in the market. (2) The elapsed time between ordering a product and receiving it.

**logistics services**   A term to encompass a combination of the following activities; storage, materials management, distribution, transport, assembly, labelling, information and inventory management.

**multilateral permit** A holder of a multilateral permit is allowed an unrestricted number of international haulage journeys between any EC member states (*see also* bilateral permit, permit quota).

**multimodal transport** A synonym for combined transport.

**multiple** A retail business with a number of outlets; by definition a minimum of five, but typically many more.

**mutual recognition** The process for gaining type approval for products within the EC. If a product meets prescribed technical or safety standards in one EC member state then all other member states are obliged to accept the product for type approval. This removes the need to gain separate type approval in each member state.

**network cabotage** Cabotage undertaken in a regular way as part of a planned system, by an operator who provides both national and international services (in contrast to casual cabotage).

**nominated haulier** When a buyer of transport services uses a specified truck operator for their inbound transport requirements, this operator is referred to as their nominated haulier.

**own-account operator** An operator restricted to carrying goods which are owned by the operator (*see also* haulier).

**permit quota** A quantitative limit imposed on the number of permits made available for use by hauliers (*see also* bilateral permit, multilateral permit).

**provider of logistics services** A term which includes companies providing a combination of services such as storage, transport, inventory control and materials management – the supply side of the logistics market (*see also* user of logistics services).

**semi-trailer** The type of trailer that forms part of an articulated vehicle. When uncoupled the semi-trailer must be supported at one end by legs or jacks.

**shipper** An exporter or freight forwarder. The shipper is essentially the 'controller' of goods in domestic or international transport, and is therefore responsible for making important decisions on how goods should be transported.

**Single European Market (SEM)** The European Commission aims to complete the SEM within the Community so that goods and services can be traded across borders without restriction. This is sometimes also referred to as the 'Internal Market' (*see also* harmonization).

**single sourcing** Buyers, especially manufacturers, have sought to reduce the number of sellers that they deal with. This both simplifies administration and improves product quality. When the buyer purchases from only one supplier this is described as single sourcing.

**supermarket** A store which sells mainly food items, and which is often located in a high street. It has a smaller sales area than a hypermarket or a superstore. The precise definition according to floorspace varies from country to country.

**superstore**  This is generally a very large store with a floorspace of over 5000 square metres. Some corner stores, however, grandly refer to themselves as superstores.

**swap body**  A body which can be detached from a vehicle or trailer chassis. When demounted, it is supported by legs.

**symbol group**  A synonym for voluntary chain.

**tracking and tracing**  Terms usually applied in the parcels and express freight sectors. Tracking refers to the ability to track a consignment throughout its journey (that is, to know where it is at any time). Tracing is the ability to establish when a consignment has reached its destination. The terms are typically used in combination, reflecting the linked nature of the activities.

**user of logistics services**  Typically a manufacturer or retailer which requires services such as storage, transport and inventory management – the demand side of the logistics market (*see also* provider of logistics services).

**voluntary chain**  A buying organization owned by a wholesaler which distributes food and other basic commodities to small retail outlets. Also sometimes known as a 'symbol group' (*see also* buying group).

**white goods**  Large domestic appliances usually intended for use in the kitchen, such as fridges, washing machines, cookers and dishwashers (*see also* brown goods).

**wholesaler**  An intermediary between producer and retailer whose main role is to channel and consolidate orders for goods. Many wholesalers are also responsible for delivering the goods to the retailers.

# US Terminology

Throughout the book every attempt has been made to use words which can be understood by readers with a background in either the UK or the US forms of the English language. Nonetheless, there are words which can readily cause confusion between the two sets of readers. As an aid to mutual understanding, the following is a selected list of US terms together with their UK equivalents:

| US term | UK equivalent |
| --- | --- |
| inventory | stock |
| private fleet operator | own-account operator |
| rail-car | railway wagon |
| railroad | (1) railway; (2) railway track |
| revenues | turnover |
| store | (1) shop; (2) warehouse |
| truck | lorry |
| trucker | haulier |

# Index

*Index compiled by Michael Heary*